Essentials of
Classroom Teaching
Elementary Social Studies

Essentials of
Classroom Teaching
Elementary Social Studies

Thomas N. Turner
University of Tennessee–Knoxville

SERIES DEVELOPER
C. Alan Riedesel
State University of New York at Buffalo

Allyn and Bacon
Boston   London   Toronto   Sydney   Tokyo   Singapore

Series Editor: Virginia Lanigan
Series Editorial Assistant: Nicole DiPalma
Cover Administrator: Linda Dickinson
Composition Buyer: Linda Cox
Manufacturing Buyer: Louise Richardson
Editorial-Production Service: Colophon Production Service
Cover Designer: Suzanne Harbison
Text Designer: LeGwin Associates

Copyright © 1994 by Allyn and Bacon
A division of Paramount Publishing
160 Gould Street
Needham, Heights, Massachusetts 02194

Library of Congress Cataloging-in-Publication Data
Turner, Thomas N.
    Essentials of classroom teaching: elementary social studies/Thomas N. Turner
        p.   cm.
    Includes bibliographical references and index.
    ISBN 0-205-14190-0
      1. Social sciences—Study and teaching (Elementary)—United States   I. Title.
LB 1584.T87   1993   93-33413
372.83'0973—dc20   CIP

Printed in the United States of America
10 9 8 7 6 5 4 3 2 1   99 98 97 96 95 94

Contents

Preface

The late Alex Haley was often asked to make speeches about becoming a writer. He usually slipped in a folksy but meaningful analogy about seeing a turtle on a fencepost. Haley would remind his audience that the turtle couldn't have gotten on top of that post without a lot of help, noting that his own successful writing career was just like that.

I, for one, had my doubts that the turtle had any desire to be on the fence post, and I certainly do not have any pretention of comparing my own writing to Alex Haley's. Even so, that turtle comes to mind when I think about this book. For some time, I have wanted to write a text about teaching the social studies. Mainly, I wanted to do it because it is something that I deeply care about and because I found other textbooks did not have all I wanted them to have or did not say it in a way that I thought really put the message across. Because I have spent a lot of years as both an elementary teacher and sometimes storyteller and as a teacher of teachers, I have some very definitive ideas about the subject.

I did not imagine, though, how very difficult it would be to get such a book all together. Without the help and patience of my secretary, Janet Coward, some grand assists from another secretary, Emily Blake, and great and loving support and encouragement from my wife, Nancy, I would never have stuck with it to the end. I want to thank them as well as my students who endured trials and rough drafts and freely gave and forgave with their input.

Essentials of
Classroom Teaching
Elementary Social Studies

1 Today's Elementary Social Studies Classrooms

LOOKING AHEAD

What is the social studies all about? Why is this curricular area in the curriculum at all? This chapter directs you to think about questions like these. It also reminds you of some growing awareness as well as a lot of changes in society that have made the teaching of the social studies even more of a challenge than it was in the past. It argues that we really need to take a different approach to teaching the social studies, a *problems approach*. Finally, this chapter focuses on the goals of social studies as perceived by several important groups and how all of this relates to both constancy and change in the social studies.

CAN YOU? DO YOU?

Can you

- Tell how the social studies has changed since you were in elementary school?
- Tell how the social studies has remained the same?

Do you

- Have some understanding of what might be meant by "a problems approach" to teaching the social studies?
- Have some idea of what a teacher needs to know about the social studies?
- Think of the social studies simply as history and geography?
- Know what the goals of the social studies should be?

CHANGE IN THE SOCIAL STUDIES

Elementary social studies has to be different today. Children's lives have changed in the last few decades. Even the problems that children face are different. To mention only a few of the differences, there has been a constant increase in the period in the number of latch key children, in child abuse, in divorce in families with children, in domestic violence, in gangs, in the use of drugs and other substance abuse among children, in the number of single parent homes, and in crimes involving juveniles, and in reported child abuse (Frost, 1986). Though less negative, there have been changes that influence children's present and future lives in other ways. There has been a dynamic, complex revolution in technology, information, and communication. There have been major shifts in society including sweeping changes related to sex roles and ethnic and cultural relationships. There have also been major changes in the governmental and economic make up of American and world society.

In a world in which change has become the norm and we have to constantly face dilemmas for which there is no precedent, the social studies needs more than ever to help children learn to deal with problems. Teachers need to take a problems approach. Though the word problems may be defined in many ways, we are going to use it to mean any task or situation for which a solution is required or desired and for which a method of solution is not provided or immediately apparent. But problem solving is more than the situation itself. Often problems involve moral dilemmas or difficulties, dangers, or curiosities for which there is no verifiable solution. Problems require that existing knowledge be retrieved and used to resolve new or different difficulties. Most importantly, intrinsic to problem solving is the ability to deal with failure and with the inability to identify easy or quick solutions in constructive ways.

Problem-solving ability is, perhaps, the most pervasive of skills from a curricular standpoint and the one skill most needed throughout life. Almost all of the situations we face as a society and nearly all of the decisions demanding personal events may be best described as problems. If children (and teachers) can develop the requisite mindset, attitudes, and skills of problem solvers, they are equipped to meet the future. If they do not, their education becomes obsolete almost before it is complete. Problem-solving ability is the essential skill for each of the disciplines. That is, a person with a problem solving mind set will be a more successful student. This is one ability that teachers need to emphasize if ever children are to become independent learners. Problem-solving ability is also the essential survival skill for school. Each teacher, each class, each other student, each school day, each assignment presents a unique intricacy of circumstances and demands. It would not be an overstatement to say that the essential life role is problem-solving.

OBSERVING THE PROBLENS APPROACH IN OPERATION
IN A PRIMARY CLASSROOM

The primary teacher who uses the problems approach is going to be constantly asking questions, trying to arouse curiosity, and having the children make decisions. The teacher will be encouraging children's questions and helping them to find ways of seeking answers. The entire environment of the classroom becomes fixed on learning how to learn. Children's awareness of problems and their ability to generate alternative solutions is heightened in this kind of environment.

Perhaps the best way to look at how the problems approach works is to look at how one primary teacher used this approach as she entered into a study of community. The teacher started her first graders into their study of the community by reading Dr. Seuss's *Horton Hears a Who*. She soon had them thinking and talking about the perils and dangers faced by the people of the tiny world in the story. The point of the story, of course, is that everybody in a community needs to work together to solve the problems, and of course these children thought themselves very clever when they figured it out.

The teacher would not let them rest on that, though. Soon she had them talking about how we come to recognize problems and different ways that the "Whos" could have solved their problem once they discovered it. One of the questions that she asked was how different television characters might have solved the problem. (Both cartoon characters and prime time heroes were suggested). She also got them thinking about how important they were in their own community and how they could not help unless they knew more about their community and its own particular dangers and problems.

The next day, the teacher took the children on a walking field trip of their community. They went only a few blocks, but as they went they began looking for different problems in the own community. Sometimes the teacher had to make suggestions and probe with questions, but always, she let the children decide if something was a problem. When they got back to the classroom they began making a list of the problems they had seen. The list included some things that were dangers and some others that just seemed to give people difficulties. Different types of garbage and litter were among the most common things that the children noticed, but the teacher tried to shift their attention to other kinds of problems. This all started to sound somewhat negative, so they also started making a list of the good things they knew about or had seen in their community.

That day the children went home with the assignment of asking their parents and others about problems in their community as well as what the adults liked about the community. The next day, in school, the children added to their lists, taking a little time to talk about the ideas that were brought in. The teacher put all the ideas on large pieces of paper, but she had left lots of room. When the list was finished she passed out scissors and old magazines and newspapers. The children worked in pairs, each pair trying to find a picture that showed one of the ideas. If they could not find a magazine picture that they thought was appropriate, the teacher encouraged the children to draw a picture. (The pictures later helped serve as reminders to these mostly nonreading children of what each sentence said.)

Later, the children built a box community on a large table. They got to decide what went into a community like theirs and to design their own buildings. The teacher and a parent volunteer helped them label their buildings. One of the questions they had been asking was, 'Why was there so much litter in the community?' To help them understand, the teacher covered the completed scene with a tablecloth. Each day for a week, every child put a single small piece of scrap paper under the tablecloth. When they removed the cover, everyone was surprised at how much trash had accumulated on the streets of their community.

The box community was used to study other community problems as well. The children had tried to follow the layout of their own community in designing it. Therefore, they were able to look at such problems as traffic congestion, and sidewalk hazards through their own model.

Soon the children decided that they needed a map of the community they began making one. The teacher started them thinking about the problems of making a map; for example, things like accuracy, relative size, symbols, and orientation.

There was a natural flow in every transition. Each situation led to a new set of questions and curiosities. Though there were some places where some children seemed to be lost for a few minutes, most often due to a lack of verbal memory, the presence of the problems was so pervasive that attention was never lost for long. The children kept wanting to be back with "the program."

OBSERVING THE PROBLEMS APPROACH IN OPERATION IN AN INTERMEDIATE CLASSROOM

In the intermediate classroom, the focus is shifting toward independence. Students can deal with problems and content that are much more distant and removed from their own experience. These students need to be more involved in the systematic development of questions and problems. Because they have more skills, knowledge, and experience, the students can be involved in a greater variety of research activities. They are more peer oriented and less teacher oriented, so group problem solving can be structured into the activities. The emphasis remains on an environment where curiosity is encouraged and stimulated. The teacher in such an environment is going to be constantly leading children to events and ideas that will set them thinking. The student in this setting is going to be "on the learn."

Looking again at a particular classroom, this time we will focus on an upper intermediate grade teacher who has launched into a study of the medieval period in European history. The teacher began by trying to get the students to systematically examine their existing concepts of the period. They talked about movies such as *Robin Hood, Prince of Thieves* as well as some things that had been picked up from cartoons, comic books, and games. Some of the children also had some knowledge that came from children's literature. There was as much, if not more, fantasy as reality in what they knew.

At about this time, the class was surprised by a visit from two people in medieval clothing. One of these men told the children that he was an architect and that he was involved in designing and building castles. The other man said that he was a knight. The men described a situation they were involved in on the coast of England near the Welsh border. King Edward had sent them there to build a castle. Now they had to decide exactly where to build it, but it was not all that easy. While the men were in the classroom, they talked with the children about the reasons for castle building, about all the problems that might be involved, and about the rudiments of castle defense.

By the time the men left, an idea had evolved. Soon the children had developed a hypothetical map of what the region would be like. At the teacher's insistence the map was quite large. In addition, the children were urged to orient their map to some real area on the English coast. The map itself was not altogether fiction because the children did some reading about the geography and geology of the area. The completed map showed a seacoast, the Welsh border, three villages for which the children made up names, and a monastery. It also showed a river, some fens or swampy land, a forest area, and a few roads. Other features were added as the children continued to read and discuss. They learned something about feudal land division and tried to reflect it in the map. Other landmarks, including a ruined castle and some churches, were added. The villages themselves began to take on detail and show differences in size and complexity. As the children researched, they decided that there had to be a feudal manor or two in the area with some kind of fortifications; these were added.

The people came last. The children's research began to reveal the different roles and social statuses that the various people at the monastery and in the villages would have had in all likelihood. The class developed a set of characters, each of whom they tried to describe in some detail. They gave them names and described where they lived, what they did and how they did it, how they dressed, and what their lives were like. They were particularly fascinated by the diet of the common people during this period. The study of daily life, clothing, and customs evolved through group work over about a week.

The students then drew names so that each could "become" one of the characters. Once more in groups, this time according to where they "lived," they continued researching their character. The groups also began talking about where they wanted the king's castle to be built. They looked into the dangers and fears that faced the lives of the people of this period.

Nearly three weeks after their first visit the two medieval men returned. For this visit, the children had planned and wore costumes of their own and the questions were almost unstoppable. The children eagerly told the visitors what they had been doing. Then each group made a presentation in which they introduced themselves in their medieval roles. The groups each made a case for one particular site for the king's castle. Some of the groups, especially the one representing the monastery, did not want the castle built right in their area. Others had noticed not only the protection that the castle offered, but the commercial possibilities that a garrison of soldiers would have for the nearest town. When the groups were finished, the architect and the knight explained where they thought the king's castle should be built. Most importantly, they showed that they had listened to the children's reasoning as they presented their own case.

This was the beginning rather than the end. The study went on into the actual building of the castle and to several follow up activities. However, this beginning had laid a foundation of interest and reason to research on which the teacher could continue to build. While the children were creating a scenario and story line as well as a setting of their own, nearly every major theme and concept of medieval life was explored.

GOALS OF THE SOCIAL STUDIES

What do you need to know about the social studies? The answer probably seems to be more than you do know or can learn. It is certainly more than you will be able to get from any textbook. As a teacher, you owe it to the generations of children that you teach to become mindfully, curiously, purposefully alive to them, to their world, to history as a thick endless blanket of stories about people and events, and to the values and rules needed for people to live together. So the real answer to the question, "What do you need to know about the social studies?" is, "As much as you can learn about history, geography, political science, sociology, anthropology, economics, psychology and, yes, about religion, too.

Social studies in the elementary school has most often been regarded as an area that should be taught, but only if there were time. Priority time in the school day, of course, has to be given to the basic skill areas of reading, mathematics, and language. It has not been that the social studies is considered unimportant, but that the basic skill areas are seen by society, by administrators, and by elementary teachers as "basics" or "fundamentals" that have to be learned first. Important as language and mathematics skills may be, they are taught only because the children will need them to live in the social world. The Back to Basics years of the 1970s and early 1980s had a strong adverse influence on elementary social studies. Separate studies by Gross (1977) and Hahn (1977) affirmed that the social studies was disappearing in the early grades. If anything, that trend continues in the presence of the whole-language movement (Goodlad 1984, Hahn 1985). Many would argue that the social studies is, after all, embedded in curriculum. This curriculum involves an emphasis on reading stories, poems, and plays, all of which have extensive social studies content. Then too, the school day itself consists of a rich and complex series of social situations and problems, ranging from homeroom to recess to lunchroom to school bus. Social studies specialists would argue that the focus in these programs is still largely on skill and that language, not social development, is the focus.

Educators and politicians may soon have to wake up to the fact that the social studies is basic and fundamental in the earliest schooling. Educational reform has not had any real impact on achievement in the basic skill areas and schools have about run out of time to take from other areas. Children simply are not likely to improve their learning attitudes. There simply has to be more attention given to help children learn about themselves and their place in and responsibility to society. The National Council for the Social Studies Task Force on Early Childhood/Elementary Social Studies (1989) has described a major purpose for the social studies as equipping children with "the knowledge and understanding of the past necessary for coping with the present and planning for the future..." The Task Force went on to say that the social studies enables children to "participate in their world" by helping them understand their relationship to other people and to social, economic, and political institutions.

Put another way, the two primary jobs of schools are to help the society by producing effective, contributing citizens and to help the children lead happy lives in which they are enabled to achieve their potential. That is what the social studies is all about, and it is also why it is so needed in the elementary school.

Though social studies specialists disagree as to priorities, the following list identifies those purposes that are most often associated with social studies programs:

- _____ Preparing responsible citizens for the nation, the state, and the local area.

- _____ Preparing students for college.

- _____ Developing awareness and understanding of contemporary social issues.

- _____ Developing healthy self concepts.

- _____ Teaching the methods of social scientists.

- _____ Motivating students to want to learn about the social studies.
- _____ Developing the ability to solve problems and make decisions.
- _____ Developing "global" citizens with a world vision.

Whatever we do as teachers is certainly done for the present, but it has to be done with an eye to the future.

In trying to help you become good social studies teachers, or good teachers of anything for that matter, it is important to get you to look at what happens if you succeed as teachers. The children you teach will, in due course, become adults themselves. They will obviously be living in a different kind of society, one that teachers must try to anticipate and prepare them for. But, beyond that, the kind of impact that teachers will have had on them and the kind of people they become are critical outcomes of education. Following are just a few of the areas where we, as teachers of elementary social studies, will have had an impact when the children we teach become adults:

- The jobs they have and the way they do their jobs
- The way they feel about themselves
- The way they handle responsibility
- The way they treat other people
- How they meet and resolve problems and difficulties
- Their motivation and overall attitudes
- What they value and how they treat the things they value
- How they relate to their heritage
- How they relate to their environment.
- How they relate to and deal with people of other cultures, nationalities, and ethnic groups.

In each of these and in other areas where teachers influence children, I think that it is safe to say that most of us would happily accept a broad variety of outcomes and still feel that we had been a positive force. The question is, "Just how much in each area can we expect of ourselves?" That is not a question that can be left unanswered. I like the analogy of putting together a jigsaw puzzle. It is always easier to do if we have a picture of what it is going to look like when we get it all together. The same holds true for teaching. From an attitudinal standpoint, I have always found it useful to envision my students 10 or 15 years into the future, and imagine them in the most positive light I can. It gives me an idea of what I am working for.

Goals and objectives should be the first and most important concerns of any teacher, especially any social studies teacher. They complement one another. Goals are distant, unmeasurable, and even unattainable. They give direction to our efforts and, if we are goal oriented and goal driven, we constantly work toward them, yet never reach a point when they are achieved. How can one reach the goal of becoming an effective problem solver, for example, or the even broader goal of being a good citizen? The essence of goals is that they describe the person we are constantly in the process of becoming (Moore 1989).

Objectives, on the other hand are short term, attainable, often measurable, and very specific. We can know when we achieve them, so they become for us milestones and markers of our progress. Goals determine the directions we want to go, but the accomplishment of objectives lets us know that we are getting there.

In education, we generally begin planning by defining our goals. Once goals are set, we try to describe the specific teaching and learning outcomes for short periods of instruction that will move students toward the goals. Goals without objectives remain as only dreams. Objectives without relationship to goals are purposeless. Objectives for the social studies tend to be decided on the basis of the specific content being taught and the group to which it is being taught. (Social studies objectives will be discussed in more detail in Chapter 2.) The broadest goals for the field have been centrally determined and defined in the United States by various groups, given authority by still larger organizations. Regardless of the group, throughout this century social studies has invariably linked to goals of citizenship education. (Jarolimek 1981, 4) The frameworks developed in the reports of the various commissions, task forces, and committees have served as models for textbook curricula and for those developed for state and local school districts.

Among the most recent of these reports, three will probably influence the direction of elementary school social studies in the 1990's and on into the twenty-first century. These are the National Council for the Social Studies Task Force on Scope and Sequence (1984), The National Council for the Social Studies Task Force on Early Childhood/Elementary Social Studies(1989), and the Curriculum Task Force of the National Commission on Social Studies in the School (1989).

The introductory, summarizing statement of the goals section of the report of the NCSS Task Force on Scope and Sequence set a problem solving focus for the social studies and emphasized thinking skills. The Task Force said, "Social studies programs have a responsibility to prepare young people to identify, understand, and work to solve problems that face our increasingly diverse nation and interdependent world." (NCSS Task Force 1984, 251). The report went on to say that the social studies derives its goals from the nature of citizenship and then organized those goals into the broad categories of knowledge, democratic values and beliefs and skills.

The NCSS Task Force on Early Childhood/Elementary Social Studies (1989) echoed much of the same tone and similar organization in its report.

The goals focused on cooperative problem solving, claiming that basic skills in reading, writing, and computing were necessary but not sufficient if children are to survive in today's world. Critical thinking and the development of positive attitudes toward self and others were given priority in this report.

The Task Force of the National Commission on the Social Studies was funded by the Carnegie Foundation, the Rockefeller Foundation, the MacArthur Foundation, and the National Geographic Society. It enjoyed the sponsorship of the National Council for the Social Studies and the American Historical Association. Over two years in preparation, the Task Force's report, titled *Charting a Course: Social Studies for the 21st Century* (1989), formulated the following goals that the social studies curriculum should enable students to develop:

1. Civic responsibility and active civic participation

2. Perspectives on their own life experiences so they see themselves as part of the larger human adventure in time and place

3. A critical understanding of the history, geography, economic, political, and social institutions, traditions, and values of the United States as expressed in both their unity and diversity

4. An understanding of other peoples and of the unity and diversity of world history, geography institutions, traditions, and values

5. Critical attitudes and analytical perspectives appropriate to analysis of the human condition

LOOKING BACK

Social studies has been throughout most of the last half of the twentieth century and will continue to be into the twenty-first century reformist in nature; that is the curriculum has been and will be in flux. This is due, in part, due to the constant changes in the social world.

The one educational need that remains constant in a world of change in that children need to learn how to solve problems. When teachers take a problems approach in social studies they work at enabling students to deal with situations where their experience and knowledge offer no ready answers. Problem solving is, perhaps, the most pervasive of all skills.

In spite of growing concern that the social studies may be disappearing at least from primary classrooms, the two main jobs of the school continue to be producing effective, contributing citizens and helping children lead happy lives. Social studies programs have a variety of purposes which relate to these two jobs. Among the most important of these is preparing students to be responsible, aware of contemporary issues, to have a world vision. In some cases, elementary social studies teachers have to be concerned about preparing students for college and even for careers in the social sciences. If they are to be successful at all, though, teachers must develop both the love of learning and the ability to solve problems.

Goals and objectives should be major concerns of teachers of the social studies. Goals are distant and unattainable, but they give direction to teaching. Objectives, on the other hand, are short term and obtainable. Objectives are the building blocks toward goals.

The National Council for the Social Studies, as the organization of teachers most concerned with social education, has constantly examined and reexamined the goals of the social studies. Recent task forces of that organization have particularly emphasized problem solving and thinking skills.

SELF-TEST

1. How would you characterize the problems approach to the social studies?

2. Why was the map-creation exercise so critical in the class where they were studying medieval history?

3. In what areas are teachers of the social studies going to have impact?

4. In what ways did the two task force groups referred to in the chapter stress the role of thinking skills in the social studies?

REFERENCES

Geisel, T. (1954). *Horton Hears a Who*. New York: Putnam, 1954.

Goodlad, J. (1984). *A Place Called School*. New York: McGraw-Hill.Frost, J.L. (1986). Children in changing society: frontiers of challenge. *Childhood Education*, 62 (March/April), 242–249.

Gross, R.E. (1977). The status of the social studies in the public schools of the Unites States. *Social Education*, 41 (November/December), 194–200,205.

Hahn, C.W. (1977). Research in the diffusion of social studies innovations. In Hunkins, F.P. (ed.), *Review of research in social studies education: 1970–75*. Washington, D.C.

National Council for the Social Studies, and Boulder, Colo.: ERIC Clearing House for Social Studies/Social Science Education Consortium, pp. 137–177.

Hahn, C. W. (1985). The status of the social studies in the public schools of the United States: another look. *Social Education*, 49 (January), 220–223.

Jarolimek, J.J. (1990). *Social studies in elementary education.* New York: MacMillan.

Moore, C. et al. (1989). Mental terms and the development of certainty. *Child Development*, 60 (February), 167–171.

NCSS Task Force on Early Childhood/ Elementary Social Studies (1989). Social studies for early childhood and elementary school children—preparing for the 21st Century. *Social Education*, 53 (January), 14–23.

NCSS Task Force on Scope and Sequence (1984). In search of a scope and sequence in the social studies. *Social Education*, 48 (April), 249–262.

Task Force of the National Commission on the Social Studies in the Schools (1989). *Charting a course: social studies for the 21st century.* Washington, D.C.: The National Commission on the Social Studies in the Schools.

SUGGESTED READING

Barr, R.D., Barth, J.L., and Shermis, S.S. (1977) *Defining the Social Studies, Bulletin 51.* Washington, D.C.: The National Council for the Social Studies.

Edelman, M.W. (1992). The challenges of the 90's: saving our children. *Social Education*, 56 (April/May), 240–243.

Longstreet, W. (1989). Education for citizenship: new dimensions. *Social Education*, 53 (January), 41–45.

Onosoko, J.J. (1992) An approach to designing thoughtful units. *The Social Studies*, 83 (September/October), 193–196.

2 Making Plans to Teach

LOOKING AHEAD

The purpose of this chapter is to help you become a better planner. Therefore, attention is given to identifying the problems of planning teaching and the structure of particular social studies teaching plans. Questions to consider as you read include the following:

- What are my strengths and weaknesses as a planner?

- What do I need to be able to do in order to plan a teaching unit?

- Am I likely to need to rely heavily on a textbook?

- What purposes do other teaching plans serve?

As in other subjects, good planning is a necessary, but not sufficient ingredient of good teaching in the social studies. In other words, good teachers are good planners, even though it does not follow that the most thorough, imaginative focused planning automatically makes anyone an effective teacher. Obviously, there is more to it than that. If you are not convinced, imagine a teacher who does not plan at all. Such a teacher has no sense of what is to go on in the classroom and quickly loses all efficacy and impact. Fortunately, few teachers fit that description, but many are just a step removed. Too often, teaching plans consist of cryptic notes in lesson-plan books referring to pages in the textbook. These kinds of plans can hardly lead to exciting, creative classrooms.

CAN YOU? DO YOU?

Can you

- Plan an instructional unit?

- Identify and describe different types of units? Write objectives?

- Establish "set" in a lesson?

- Identify the steps in a case study?

Do you

- Have experiences in collaborative planning?
- Know how to go about choosing a unit topic?
- Know how much freedom teachers have about what they teach?
- Know what is meant by the term *webbing* when referring to planning?
- Have an understanding of the concept of instructional objectives?

FOCUS ACTIVITY

Before reading this chapter, you might try this activity as a class.

SOCIAL STUDIES PLANNING: PEOPLE SCAVENGE

You may remember going on a scavenger hunt as a youngster. You were given a list of often strange items to bring back. Probably you competed in teams within a time limit. A *people scavenge* is very similar to the familiar scavenger hunt. The major differences are that (1) instead of objects, you are searching for people with certain experiences or knowledge; and (2) the whole activity is done in the classroom.

Following are fules for people scavenge:

1. Your job is to get the initials of someone in each blank on the list that follows. You find out who has the knowledge or experience named simply by asking questions of each classmate.

2. Everyone in the classroom (including yourself) is eligible, but you can use each person for only two items.

   - _____ Can define *social studies* in 25 words or less
   - _____ Has a social studies topic that they have studied as a hobby
   - _____ Knows the difference between a goal and an objective
   - _____ Can tell the difference between a teacher activity and a lesson
   - _____ Can name the largest teacher aggravation of social studies teachers
   - _____ Has made a lesson plan and taught from it
   - _____ Knows what a unit is
   - _____ Can name 5 social sciences
   - _____ Has looked through at least one copy of a journal for social studies teachers

- _____ Knows the names of 5 journals or magazines for teachers
- _____ Has helped a teacher prepare a unit
- _____ Can give three reasons for planning what you teach
- _____ Can remember 3 social studies units from his or her own elementary school days
- _____ Has been to at least one conference meeting for teachers
- _____ Can name 2 publishers who publish a series of social studies textbooks
- _____ Can give 3 excuses teachers might have for not spending enough time planning
- _____ Can tell the difference between a resource unit and a teaching unit
- _____ Has observed a social studies lesson being taught in the last year
- _____ Knows the difference between a fact and a concept
- _____ Has ever had to make a choice about a topic to teach

After the instructor ends the search, discuss the list. This people scavenge technique can also be used with elementary school children with almost any topic as (1) an icebreaker, (2) a way of assessing readiness or background on a topic, or (3) a way of grouping.

FINDING FOCUS AS YOU READ

Why Is Planning Important?

Planning has special importance in broad areas like the social studies where there is so much information. Because of the breadth of the field, teachers cannot know enough to teach social studies without some help from a number of resources. One of the major elements in good planning is finding and collecting those resources and organizing them in a purposeful way.

Except for kindergarten and perhaps first grade teachers, the starting point for planning will most likely be a textbook. Additional guidance and direction may come from a curriculum guide provided by the school district (Woodward, Elliott and Nage 1986). New teachers may also obtain help from a mentor teacher in some areas. A team leader, a department chair, or an entire group of grade level colleagues may also have input. Because state governments are legally responsible for the schools there may also be state guidelines, rules, regulations regarding what is taught.

National teacher organizations may also provide input about what goes on in the social studies. (NCSS, the Association for Supervision and Curriculum Development, and the National Education Association are among the largest of these organizations. The NCSS alone publishes two useful journals, *Social Education* and *Social Studies and the Young Learner*.)

One problem with all these resources, and, remember, these are only the beginning points, is that they tend to create a wall of print that only further confuses new teachers. Novices then retreat to the safety of that first one, the textbook. Staying strictly with the text becomes their pattern and that is where they may stay for the rest of their careers. It is a natural thing to do. It lessens the thinking involved, and leaves the difficult decisions of planning to the so called experts.

There are a few reasons why reliance on textbooks is not the best course. (1) Following this route means that the teacher, the social studies, and the classroom are not likely to be very exciting, interesting, or enjoyable for the children. If the whole point of schooling is to make independent learners, and I think that it is, this is surely the last kind of atmosphere one would want to create. (2) "Read and answer the question" social studies, which is the type of teaching the textbook approach is likely to produce, is not likely to be very meaningful or seem very purposeful to students. Almost a corollary to reason #1, not only are they not going to enjoy it, they are not going to learn from it or understand why they are doing it. 3) There is little teacher satisfaction gained from such an approach. In fact it is boring and unrewarding to teach that way. No wonder teacher burn-out has become a national epidemic in our schools (Walsh 1979).

SETTING THE STAGE: CREATING THE ENVIRONMENT

Let us suppose that you are going to avoid the textbook pitfall. How do you begin to plan? Curiously, both the planning process and the actual planning product that flows out of this process involve a good deal of scene setting. Doing social studies in the classroom is almost like doing theater. We are trying to create a dramatic climate, one with just the right tension and sufficient excitement for learning to occur. With effective planning in the social studies, that climate is there and it can be identified by some predictable hallmarks (Brophy and Good 1978).

These include

1. A sense of anticipation or expectancy on the part of the student audience: They know that something special is going to happen and they have a fairly good idea of what it is, with just enough uncertainty for the sake of anticipation and suspense.

2. A feeling of purpose and direction: Students know why they are there and what the class is all about.

3. An awareness that is more than knowledge of continuity" What is done today relates to yesterday as well as to tomorrow. Not only are there connections that give lots of satisfied "Aha!" moments, but there is a wholism that in itself adds to the meaning.

4. An atmosphere of involvement or participation in the planning process itself and how the plans flow into the doing: There is a sense of community or even family that acknowledges that "we are in this together."

5. An awareness of leadership: To a degree, this seals off or at least pulls the reins to control conflict and it keeps a sense of urgency allowing flexibility but keeps at the job.

HOW EFFECTIVE PLANNING BREAKS DOWN

It may seem negative to approach planning from a "why don't teachers do it?" perspective, but it may be important to look at some of the reasons for not planning effectively. This may be helpful when we examine some of the planning tools that are used in the social studies. First, we have to recognize that we must deal as much with teachers' perceptions of reasons. In fact, their feelings may be more the reasons themselves. There is a growing belief that time management is an area in which simply understanding the problems and deterrents may help the teacher in overcoming them. Here, then, are a number of reasonable conclusions about the factors involved in teachers' failure to plan.

1. Not enough time: Teachers have crowded days often filled with unavoidable trivialities, both planned and unplanned. Clerical tasks, children demanding attention, classroom accidents, discipline situations, paper grading, and many others compete to more than fill every minute.

   "Not enough time" could really be used as reasons one through five why teachers do not plan sufficiently. Most teachers will cite that as the major reason they do not spend more time planning and may be very defensive about it.

2. Failure to set time priorities or give priority to planning: Because teaching is time intensive, teachers to be very careful to choose what they do and do not give priority time use. I become involved with what I like to call "time traps." There are legitimate activities to which I find myself giving more and more time. One of these is grading papers. If I am not careful, I find myself drifting toward spending more and more time outside of class grading papers. When grading cuts into planning, something is wrong.

3. Depending on previous material: Once teachers have taught a topic a few times, they begin to accumulate a quantity of "stuff that works."

There are obvious advantages to this and the old adage, "if it isn't broken, don't fix it," comes to mind. But there are also dangers, including creeping staleness and a tendency to get behind the times. There is a strong likelihood that the teacher will get tired of the material or will spend insufficient time reviewing it and planning a fresh approach.

4. Procrastination: For some of us, the whole problem is reduced to being slow about getting around to things. Then there is simply not enough lead time to do the preparation or obtain the needed materials.

5. Failure to communicate: There is a cooperative element even in teacher planning. Good planning means letting involved people (parents, resource people, school officials, other teachers, etc.) know what they need to know and what they need to do in advance. If there is no clear understanding on the part of the people who may help in the preparation, the planning process breaks down.

6. Experience: Experience itself may stand in the way of effective planning. Teachers can develop patterns and habits very quickly that are counterproductive, and these may persist and transfer. The way we do one thing may be because of the way we did something else or because of the way we have always done things. Bad habits are easier to make and more difficult to break than good ones.

7. Lack of interest or enthusiasm or content fear: Some individuals will say that they do not like the social studies. They may even relate a terror of history and geography classes they had to take in college. Because good preparation involves immersion in content, this can present a real problem. If they teach the content at all, they are likely to communicate their own fear or dislike of it. They are also likely to repeat the kind of negative, unprepared teaching that turned them against the subject.

8. Low energy: Many teachers say that they just do not have the energy, psychological or physical, to plan. Planning does take drive and excitement, and these people claim that teaching drains them leaving nothing left over to put into getting prepared.

9. Inability to deal with peer pressure: Teachers want to be approved of and liked by other teachers. To gain approval they try to act in ways that the old timers approve. They model their behavior on experienced teachers. They try to follow their advice. When older teachers tell them that things that they learned in college were idealistic and have nothing to do with the real world, they nod their heads and act accordingly. The impact of all this on planning is that the new teacher runs the gauntlet of bad models, bad advice and fear of being rude or being ridiculed and is likely to form bad planning habits as a result.

There are no easy ways to deal with all these forces that work against planning. Obviously, self-discipline and a firm sense of purpose are what teachers need. There are also some strategies that teachers can use to improve their planning habits and skills. Not all of the following suggestions will work for everybody, but they are worth a try.

1. Budget your time, and that includes scheduling planning time and sticking to the schedule as though a planning time were a meeting with the president.

2. Make lists of planning jobs and prioritize the lists.

3. Examine and change your patterns of behavior. Little things make big differences. Whose room you walk past or when you arrive and leave school or how you avoid and don't avoid distractions can add or subtract significant amounts of planning time.

4. Do the "worst first," meaning complete that which you most dread and want to put off *before* you do the easier or more satisfying things.

5. Learn to be rude politely and without feeling guilt, turning off and away those who would interrupt your planning time.

6. Record and celebrate your planning successes in ways that you can remember and then repeat. (If it works, make sure you can do it again.)

TYPES OF PLANNING FOR INSTRUCTIONAL UNITS: WHY SOME UNITS ARE ESPECIALLY SUITED FOR SOCIAL STUDIES INSTRUCTION?

As I said earlier, textbook teaching is an easy pattern to set and be stuck with. One reason is that nearly all teachers had to do some of it. There are good reasons for this.

Textbook Units

Social studies textbook series are structured into units covered by single chapters or, occasionally, series of two or more chapters. Teachers' editions provide such material as vocabulary lists, activity ideas, day-by-day lesson plans, and even lists of additional resources. Publishers may also make available numerous supplementary materials including such items as blackline masters from which student handouts can be made, posters, maps, and charts.

Teachers who rely heavily on the textbook for at least part of their social studies program need to be especially concerned about purposeful teaching. A regimen of careful planning can help reduce, if not totally avoid the pitfalls usually associated with textbook teaching. The following steps might be considered by the less experienced teacher:

1. Try to get the big picture. Find out what the goals of the textbook program are and how it is organized.

2. Think about the calendar for the school year in terms of the amount of time you want to give to the various units in the program. As you do this, be sure to consider unequal treatment (giving more time to some topics than others) and to omitting some topics.

3. For each unit, use the teachers' edition guide materials judiciously to plan activities to introduce the topic and then to help students achieve the objectives and reach a holistic understanding of the topic.

4. Maintain a high level of sensitivity to reading difficulties students may encounter and be ready to adjust instruction (There will be more about avoiding and helping with reading problems in Chapters 3 and 4).

5. Enrich the textbook's suggestions with supplemental activities. Try to establish a balance of new versus repeated instructional activities from chapter to chapter. This gives students both the security of being able to learn a set of expectations about how to do things and the motivational freshness of activity variety.

6. Examine and use evaluation materials provided by the text, but only after seeing their relationship to the teaching objectives. This usually means that you see what information, concepts, and basic skills are being tested. Make sure these do not have errors. (For example, it is worth the time to do tests yourself first, just to see if the answers *are* there.)

Collaborative Units

In many school districts, teachers work in teams to prepare units. The arrangements for doing this vary. In some cases, there are structured formal efforts across entire school districts by appointed groups of teachers. Another formal arrangement may involve a head or coordinating teacher or a mentor teacher relationship in a single school. There also may be both formal and informal teaming of teachers in a grade level.

The kind of units produced and the ways that teachers are expected to use them display almost as much variety. In most instances, the intent is to combine talents and save individual teachers planning time while producing some consistency throughout the school or system in the content that is taught. The units may in some instances even be developed to ensure that all teachers will be following some preplanned course of action. It is more likely then that such efforts will produce resource units which can be shared among teachers. Resource units systematically delineate common objectives, identify the most appropriate and useful available resources for teacher and student use, and create and share plans for activities (teaching strategies). Resource units may also plan out tests and other evaluation procedures.

In some instances, units that are planned by collaborative effort may be regarded as teaching units. These will have specific activity or lesson plans with few, if any, alternatives. Teachers may be expected to follow such units entirely, or they may have the option of doing the prescribed lessons or developing their own plans.

Teachers moving into a grade level and school where such collaborative units are used may want to consider the following as guidelines:

1. Find out what degree of conformity and collaboration is expected from you as well as the extent to which you are expected to use units already prepared. At this step and all others it is good to establish an advice seeking relationship with a mentor teacher or the lead teacher if possible. (At the same, time you can find out how much creativity is encouraged.)

2. Become familiar with available units, paying particular attention to the goals and objectives. (Make sure that you understand and follow the pattern of intent.)

3. See how the collaborative units relate to the textbooks that are in the classroom (if there are any).

4. Browse through the activities looking for the overall motivational and teaching quality as well as particular outstanding ideas and plans.

5. Look for ways to augment, embellish, and improve the activities and lessons in the existing collaborative plans.

6. If the school allows, plan alternative activities and lessons to substitute for those that you see to be weaker.

7. Work through and implement the plans provided. Keep an open mind, but review effectiveness and possible alternatives.

On Teacher-Developed Units: Why and When

The word *unit* is used with a lot of different meanings. Basically, a unit includes everything a class does to learn about a particular topic. What unifies the study or makes it a unit is the topic itself, whether it is a general category (such as Transportation), a concept (such as Democracy), a time period or event such (such as The Age of Exploration), or a question (such as, What can be done to reduce pollution?). When we talk about units in teaching, we are usually talking about the teaching plan for that topic. Such plans vary in length, in amount of detail, and even in their source of creation. A unit may attempt to plan for a week or for six weeks of work. Some people think that children ought to learn more about each topic they do study, while others are convinced that we need to cover more topics. For most teachers a unit plan will be for three to four weeks, but early primary units tend to be for shorter periods.

A pressing question at any level of experience is when and how should teachers develop their own teaching units. The prevailing pattern, especially in the upper grades, is to stick to the textbook partially because beginning teachers have the feeling that this is what they are supposed to do and partly because this route is secure and easy. Textbook teaching is an easy pattern to set and be stuck with. Nearly all teachers, pressured with too much to do and too little time, find it absolutely necessary to use textbook units or some other pre-prepared instructional plans.

As a rule of thumb, I think that teachers should, if they have the option, develop at least one new unit of their own every school year. I believe that teaching is a creative profession and that creative teachers will want to be constantly developing new ideas themselves. However, given the amount of time required to find, adapt, and develop resources, one new unit is probably all that any teacher can do well. Of course, this does not mean that there cannot be constant additions, adaptations, and alterations to existing units. The unit developed in any particular year would depend on such factors as (1) current teacher interests and concerns, (2) calendar events occurring in particular years, (3) materials that the teacher discovers, (4) major perceived weaknesses and gaps in the units available, and (5) current interests of children.

Teacher-made units may take practically any form, but whatever form they take is almost certainly going to mean more work for the teacher than simply following a prepared unit plan. Why do them then? Well, if the answer is not that planning such units will mean better teaching, then they are not worth the effort. However, there are several arguments supporting the view that teacher-made units are worth the effort. First, there is the contention that the teacher can plan them to fit particular needs and abilities of a particular class. Teacher-made units can take into account resources that are the teacher's personal possessions as well as those that may be part of an individual teacher's classroom collection. Such units can also reflect a teacher's individual abilities, talents, personality, and teaching style. Most important, perhaps, is the argument that planning a teaching unit can be creatively and personally satisfying. It can provide teachers with that sense of accomplishment that is so important for retaining a positive attitude and avoiding burnout in any profession, most especially one like teaching.

Individual teaching units have the tailor-made quality of being uniquely suited to achieving what the teacher thinks to be most important in the very ways that seem most suitable for the people most directly involved.

DECIDING ON UNIT TOPICS

There may be as many as three options open to teachers who want to plan their own units or at least some of them. The teacher may go to a set of curriculum guidelines or to a curriculum guide where a course of study is outlined. In some instances, teachers are required to stick to the topics described in such a guide but have the freedom to develop their own interests. A second option that teachers may have is to plan in conjunction with other teachers on their team (either grade level or some other configuration) so that all children are exposed to similar topics or themes the same topics or themes. The final option involves teacher-guided group planning through which interests, needs and problems identified by the children are explored.

Whether the teacher is planning the unit him or herself or helping students to plan, a similar process occurs. Sometimes a wonderful, exciting idea seems to almost jump out. The teacher or the class experiences some stimulating, motivating event that generates enthusiasm and curiosity. For example, something in the news, an event on the calendar, a happening in the neighborhood, or something someone reads or sees on television grabs attention and makes some topic seem a perfect study for the class. More often though, the teacher may be searching for a topic. For such searches< thinking seems to go through four stages: (1) coming up with some possible topics, (2) narrowing the field and finding particular focus, (3) identifying a particular topic and refining that selection into a title that adds zest and uniqueness (takes it out of the boring and mundane class), and (4) deciding on the directions and structure that studying that topic ought to take.

Obviously, the beginning teacher first needs to have an idea of what classes of things are appropriate as unit topics in social studies. It would be true, but not very helpful, to say that the range of topics almost defies description. Looking at one or several textbook series may give some idea of the types of topics that might be appropriate. This is going to provide a limited notion, at best, and probably an unimaginative one. To get a broad picture it might be suggested that, among the classes of things studied as unit topics, the following are typical: countries or groups of countries, regions, civilizations, specific places or types of places, eras, specific time periods, events or series of related events, processes, phenomena, problems, historical figures, historical developments, and issues.

To show how the evolution of selection can take place, it might be useful to take the example of a fourth-grade teacher who has already gone through part of the agony and indecision, and that is exactly what such often frustrating activity is. The first level of decision making has already been passed and the decision was to teach a unit dealing with Africa. But what about Africa? The topic is still far too broad, bland, and unfocused.

At stage one the teacher, perhaps using a few resources and even talking with others about it, comes up with a list of topics such as the following. It might be noted that there is great variation in the quality and appeal of the topics as well as in the focus.

The Many Faces of Africa

African Folk Tales

African Glories: African Civilizations of the Past

Animals and Plants of Africa

Explorers of Africa

African Ports of Call

The Gold Coast of Africa

European Colonial Empires in Africa

The Many Countries of Africa

Regions of Africa

Shaka: King of the Zulus and British Colonial Africa

Third World Countries in Africa

The Riches and Resources of Africa

Colonialism, Tribal Cultures, and National States in Africa

Leading Nations of Africa: Egypt, South Africa, and Kenya

Rain forests of Africa

Desertification of Africa

Modern Governments of Africa

Animals and Plants of Africa

Africa: Myths and Truths

Cities of Africa

South Africa and Apartheid

The Slave Trade in Africa from Earliest Times through the Founding of Liberia

Once a satisfactory list is formed the narrowing process begins (stage two). The individual topics are weighed in the balance of questions such as:

- How does this fit in with the other units that are being taught?

- How does this relate to the overall goals and purposes for the class?

- Is this something that this class might really get excited about?

- Is this broad enough (or narrow enough)? Is it too general (or too specific) in the focus it allows?

- Are the right kinds of resources available to teach this?

- How does this approach fit in with the way we are handling other topics in the class?

- How excited could I get about teaching this topic?

Through this narrowing process, our hypothetical teacher may decide that the basic emphasis that he wants is geographic as opposed to historic and that, for one reason or another, too specific a topic may limit the directions that children can go with their explorations. With these criteria in mind, he is able now to reduce the list to five or six items.

Now the teacher moves to stage three, deciding on Myths and Truths about the Dark Continent as a title. It seems provocative, creates curiosity, and yet leaves room for some of the geographic focus he wants. But it is precisely because of that openness that stage four is necessary.

Stage four involves fleshing out some sense of direction. In this case, let us assume that the teacher wants to deal with areas where children lack accurate knowledge about Africa. He must identify a series of problems such as the following:

- The belief that Africa is a country

- The belief that all Africa is jungle

- The idea that Africans are primitive savages

- Ignorance about modern African cities

- Lack of knowledge about the variety of people and products of Africa.

DEVELOPING THE UNIT PLAN

Once a focus has been found, effort can be directed at developing one of three types of units. The teacher may decide to develop his own resource unit. The kinds of work that this involves is mainly creating, collecting, gathering, and ordering materials, teaching ideas and activities, much as a team of teachers would do in developing a collaborative resource unit. One major difference is that the teacher can include personal resources that would not be available to everyone in a collaborative unit. The other two options, sketch units and teaching units, differ from one another most in the extent of development and in the amount of attention that is given to detail. Sketch units are of greatest use to teachers who are trying to form a broad overview of the teaching content, sequence and activities, and who then use the sketch unit as a basis to gather resources and do more specific planning later on. These outline plans are also useful to teachers who find it convenient to rely heavily on textual materials, but who want to have the control of doing their own basic planning.

Teaching units are more thorough and fleshed out in greater detail. They offer teachers the advantage of a plan of study that needs only calendar and success-failure adjustments as the actual teaching evolves. That is, the teacher has to do very little planning other than to make those adaptations that become necessary when teaching sequences take more or less time than planned and those where careful monitoring indicates a need for additional activities.

Whether the teacher is doing a sketch unit or a teaching unit, the next step in planning is to get some kind of clear and specific picture of the desired learning outcomes. This is going to help in at least two ways: it will give directional focus and it will help limit the scope. This targeting tells us what to teach, while, at the same time, it keeps us from the pointless and sometimes frustrating activity of trying to teach everything about often broad unit topics.

There are several ways to attack the problem. The teacher may choose to begin by developing a set of instructional objectives. Another starting place is the content itself. Some teachers prefer to start with a content outline or a content organizational chart in which a list of generalizations serves as headings. A newer idea is a kind of visual representation called a *web* which shows the interrelationships of the different concepts and/or elements to be covered in the unit. Let us examine objectives, content outlines, and webs.

INSTRUCTIONAL OBJECTIVES

At some point in planning, a teacher needs to be concerned with the learning outcomes that he or she wants to occur as a result of the instruction. Educators usually refer to these outcomes which are given special focus as objectives. A social studies centered unit will have multiple objectives. In fact, most social studies activities have several objectives in addition to much incidental learning.

Objectives are targeted gains in knowledge or skills and desired changes in affective areas like aspirations, attitudes, values, and feelings. Since they are targets, objectives need to be identified as specifically as possible. A well-stated set of objectives should give clear direction to the teacher and be of help in planning activities. Specific objectives are also helpful to teachers and students in evaluating learning. By clearly identifying what the outcomes should be, everyone can tell when they are achieved.

For this reason, many school systems insist that teachers use what are referred to as *behavioral objectives*. Behavioral objectives are even more precise. They identify specific acts that students can perform that will show that the desired learning or change has occurred. Such objectives are observable and the standard of successful achievement is identified.

Language is very important in writing behavioral objectives. Words and terms that suggest that the teacher would have to know what was going on inside a child's mind are simply unacceptable. A properly stated behavioral objective would never suggest that the child would "know" or "understand" something. Following are parallel examples of objectives. In each set, the first objective uses acceptable behavioral objective language while the second does not. It should be noted that behavioral objectives cannot be written simply by referring to some word list of strong specific action verbs. Teachers who do this may fall into the trap of focusing on trivialities or identify activities rather than desired learning outcomes. Words and phrases in isolation may be deceptive. It is the specific identification of an observable action that actually shows a learning that defines an objective as behavioral. It should also be noted that an objective can be very specific, important, and valuable for teaching, yet not be behavioral.

EXAMPLE SET 1
Behavioral: After a study of the maps of Africa, the student will be able to name five countries in Africa.

Nonbehavioral: Students will know that Africa is a continent made up of over 40 nations.

EXAMPLE SET 2
Behavioral: The student will be able to correctly identify areas of high population density on a population map.

Nonbehavioral: Students will understand how to use a population map.

EXAMPLE SET 3
Behavioral: After a study of the Middle Ages in Europe, students will be able to list three provisions of the Magna Carta.

Nonbehavioral: Students will realize the significance of the Magna Carta.

EXAMPLE SET 4
Behavioral: After studying the community and the people who work in it, the students will be able to match pictures of ten community helpers they have studied with their place of work on a pictographic map of the community.

Nonbehavioral: The students will become aware of the workplaces of community helpers.

EXAMPLE SET 5
Behavioral: Given a cup of multiple colored candies, the children will be able to correctly make a graph showing the distribution by color.

Nonbehavioral: The kindergarten children will learn to graph using one criteria.

CONTENT OUTLINES

Content outlines help the teacher determine what is most important to teach. The beginning point may be as simple as the content flowchart such as the following for a unit on Egypt. Such a flowchart not only identifies the areas of study but begins to suggest the order of the teaching itself.

Content Flow Chart

Unit Topic: Egypt

Locating Egypt

Physical Features

Cultural Sites

Current Government, Political Situation, and Events in Egypt

Historical Significance and Background

Importance of the Nile River

Ancient and Medieval Civilizations of Egypt

Such a topical flowchart offers little more than broad and general headings. The teacher will undoubtedly want to develop a much more detailed outline before proceeding further if this approach is followed. Nonetheless, as nonspecific as the flowchart may be, it begins to provide the unit with direction. Building at least a mental content flowchart of a unit is an effective way for the teacher to develop a very helpful mental picture or what might be referred to as a *cognitive map* even for textbook-centered teaching.

Those with a strong content orientation might prefer a much more detailed content outline as the beginning point for mapping a unit of studies. Others might prefer a cognitive-elements chart such as the one that follows for a unit on the Middle Ages.

Major Ideas	Essential Concepts	Synopsis Statements
The church preserved and provided unity for Europe in the Middle Ages.	Monasteries Empire Catholic Scriptorium	Following the learning destruction of the Roman Empire, Europe was in chaos. The only single unifying force was the Christian church.
The feudal system involved service and loyalty and became the dominant pattern in Europe in the Middle Ages.	Feudalism Vassals Vassalage Hierarchy Serfs Fief	The feudal system in Europe was a complex order that detailed the relationship of nobility. A noble owed service to his lord who, in turn, owed him protection. The service included both military service and a portion of what the noble produced on his land.

Major Ideas	Essential Concepts	Synopsis Statements
In the late Middle Ages, merchants, craftsmen, towns and trade grew in power and importance.	Guild System Trade Routes Apprenticeship Patronage Crusades	The growth of towns gave markets for the movement of goods. The Crusades and the travel of merchants increased trade and demand for goods and services.
"Barbarians" or non-Christians threatened and invaded Europe throughout the Middle Ages.	Barbarians Islam Moors Norsemen	From the sixth-century, Islam was a constant threat to Christian Europe. Viking sea raiders were a threat in the north, especially the ninth century
Nation states began emerge in the late Middle Ages.	Nations Nationalism	Beginning with England and France in the late twelfth-century, the power of the king or royal house grew. The power of the feudal barons diminished.

CONCEPT WEB

A more recent device that teachers can use to frame the big picture of a unit is called a web, and its appearance bears a strong resemblance to a spider's work. Basically, a web shows how the various concepts covered in a unit are linked or interrelated. Near the center of the web are the broad topics and most important ideas. Peripheral layers show the subordinate and less important ideas. Unit webs are better evolved in two stages. The first stage is simply brainstorming and choosing topics to study. The second stage arranges these topics according to priorities (importance) and relationships. Webbing is a better tool when the teacher has a comfortable familiarity with the unit topic and therefore knows the content. Because brainstorming is involved, it is a good technique to use in collaborative units or with a mentor or friend. The illustration on the next page shows a web for a unit on computers.

MOVING TOWARD THE DEVELOPMENT OF ACTIVITIES

As the teacher is building toward this mental picture of the unit, a lot of other things need to be going on simultaneously. One thing that is very important is that the teacher needs to be constantly on the look out for re-

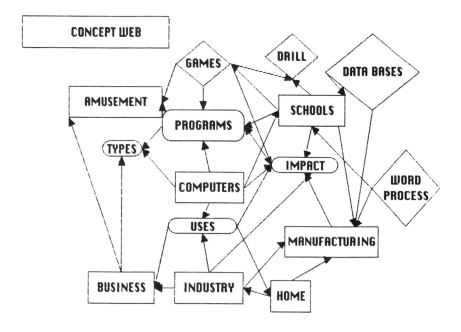

sourccs. In our very mediated world the list of possibilities is overwhelming and includes such things as books and magazines with good teaching
activities, fiction and nonfiction books and stories that children will want to
and be able to read, information resources both for the teacher's use and
that of the children, films, filmstrips, videotapes, slide sets, pictorial materials, computer programs, music, and artifacts.

These tools of teaching soon will accumulate until there is a problem of
selecting the best, most appropriate, and most useful. The resources, along
with the overview of the content and the development of the objectives,
begin to shape the kind of learning activities that will form the unit itself.

The dramatic element of the classroom was alluded to earlier. The sequencing of the teaching-learning activities in a unit is very much like
structuring the drama itself. Much like a play or a movie, if you can imagine a very long drama, the unit unfolds over several days or weeks. Like a
drama, the earliest stages of the unit have to grab attention; provide a sense
of direction and purpose; create excitement, interest, and suspense; and
give a great deal of background information. This is often referred to as the
initiation stage of the unit and teachcrs usually have just one or, at best, two
days to accomplish everything I have described. During that time, teachers
also have to discover something that dramatists can only guess at when
writing plays, what their students already know and what background
they are bringing to the study. If a playwright guesses wrong, the show
flops. If a teacher misjudges, but remains sensitive and alert to student re-
actions early on, there is still time for adjustment with a minimum waste of
student and teacher time, education's most valuable commodity.

Once the unit is launched, the body of the unit can be built of activities that are aimed at developing the objectives and maintaining and extending interest. These activities, which form the greatest part of the unit, are sometimes referred to collectively as the *developmental phase* of the unit. Most of the research, information gathering and sharing, problem solving, and extension and enrichment of the unit goes on during this developmental period. In other chapters in this book, various types of activities and activity building will be shown.

The final phase of a unit, called the *culmination phase*, serves multiple functional purposes. At this point, it is fairly obvious that closure is needed, some activity or activities that will give the children a sense that they are finished with this particular study for now at least. Going back to the drama analogy, a unit needs a climax and the culminating activities need to provide this. It may be that the children will show what they have learned by sharing their knowledge with someone else: parents, the principal, other classes, or even each other. So, one type of culmination activity might be a program, a festival or cultural celebration, the making of a videotape by the class, or some similar activity. The culmination of the unit also serves as a summative overview and a drawing together of all that has been learned. It should be, in fact, the time when the teacher helps the children to comprehend the significance of what they have been studying. If the children have been working on a problem or a group of problems, this is the point where solutions are offered and findings and conclusions are reached. Not surprisingly, the culmination of a unit is also the place where the teacher needs to take stock or make the final evaluation of what has been learned. Of course evaluation should be ongoing and present in every activity, but it is again at this culmination level that the teacher needs to make the final assessment. One last set of functions that the culmination of a unit may serve is that of maintaining or even stimulating interest in the topic that has been studied while providing a transition to some new area of study. While it may seem strange to try to create interest just as you are leaving an area of study, this is the very point at which we want to be saying to children, "We've spent all the time we can, but there are a lot more interesting and exciting things for you to learn if you want to go on your own. Now here are some other ideas for you to look into and here are some great resources you can use." The transitional function is equally logical when you think about how children learn. Basically, they understand new experiences by comparing them to things they already know about. So the transitional aspect of the culmination is simply the beginning of showing relationships, similarities, and dissimilarities with the new area of study.

The format of a unit may be developed in many different ways, no single one being *the* correct method. To mention a few, units may be organized as sequenced daily lesson plans with lessons of varying duration each structured around one or more specific objectives; as sets of lessons each teaching specific concepts, generalizations or subtopics; or as subsets of activities reflecting the various curricular areas from which the activities are drawn (art, music, language arts, etc.). Regardless of the format that shapes the unit, all unit plans need to show reflection on certain necessary elements. These are shown in the format that follows. A short (one week) unit follows, illustrating how this format may be used.

UNIT ELEMENTS FORMAT

1. Descriptive and identifying information
   A. A title (This may be in the form of a statement, a problem statement, an issue description, or a descriptive and appealing title.)
   B. Grade level(s) of students toward whom the unit is directed
   C. Estimated or allotted duration (the time in weeks with some description of how much time is to be spent each week)

2. Rationale
   A. Overview statement of the importance of the area of study both regarding both content and the approaches used
   B. Arguments and assertions regarding the significance and the appropriateness of the topic of study

3. Unit objectives
   A. A list of the most important targeted learning outcomes of the entire unit (These may be categorized in some way, the most common classification being cognitive or knowledge objectives to include facts to be remembered, concepts and generalizations to be understood, etc.; affective objectives to include values and attitudes to be developed, beliefs and aspirations to be gained, appreciations to be cultivated, etc.; and psychomotor or skills objectives.)

4. Content description (This may be embodied in the objectives and not needed as a separate entity.) Content description may be presented in several ways including the following:
   A. A list of generalizations
   B. A sequenced content outline
   C. A concept web of the unit
   D. A list of concept definitions

5. Activity sequence
   Again, there is more than one way to present this area including the following:
   A. An ordered set of lesson plans with initiating, development, and culminating activities in order
   *B. Activities arranged according to the subject area with which the social studies is being integrated (art, music, language arts, etc.)

---

*These activities will require separate planning sections for initiating and culminating activities

*C. Unit activities organized into subunits each representing a subtopic, a generalization, a key concept, or some other content heading

*D. Unit organized around key activities with contingency alternatives stemming from each of these

*E. Unit organized into key activities with enrichment activities and skill and background activities plans in a needs basis (Often this will be done in the form of Learning Centers.)

6. Description of the unit evaluation process. Development of the evaluation or assessment design as it is built into individual lessons and activities. Ways of assessing to what extent learning outcomes have been achieved detailing evaluation strategies, including any unit test(s)

7. Resources. This cataloging effort may take the form of a simple bibliographic listing or a more useful but more time-consuming series of annotated bibliographic entries. One convenient organization pattern for resources is division into teacher-resource and student-resource sections. It is also useful to create subcategories based on resource type (e.g., audiovisual materials, games and computer resources, reference materials, enrichment trade books, etc.)

An Illustrative Primary Grade Unit

Unit Title: Why Do We Have a President and What Does a President Do?

Grade Level: First or second Grade

Allotted Time: One to two weeks with follow up sessions throughout the year.

Rationale: It is very important for children in this society to begin learning about the office of the president in the government of the United States. Children constantly hear and see presidential references from parents and other adults, on television and in movies, and even as they look at money and stamps. The president is the most important single figure in the government and presidential decisions and policies influence everyone's life.

This unit is an introduction to the presidency that will be an aid to understanding in future years. The focus in the initial unit will be on the office itself and the current president. The follow-up to the unit will involve an introduction to the presidents of the past.

Conceptual Areas and Concerns

The concept of president

Who the current president is

The president's jobs

The White House as the home of the president

Unit Objectives
The students will

- Know who the current president of the United States is and what that person looks and sounds like.

- Learn what the president's jobs are.

- Gain an idea about where the president lives and how the president travels today.

- Learn about the different jobs and the work of the president.

- Know about some of the past presidents.

Activities

Initiating Activity

Objectives

- The students will be able to recognize and identify a picture of the president of the United States and name the president.

- The students will be able to name some of the jobs of the president in the government.

- The students will know that the name of the president's home is The White House and have an idea of its location.

Procedure

Begin by showing the children a series of pictures of the President. In many classes, some children will be able to make an identification at least by title. Make sure that the word president and the president's name are mentioned several times as you talk about what the president is and what the president does. If possible, find a recording of "Hail to the Chief." Talk about why the bands play that song sometimes when the president arrives. Play any available videotapes of the president in the news. (Avoid recordings that will be too boring, especially long speeches.) Tapes showing the president signing bills or making official visits will be useful. Talk with children about what they know about the White House. Again show pictures. If you think they are ready to learn about location and to do U.S. map work, ask if the children know where the White House is and show them Washington D.C. on a map of the United States.

Use a pattern for a stack of four labeled hats, one for each of four specific jobs of the president.

Uncle Sam hat: Chief of State

Army hat: Commander in Chief

Top Hat: Director of Foreign Policy

Hard Hat: Guardian of the Economy

Have the children color each hat and then practice saying the role and stacking the hats. End the activity by having the children identify the president by name and title and the White House from pictures, and rename the four jobs of the president.

Developmental Activities

1. Make a presidential library in the classroom. This will include a bulletin board, a scrapbook of newspaper and magazine clippings (especially those with pictures). It will also have a browsing table of activities and books about presidents.

2. Look at presidents' pictures on money, stamps, and so on.

3. Show pictures of the First Lady and talk about who she is.

4. Have each child tell what he or she would do if he or she were president.

5. Have children all tell something that they would like to say to the president if the president should come to visit their class.

6. Have each child suggest something they would like to show the president about the school.

7. Let the class try to come up with the following information about the president:

   • How tall is the president?

   • What is the president's favorite food?

   • What food does the president not like?

   • What are the president's hobbies?

   • Where does the president go to vacation or rest?

   • What are the president's favorite sports?

   • Does the president have a favorite movie or television show?

8. Choose two popular cartoon or television characters and have an election for president in the class. Have children try to tell why they think that each would be a good president. Then go through the exercise with written ballots and a voting booth.

9. Show pictures of the Oval Office and talk about it as the president's office. Present a trash can and ask the children to imagine that it is the trash can from that office. Ask them to think about what items might be found in it at the end of a work day for the president?

10. Keep a yarn map showing where the president travels. If possible, show television news showing the president's visits to different places.

Culminating Activity
Assign the children one sentence each about the presidency and have them draw a picture showing their sentence. After all the pictures are drawn, use a camcorder to record the children showing their pictures and telling about them. Show the videotape both to the children and to a gathering of parents.

Sentences

- _____is the_____(number) President of the United States.
- The president has many jobs.
- Some of the people who help the president are called the cabinet members.
- The president lives in the White House.
- The White House is in the city of Washington, D.C.
- _____, the president's wife is called the First Lady.
- If the president should die, the vice president would take over the job.
- The president works in the Oval Office.
- The Secret Service guards the president.
- The president is commander in chief of the Armed Forces.
- The president is the head of the government.
- The president is the director of foreign policy.
- The president is the chief ambassador to other countries.
- The president likes _____.(Favorite food).
- The president sometimes travels in a plane called Air Force One.
- I like the president because_____.
- One of the things that the president likes to do is _____.
- The president makes speeches.
- When the president signs bills, they turn into law.
- The president meets people.
- The president makes decisions.
- The president tries to decide what is best for the country.
- The president gives orders.

- People follow the president.

- George Washington was the first president.

Follow the unit by presenting and talking about one president every week. Keep a cumulative bulletin board with pictures of each president as they are discussed. Each week, have the children try to rename all the presidents that have been previously covered as a group choral exercise.

An Illustrative Intermediate Grade Unit

Unit Title: The Acquisition of the Louisiana Territory

Grade Level: Fifth Grade

Allotted Time: Five 50 minute class periods spread over less than 2 weeks.

Rationale: The unit will deal with the acquisition of the Louisiana Territory by the United States and the subsequent exploration of that territory. Because the class is studying the history of the United States throughout the year, the study of a particular historic episode in more detail is especially useful to show the human side of history. The Lewis and Clark expedition shows the hazards and some of the difficulties faced by pioneers without the violence or sensationalism. The journal of the expedition is a complete and detailed primary resource that the children can read with understanding. The members of the expedition exemplify courage, resourcefulness, a sense of responsibility and duty, and other desirable character traits. The purchase and the exploration of the Louisiana Territory nearly doubled the territorial size of the United States, thus having tremendous impact on the young nation.

Objectives:
The students will

- Be able to identify the importance of the Louisiana Purchase.

- Know the major details of the Purchase.

- Be able to identify purposes for the Lewis and Clark expedition.

- Be able to name several of the difficulties that the expedition encountered.

- Be able to trace the approximate route of the expedition on a map and know about how long Lewis and Clark spent on the trip.

- Be able to make comparisons to other explorations.

Content Outline:

I. Events leading to the purchase
   A. The need of Americans on the western frontier to be able to use the port of New Orleans
   B. The acquisition of Spanish territories by France and the closing of the port of New Orleans
   C. Monroe and Livingston appointed by President Jefferson to go to France
   D. The personality and motivations of Napoleon
      1. Need for money to finance his military efforts
      2. Lack of desire to defend large distant territories against a powerful British navy
   E. The vision and opportunism of Monroe and Livingston to exceed their authorization

II. The Lewis and Clark expedition
   A. Purposes of the expedition
      1. Gathering of scientific information
      2. Contact with the natives
      3. Proving the feasibility of travel
      4. Exploring and mapping
   B. Difficulties and dangers
      1. Environment and weather
      2. Travel hardships and problems (including the danger of being lost)
      3. Possible encounters with hostile natives and wild animals
C. Impact of the expedition

Activities

Initiating Activity

Objectives

- Know the events leading up to the Louisiana Purchase and the terms of the Purchase

- Be able to identify the major purposes of the Lewis and Clark Expedition

Procedure
Present the background to the Louisiana Purchase as a series of problems in a storytelling context getting the children to respond.

Problems
If you are in a business, what do you have to do? (Sell the goods or services.)
     Now, if you have something to sell and you and your product are one place and the people who want it are hundreds of miles away, what is your problem? (To get it to market as quickly and cheaply as you can. Give the

background on the furs and other goods Americans had to take down river to New Orleans.)

Well, what happens when the officials in New Orleans will not let you bring your goods through any longer? (Guide discussion to the eventual involvement of President Jefferson.) What do you think the president will do?

The next step is to lead into a role play activity in which two students portraying James Monroe and Robert Livingston are given their commission by the president and Congress to buy New Orleans and Florida from France for $2,000,000. They meet the Emperor Napoleon who was, so the story goes, in his bath at the time of the interview. (Napoleon should be portrayed by the teacher, another adult, or a very well coached student.) At the point where Napoleon makes his offer, interrupt the role play to discuss with the class the implications and the reasoning of all parties. Explain to the students that the final terms were worked out, not by Napoleon himself, but by the French Foreign Minister whose name was Talleyrand Périgord and by the Treasury Minister, Barbé-Marbois.

Tell them that these two ministers got more money out of the Americans than Napoleon expected. Have students guess how much more money (It was $5 million.) Ask the students about who they think got the better deal. Then bring closure.

Tell the students that at this point Jefferson and the United States had bought "a pig in a poke." Hold up a cloth or leather bag and explain the expression. Tell them that Jefferson knew there was a big river involved (pull a long crooked strip of blue paper out of the bag) and an important port city (pull out a number of Monopoly-type houses and tiny toy ships.) But all Jefferson or anyone else knew about the rest of that purchase was that there was a lot of it. (At this point, empty the bag which is filled with the jigsaw puzzle pieces representing the current states that were eventually carved from the Louisiana Territory. Tell the students that Jefferson was not the kind of man who would leave something like this alone. Lead into the commissioning of the Lewis and Clark expedition and its purposes.

Close by announcing the objectives of the rest of the unit and then reviewing the details of the purchase, using a large wall map and tracing the expedition's route very quickly.

Developmental Activities
Review the Louisiana Purchase. Tell the children that this amounted to a cost of about 2 cents per acre. Have them figure the number of acres and square miles. Possibly have them figure cost using inflation (about 200 fold).

Explain the purposes of the Lewis and Clark expedition by reading or having children read portions of the Lewis and Clark journals. Discuss the importance of the expedition.

Using the journals and maps, have the students make a carefully measured time line of the 28 month journey. Also have them use string measures (pieces of string cut and marked to fit map scale) to measure various segments of the journey. Discuss the reasons some distances would take longer.

Discuss the hardships, dangers, problems, and difficulties that the students imagine the expedition might have encountered. Then have the students do the following in-basket activity which is based on actual incidents during the expedition.

UP THE RIVER WITH LEWIS AND CLARK

For the Teacher

Student Objectives

*   Students will understand the dangers and difficulties faced by Lewis and Clark.

*   Students will be able to recognize differences in significance and urgency among frontier situations where outside help could not be available.

Opening Activity

Have students work in pairs playing the roles of Lewis and Clark. The role-play activity should be done in the following steps:

1. Let students examine a map showing the route of the Lewis and Clark expedition. Explain the reasons and purposes of the expedition.

2. Pass out Student Handout 1. Have students work through the 15 situations prioritizing the need for action and finding solutions. You may want them to write down their solutions. Some will be obvious, others will require some creativity.

3. Discuss the various ways students have ordered the situations and compare solutions.

4. Distribute Student Handout 2 and have students compare their solutions with what Lewis and Clark actually did.

5. Pass out Student Hand-Out 3 and have students discuss how their priorities differ and compare with a historian's views. (Note: You may prefer to use only a teacher copy and present them orally.)

6. Have students discuss what they learned from the activity. You might discuss why most native Americans were so friendly which is very different from the picture painted by movies and television), other dangers that might have come up, the length of the journey and the time it took.

Student Handout 1: Up the River with Lewis and Clark

Following the Louisiana Purchase in 1803, President Jefferson planned an expedition to discover the course and source of the Missouri River and the easiest water route to the Pacific Ocean. Jefferson's private secretary, Captain Meriwether Lewis, and Captain William Clark of the U.S. Army, whose roles you will play, were associated in the command of the expedition. The party consisted of nine young men from Kentucky, fourteen soldiers of the U.S. Army (who had volunteered), two French boatmen, an interpreter and hunter, and a black servant (a total of 29, including Lewis and Clark). The party started with keelboat, two French pirogues (canoes), and two horses.

You should first decide which of you will be Lewis and which will be Clark. This simulation activity involves 15 situations actually encountered by Lewis and Clark on their expedition.* Of course, Lewis and Clark did not have to deal with all these things at once but for the purposes of this activity you are to pretend that you are faced with all of these situations on the same day. As co-leaders of the expedition you and your partner must do two things. First, you have to decide which situation you must react to first, second, third, and so on, and number the situations accordingly. Second, you need to come up with a course of action.

- _____ The hunter has brought several fresh killed deer into camp.

- _____ The last of the candle supply has been used.

- _____ Two of the men who have been absent without leave have just sneaked back into camp.

- _____ The keelboat has hit a submerged log and swung broadside onto a snag, and is in danger of being stove in.

- _____ A very bad half mile of the river, called the "Devil's Race Ground" lies directly ahead filled with rapids and jagged rocks.

- _____ Heat has become unbearable.

- _____ A man has developed a "tumor" (really a boil) on his chest and it has become painful.

- _____ A band of Native Americans has asked to come on board the keelboat.

- _____ Because of fear of being attacked, the men have lost sleep and are very tired.

- _____ The anchor has been cut loose accidentally and is buried in the sand and lost.

- _____ The president has indicated that he will expect careful maps and specimens of plants.

- _____ A French trapper, unknown to the party, has come up asking to be hired as an interpreter.

---

*The sources of information for the simulation is *The Journals of Lewis and Clark* edited by Bernard DeVoto. New York: Houghton Mifflin, 1953.

- ____ A group of French traders coming downriver have reported that the Osage Indians, upriver, will not believe that the Americans now hold the land.

- ____ The Omaha Indians, a wandering tribe, are reportedly stopping every river party and plundering or taking tribute.

- ____ The party has spotted packs of huge wolves and huge bears several times larger than any seen before.

Student Handout 2: From *The Journal of Lewis and Clark*

Here is what Lewis, Clark, and their men did when they faced these problems.

- ____ All meat not eaten right away was jerked , or cut into strips and dried in the sun within a day or so.

- ____ This happened on January 18, 1806. They had brought molds and wicks and new candles were made from elk tallow.

- ____ On March 17, 1804, two men were court-martialed for being gone without leave and sentenced to receive 25 and 50 lashes, respectively. Captain Clark then suspended the sentence.

- ____ This happened on June 9, 1804; with oars and tow ropes they managed to free the boat.

- ____ The expedition tried to send one canoe through, ran onto a sand bar, broke a tow rope, and nearly capsized. Finally, swimmers pulled the canoe to safety. The men then carried boats, equipment, and all by land across the entire half mile.

- ____ At times they made awnings to keep out the sun.

- ____ Clark lanced this growth and drew out the fluid.

- ____ The party allowed native Americans on board the keel boat on several occasions.

- ____ They had to find an area where friendly Indians and good weather would allow them to rest up.

- ____ A substitute anchor was made out of stones.

- ____ Lewis, especially, collected samples of plants and rocks. Clark did the large part of the mapping each night. Native Americans provided added information.

- ____ Charbonneau, the Frenchman's name, joins the party. With him is his 16-year-old wife, Sacajawea. (She can speak Shoshone and this becomes essential upriver.)

- ____ On August 3, 1804, Lewis and Clark called several tribes together, gave them presents, including an American flag and some medicine, and made speeches. Similar meetings occurred later on with other chiefs. At the meetings, they convinced the tribes that the United States, not France, must be dealt with.

• ____ The Omahas are nearly wiped out by smallpox before Lewis and Clark arrive and the threat is reduced.

• ____ Lewis and Clark were amazed at both the bears and the wolves. It took ten musket balls to kill one big bear.

Student Handout 3: In What Order?

There is no correct or incorrect order for these situations. The following order is suggested based on the ideas of a frontier historian. The numbers reflect the order in which the problems are listed in Handout 1: Up the River with Lewis and Clark The major things to consider are the urgency of each situation and the impact on the expedition of acting or not acting right away.

• _7_ The meat will spoil very quickly in the heat.

• _10_ Candles were needed that very night for light.

• _6_ This is ranked fairly high because it is necessary to act quickly. To fail to do so might cause discipline problems later.

• _1_ Obviously, they had to act immediately to keep from losing the boat and supplies. The expedition would probably be finished if this happened.

• _2_ A decision would need to be made before entering the risky waters.

• _11_ Not much could be done about the heat, but it could sap strength and slow the expedition.

• _5_ A man unable to travel would slow the expedition down. There was no need to rush, however.

• _3_ Native American courtesy is the problem here. The risk of offending native Americans was one that the expedition leaders did not want to take.

• _4_ It was very important that all were in fit condition to face the dangers and difficulties. Lives could be lost otherwise.

• _8_ Without an anchor, the boat had to be beached each night.

• _12_ This was done regularly and automatically by both leaders as a part of the daily routine.

• _9_ The decision had to be made while the man was there.

• _13_ This was a problem to plan for, but there was time.

• _14_ Mostly still rumor, but there was a need to be prepared to defend.

- _15_ More something to keep the party alert and together than anything else.

Introduce the "Magic Gun", one of the earliest air rifles, which Lewis and Clark took with them. It fired a 28 caliber bullet and once charged with compressed, air could fire repeatedly. Though the gun was not much good for hunting, it was very useful to the expedition. Discuss the reasons for the gun's usefulness. (It impressed the native Americans.)

Have the students plan, write, and rehearse a program to be presented to parents or another class about the Louisiana Purchase and the Lewis and Clark expedition.

As a follow-up activity, give the students a list of other explorations that they might like to read about and study

- The voyages of Columbus

- LaSalle's trip down the Mississippi River

- NASA space explorations, including Neil Armstrong's moon landing

- Leif Ericson's voyages

Have children discuss how these were like and how they were different from the Lewis and Clark expedition.

Culminating Activity

Have the students put on a program consisting of:

- A reenactment of Jefferson's decision to send emissaries to France and the meeting between Napoleon and Monroe and Livingston

- A Living Time Line in which children costume themselves as events in the Purchase Purchase and Lewis and Clark expedition, each describing his or her own event

- A floor-map activity in which guides lead guests along a large floor-map representation, showing guests the route of the expedition

Evaluation

Evaluation is built into every activity in some way. A final unit test might consist of the following questions:

- From what country did the United States purchase the Louisiana Territory and what was the price?

- Name two dangers faced by the Lewis and Clark expedition.

- Give one reason why the Louisiana Purchase was important.

- Give one purpose of the Lewis and Clark expedition.

- On an unlabeled map, trace the route of the Lewis and Clark expedition naming the rivers they traveled.

Resources

Adams, A.B. (1981). *The disputed lands: a history of The American West.* New York: Putnam.

Barnard, E.S. (1987). *Story of the American West.* Pleasantville, N.Y.: Readers' Digest.

Coit, M. L. and the Editors of *LIFE*. (1963). *The life history of the United States: the growing years.* New York: Time.

DeVoto, B. (Ed.) (1953). *The journals of Lewis and Clark.* New York: Houghton Mifflin.

WHAT MAKES A UNIT PLAN SUITABLE FOR SOCIAL STUDIES?

The utility of any type or format of unit plan in bringing about effective social studies instruction will vary with the teacher and the school situation. Organized, highly structured teachers who are capable of and comfortable with precise, long-in-advance planning and follow-through will probably do well with the daily lesson plan approach to planning. Teachers who want to provide maximum flexibility to adjust to student interest may find this style uncomfortably rigid.

Any type of unit plan is most likely to help bring about effective social studies instruction if it does the following:

- Helps the teacher keep a focus on the intended learning outcomes

- Aids the teacher to gather the best available resources quickly and efficiently

- Aids the teacher in assimilating social studies within the whole of students' learning

- Helps the teacher in building in motivational, creative teaching ideas

- Reduces the time needed for the teacher to plan effectively

FINDING AND USING PREPARED UNITS

Teachers may feel, usually with justification, that they do not have the time, energy, or ingenuity to prepare elaborate and extensive units of their own for the entire school year. At the same time, they may not want to fall into the pattern of teaching directly from the textbook.

There is an alternative available to teachers even if there is no established district or school curriculum guide complete with authorized, already prepared units and even if there is no easy collaborative planning or sharing going on in the school in which they teach. That alternative is to "borrow" premade units from some source outside the school.

The maxim of unit "borrowing" ought to be, "If you are going to 'borrow,' then take the best!" But how does a teacher with little time to search (if you had the time, you would have planned your own unit in the first place) find the best?

Two rules seem to apply here. The first is that the best place to search is among the professionally, even commercially prepared materials that have already undergone the scrutiny of selection and the polishing of rewrite and editing. A starting place among these is the commercial teaching magazines such as *Instructor, Teacher, Learning,* or *Mailbox.* Professional journals such as *Social Education, Social Studies and the Young Learner,* and *The Social Studies* will be worth a look through, too. A trip to a university library where a browse of indexes and ads may be very fruitful. The desired topics may jump out at the teacher in the first few minutes or it may take several hours, but it is time well invested if it saves days and weeks of planning. It would be a smart idea to check out the text series other than the one(s) in use in your school,too. The teachers' editions may hold some pleasant surprises. Certainly, any gems found in these textbooks will require some adaptation, but that will be true of most any "borrowed" materials. One other resource worth a look through in a university library will be other methods texts in social studies. Some of these contain provocative unit ideas.

The second rule is, "Always be on the lookout for materials for teaching." At conventions, in the rooms of other teachers, at the teacher center (if your system is lucky enough to have one), or even in the dentist's office, the very thing needed may be waiting for the alert person who takes the initiative and the time to nose through the available material. One of the resources for teacher prepared units is The Association for Supervision and Curriculum Development which publishes a list of available units and curriculum materials available for school systems.

To use prepared units effectively, the key concern is adaptation. The focus in adaptation has got to be on the intended learning outcomes. If the teacher begins with concern for how a unit plan can bring significant learning, then all other kinds of needed change fall into place. A second and related focus has to be on the vitality and motivational appeal of the activities for the children. Will the children be excited, interested and stimulated by these activities? A third related concern to the teacher has to do with whether or not the necessary resources are available successfully bring off the activities. This may have to do as much with a realistic self-assessment of time, energy, and initiative as with material resources, but both are needed.

PLANNING FOR SHORTER INSTRUCTION SEQUENCES

The most useful and important among shorter instructional sequences is, of course, the single lesson plan. A lesson plan is in many ways a unit in miniature, and lessons contain similar key elements such as objectives, procedural descriptions of activities, and identification of resources.

Any lesson plan design which is going to be particularly useful will be one that will be structured to aid retention. The Hunter (1990-1991) lesson sequence has been a helpful model, especially for teachers in the early stages of their development, because it is structured in distinctive steps. A lesson design adapted from elements in Hunter's design follows:

1. Get the learners' attention and prepare them for what they are going to learn. The teacher needs to think of some way of capturing interest and focusing that interest on the topic of study. This part of the lesson may review previous learnings, be a practice session, or simply develop readiness for the new material.

2. Explain the objective(s) or purpose(s). A key element in the Hunter approach is that the students have a good idea of the ends the teacher has in mind. This step includes a clear communication of what the teacher intends to accomplish. In a sense, though, it is something more than that; if possible, the teacher and the students need to reach a consensus so that there can be shared goals that are understood by both.

3. Do direct teaching. In this step, the teacher is communicating the new information of the lesson, teaching concepts, and so on, using a variety of techniques.

4. If appropriate, demonstrate or model what you want the learners to do. Though not all lessons require this step, in many it is essential. Basically, it involves demonstration or the completing of examples by the teacher. The teacher shows the students how each step in a process is completed (e.g., finding a location using map coordinates).

5. Check for understanding. This is sometimes referred to as the *monitor and adjust* stage. It is a point at which the teacher determines if the students understand what the lesson is all about. It requires some activity in which students give and receive feedback. This may involve a signaling device in which all students participate, a questioning technique using selected students, or individual responses from every student.

6. Provide guided practice. The teacher gives students a chance to use new skills or concepts. Again the emphasis is on monitored practice with feedback from the teacher.

7. Provide opportunity for independent practice.

Though this lesson planning model will not and should not be suited to every lesson, it can provide a useful pattern for many. As a model the steps in the lesson plan show very clearly the importance of developing detail, specificity, and sequence in the procedure of a lesson plan. Following is an example of a plan developed along the lines of the model.

Lesson Plan Title: African Nations

Level: Fourth Grade

Objective: Students will learn the relative locations of the African nations.

1. Get the learners' attention and prepare them for what they are going to learn. Show a large wall map of Africa. Ask a series of questions about the countries, such as: How many countries are there? What is the largest? The smallest? Where are some of the countries that have been in the news? What nations are in the North? The South? The East? The West? At appropriate times, point to the appropriate countries or have children locate them. At this point, remove the labeled map, replacing it with a large, laminated unlabeled map. Ask how many could label some of the countries. If there are any hands, allow a few trials. End this portion of the lesson by saying that it might be useful to get a better idea of where the nations are located.

2. Explain the objective or purpose. At this point, tell the children that the purpose of what they are going to be doing is to become more familiar with the names and the locations of African nations.

3. Do direct teaching. Explain the materials and the activities. In advance, prepare a series of transparencies all of the same scale, which together form a complete map of Africa. Assign each child a nation or a set of contiguous nations so that all the nations are divided among the children. Either by scheduling or some other design, have the children in pairs use the transparencies to draw enlargements of their nation(s) on sheets of butcher paper. A taped mark on the floor will, with a little reminding, keep the maps the same scale.

4. If appropriate, demonstrate or model what you want the learners to do. Explain to the children that you want them to know as much as they can about the location of their countries. Use one nation as an example. Locate it on the map. Give other locating information (what countries border it, how it relates to landmarks such as coasts and major rivers, etc.).

5. Check for comprehension. When all maps are drawn, have the children take their own. Go to a gym or any large open area. (Outside is fine if the wind is not blowing.) Use a line or some other marking. Go through a series of question and response discussion-adjustment exercises based on the following kinds of tasks:

   • Every nation south of the Sahara desert stand to the left of the line; all others to the right!

   • Name a nation and ask all children holding nations that touch it on the map to stand to the left of the line.

   • All nations on the West coast of Africa stand to the front of the rest.

6. Provide guided practice. Return to the classroom. Have each child in turn use a pointer to show his or her own nation(s) on a large unlabeled wall map. Play the "Name 5" game. Divide the class into two teams. In turn, each team's members get to name and label up to five

countries (using a felt-tip marker). The team gets a point for every nation that is right, but it loses 2 points for wrong guesses.

7. Provide for independent practice. Give each child an unlabeled map of Africa. Using one another as resources, have the children label their own maps, then check them against a labeled map. Cut out and laminate the children's maps. Have children continue to practice as a free-time activity using these maps as part of a large jigsaw puzzle.

ADDITIONAL AND SUPPLEMENTAL TYPES OF PLANS

Teachers may find it useful to have alternatives to unit and lesson plans. Schedule pressures may seem to prohibit use of extensive units, while single lessons offer seemingly isolated learnings that are not easily envisioned as part of some larger learning sequence.

One alternative is a type of planning package that is referred to as a *module.* Modules provide for one to a series of lessons, sometimes consisting of several activities centered around one or a series of closely related ideas, usually concept statements or generalizations. Modules may be used in isolation, as part of or in conjunction with a unit, or in clusters. Built into modular teaching is the notion of *mastery.* Mastery, in this case, means that the module teaches the idea to a point where some specified or at least defined level of understanding is reached. Evaluation and reteaching, then, are necessary for module construction.

As the following examples of topics for modules might indicate, modules may aim at developing definitional understanding of concepts, at helping students reach evaluational judgments, or at providing experiences that cause students to arrive at a commonly shared generalization as a way of thinking. The following are examples of definitional topics:

- A *map* is a model representing some part of the surface of the earth or some other area and it is subject to various inaccuracies.

- A *president* is the head of a nation, organization, or business, having specific executive functions and powers for a defined length of time and under restricted conditions.

- *Laws* are rules recognized by a governing body as binding upon the members of the group.

Evaluation Judgments

- A good country

- Responsibility

- Playing fair is more important than winning

The following are examples of generalizations:

- Urban communities tend to change more rapidly than rural communities.

- Though all members of a community are consumers, only some are producers.

- A single event may have several causes and produce more than one outcome.

Once the topic is identified, the module itself consists of an array of activities including examples and identified nonexamples along with identifying experiences. The activities have the express purpose of bringing an understanding or mastery of the topic.

Case studies provide another alternative to units. Case study approaches have become increasingly more viable with the development of computers and data bases. The term *case study* implies a kind of intense examination of a particular event, person, or thing, or a grouping of these. The one case is looked at as an example or model that can be studied in depth and even intently over time. In medicine a doctor might study the medical history of a few patients. From these selected cases, it is hoped that insights about others who have similar medical history may be derived. In law, a case study may be chosen because it represents a landmark decision or provides a precedent in court procedure. Sociologists, historians, and psychologists may construct fictional cases to demonstrate typical behavior. In fact, the case study approach is used by almost all professions looking at human behavior simply because of the complexity of the human thought and action.

A case study is an intensive use of example(s). The example(s) provides a data base for inquiry and concrete illustration(s) of principles, concepts, and ideas.

Case studies used in the social studies can be a way of helping the students see the personal and human aspects of a culture or of a time. Students look at one person, one family, one village rather than reading generalizations about a country, culture, or period of time. Human qualities seem less abstract. The short unit on Lewis and Clark presented earlier in this chapter differs from a case study only in the approach used. Essentially, it was the teacher not the student who used the data base. So, instead of being a student-directed study of the details of the expedition related to a single problem or a set of problems, the unit is a series of teacher-controlled activities in which students only use the Lewis and Clark material as content.

Procedure in Preparing a Case Study

1. Identify the problem to be studied and the purpose to be accomplished.

2. Tentatively identify a research procedure for students to follow.

3. Select the appropriate example (or case).

4. Develop detailed procedural plans.

5. Collect resources related to the case. Examples of resources include

    • Maps of varying sorts

    • Background information sheets

    • Interviews on topics related

    • Letters

    • Descriptions of objects

    • Diaries and journals

    • Records and public documents

    • Newspaper clippings

6. Organize the data bank of materials and data related to the case. For example, one usable pattern of organization consists of

    • A single narrative or a series of narratives describing the facts of the case. These may include first-hand accounts, scholarly summations, and even slanted or biased descriptions.

    • First person (witness) interviews with principals in or witnesses to the case (transcripts or tapes of these)

    • Pictures (photographs, drawings, etc.), films and other media visualizations (including actual film coverage of an event) of the setting, the people, and the chain of events in the case across the time period involved

    • Exhibits (artifacts, realia)

    • Maps, graphs, charts

    • Background information (including anecdotes)

7. Plan activities and materials structured to help or guide students as they examine the case or inquire into the evidence.

Three Types of Cases To Be Used or Studied

Using Hypothetical or Simulated Cases

Description: Hypothetical cases
The information is all made up (imaginary, fictitious). Characters, events, and even settings are created. Often this information is similar to, adapted from, related to, or analogical to real-world and real-life situations.

Advantages

It is *impossible* to create false, or erroneous facts. Time passage *fits* teaching purposes. Historical examples are

neither distorted nor distorting. The created case permits one to simplify and focus on the really significant. Prejudices and biases influencing thinking are diminished. This approach allows more structuring. Impressions and mood can be much more carefully controlled. Added data can be manufactured. Readability can be controlled.

Disadvantages or Problems

The data are always limited. There are no surprises. Reality questions are confusing and distorting. Time is wasted in learning facts with no value.

Using Well-known Significant Individuals and Events

This approach focuses upon the great and famous.

Description: Famous Cases

Advantages

Historical knowledge about famous people is generally attainable. Better records are kept and preserved for major events and of the lives of people who are famous during their own lifetimes. We know more about Leonardo da Vinci (1452-1519), for example, than we know about VanGogh (1853-1890), simply because DaVinci was a celebrity during his own lifetime while VanGogh was an unknown. More is written about the person, more is saved, and, even over centuries, more remains for future generations of historians.

Studying such individuals allows the student to examine the nature of and reasons for their greatness. At the same time it helps to cut these figures to human size rather than to hold them on a pinnacle of loftiness. They become real, alive, and three dimensional. Since figures are in the public eye more is known about them.

Disadvantages

Current and historical biases and prejudices may influence thinking. Today, for example, we tend to view Richard III of England as a wicked king mostly because our knowledge of him comes to us through people who supported and feared the Tudors who overthrew him in order to establish their line on the throne of England. Many of the stories about such figures as Lincoln and Washington are almost pure fabrications. With famous cases, it is often difficult to distinguish the truth from the existing stereotypical images, legends, and apocryphal stories.

Studying Case Histories of Typical Examples

Description: Typical Cases
These types of cases are selective and usually factual. The cases of relatively unknown people and events are selected. The very distinguishing feature of each case is either that it is very like the average case or that it is representative of the extremes of the problem being studied.

Advantages
By looking at average typical cases the student can explore
a more unknown area allowing freedom from bias. Such cases are less distortive of the normal reality (not as likely to mislead). Students can more closely identify with the cases in terms of their own experiences. More generalizable understandings about normal existing conditions can be gained. These cases serve the double purpose of allowing children to learn significant facts while looking at a case for other reasons.

Disadvantages
Students may be influenced by misinformation, untrue stories, single experiences, and ignorance about entire groups of people and about entire civilizations. The major problem is, of course, not having all of the important data. Then, too, there may even be great difficulty in finding data when the cases are historical. (The great are preserved, the insignificant are forgotten.) Important variables may be passed over or ignored. An additional problem is that no individual is totally typical. Finally, studying the typical case in contemporary settings may involve invasion of privacy. The approach invades personal lives of individuals chosen as cases. Data are not always accessible.

A Few Types of Activities to Use With Case Study Material

- Research-based discussions and individual reports of controversies

- Problem-solving situations calling upon data in the case

- Role plays involving the principals of the case

- Developing reports or answering questions in which they draw from data.

- Debates involving controversies or points of view regarding the same or related cases

- Creative writing to or about the principle characters in the case (e.g., letters, hypothetical diaries, fictional stories, etc.)

- Question generating sessions

- Data-generating sessions to build additional cases or to extend data bank

- Reenactments of events

- Artistic endeavors (e.g., murals, models)

- Projective analysis (What are outcomes to be anticipated beyond the data?)

- Analysis sheets and questions to be answered by studying the data

LOOKING BACK

The quality of planning makes a difference in the quality of teaching. Teachers fail to give adequate time to planning for a variety of reasons, but by determined systematic effort, planning can add to teaching effectiveness and satisfaction.

The term *unit* is most often used to describe the long-term planning a teacher does to teach a topic to a group of students. The teachers' editions of textbooks also use the term to describe the activities provided for teaching particular content, usually chapters. Whether a textbook unit or a teacher-made unit, considerable planning is involved. Teacher-made units may be of several types, including collaborative or team units, which are usually resource units: teaching units, which are prepared with a specific case and sequence of activities; and sketch units, which are less thorough and usually require much more additional planning later. Each of these types of plans has its uses.

Short-term planning most often takes the form of lesson plans. An appropriate lesson plan format for teachers in their early development should be one that helps them with the sequence of the lesson and stresses learning retention.

Alternative types of planning are also sometimes useful to social studies teachers. Among these are modules, based on mastery learning principles, and case studies which reflect inductive learning. The questions and activities which follow may be used to help you think about what you have read in this chapter.

- Brainstorm a set of unit titles and topics related to technology or some other area where science and the social studies are better integrated.

- Review some textbook units. Identify their strengths and shortcomings.

- Profile your own planning abilities. What are your assets and what are the areas where you need improvement?

- Design a single activity to teach the concepts of city, state, and nation.

- Design a survey to discover how often teachers prepare their own instruction units. Discuss the findings.

- Identify several types of quality lessons that could not be fitted to the model presented in the chapter. Determine the reasons that this model does not work for every type of lesson.

- Practice webbing a unit topic.

- Make up a People Scavenge for the unit included in this chapter.

SELF-TEST

1. What are some reasons that teachers cannot always plan as effectively as they should?

2. What are some of the characteristics of a classroom where good planning is going on?

3. How do the varying types of units discussed in this chapter differ?

4. What is a collaborative unit?

5. What are the elements necessary in a unit plan?

6. What is a case study?

REFERENCES

Brophy, J., and Good, T. (1978). *Looking in classrooms.* New York: Harper and Row.

Hunter, M. (1990-1991). Hunter lesson design helps achieve the goals of science instruction. *Educational Leadership.* 48 (December/January), 79-81.

Walsh, D. (1979). Classroom stress and teacher burnout. *Phi Delta Kappan,* 69 (December) 253.

Woodward, A., Elliott, D.L., and Nagel, K. (1986). Beyond textbooks in elementary social studies. *Social Education,* 50 (January) 50-53.

SUGGESTED READING

Kindsvatter, R., Wilen, W., and Ishler, M. (1988). *Dynamics of effective teaching.* New York: Longman.

MacDonald, R.E. (1991). *A handbook of basic skills and strategies for beginning teachers.* New York: Longman.

Meyen, E. (1981). *Developing instructional units.* Dubuque, Iowa: Winitzky, N.E. (1992). Classroom organization for social studies. In Shaver J.P. (ed.), *Handbook of research on social studies teaching and learning.* New York: Macmillan (pp. 530-539).

3 The Social Studies Program

LOOKING AHEAD

What topics and themes are to be taught? What is to be taught about these topics and themes? Questions such as these are constant and troubling for those involved in social studies education. Though there is little disagreement that the selection ought to be related to carefully selected goals and that the teaching itself should be done in a purposeful way, what is taught and what materials are used are ongoing problems to be solved in the social studies. In this chapter, we will look at some of the forces influencing the social studies program. We are going to look especially at how those forces have changed the social studies. The major reason for doing so is because you need to be aware of how these developments have affected you and of the far reaching effects on how you teach and what you will teach. It will help you understand the way that the social studies curriculum is evolving.

Recognizing that the social studies has a strong knowledge base, we will also want to look at the social science disciplines. These disciplines all examine the world from a different perspective, with different emphases and foci and, often, using different scholarly tools. The social scientists working in these disciplines provide the scholarship, methods, concepts, and information that are the basis for the social studies curriculum in the elementary schools. The better we understand them and their relationship to one another, the better we can utilize and select from what they have to offer.

CAN YOU? DO YOU?

Can you

- Identify reasons why there is controversy in the social studies?

- Describe the Expanding Environments curriculum?

- Identify the social sciences and tell how they relate to what children learn in the social studies?

- Name the social sciences and tell what each one is all about?

Do you

- Know how the social studies curriculum is organized?

- Know what an instructional theme is?

WHY IS THERE CONTROVERSY OVER SOCIAL STUDIES PROGRAMS?

Social studies has been and will continue to be constantly under attack by critics. What is taught in the social studies is constantly under examination with real concern for what needs to be changed. The root reason for this is that learning social studies is a lot more complex than developing an ability or skill that remains as the major purpose of curricular areas such as reading and mathematics. Beyond skill or knowledge acquisition, there are at least five factors to account for controversy over social studies programs.

1. The imperfect nature of anything that human effort produces: Before we even get a curriculum together, we and others begin to see the flaws and problems. When we put something into use, those flaws become glaringly apparent to us.

2. Cultural change: We live in an era of immense societal complexity and rapid change. As rapidly as we develop a program, changes occur that require adjustments. Social studies curricula are responsive to changes in the social climate. Changes in emphasis are likely to reflect the times. Wars, depressions, periods of prosperity, international relationships, and a host of other things that influence the public climate impact the social studies.

3. Different values and viewpoints: The social studies is not just a skill subject. In a democratic society, there is little likelihood of long-term consensus and none at all of universal agreement on what ought to be taught and from what viewpoint.

4. The influence of special-interest groups: In our society there are pressure groups with their own agendas and expectations. They want to influence or even control what is being taught in the schools.

5. The enormity of the changing body of knowledge that the field of social studies encompasses: The social studies simply defy coverage or even adequate sampling. We can never have enough depth or breadth. The term *social studies* is, to a great extent, a product of the twentieth

Century. It was officially adopted as the name for the curricular area in 1916 by the Committee on Social Studies, a subgroup of the Commission to Reorganize Secondary Education, which had been set up by the National Education Association (Jarolimek 1981, 5). That committee also recommended the following curricula for grades five through eight, which were traditionally considered part of elementary or grammar school.

Fifth grade	American History
Sixth grade	World History (Western Civilization)
Seventh grade	Geography
Eighth grade	American History

In the late 1930s, Paul Hanna proposed a sequence of instructional topics that was to revolutionize elementary school social studies. This framework, known as the Expanding Communities Model or Expanding Environments curriculum, was based on a theory that children's ability to understand their world progresses through a series of developmental stages and that social studies programs should be structured to coincide with those stages (Hanna 1957, 1963). The progression was from a study of the children themselves and their homes and families through increasingly larger communities which were more remote and abstract to children's thinking.

In spite of all the pressure for change, the Expanding Environment concept has been the major influence on social studies curriculum for over 50 years. The first eight grades of the twelve-grade Hanna model are shown in the following list.* Along side it the dominant pattern of curriculum organization currently used in textbook and school curricula is shown.

Grade	Expanding Environments Model	Contemporary Curricula
Kindergarten	(Kindergartens were not mandatory at this time.)	Self, school, home, families, community
First	The child, the home, the family, the school	Families, community
Second	The neighborhood, neighborhood helpers	Neighborhoods
Third	The larger community, cities	Communities
Fourth	The state, the region	State history, geographic regions
Fifth	The United States and its neighbors	American history
Sixth	The world (Western civilization)	World cultures, the Western hemisphere
Seventh	World geography	World geography
Eighth	History of the United States	American history

*Information for the list above was adapted from Hanna (1957, 1963) Superka et al. (1980), and from a survey of contemporary social studies textbooks.

The beauty of the Expanding Environment model was its logic. It made sense to a lot of people both from the standpoint of its reflection of a reasonable pattern of child development and as a logical way to organize the social studies. Hanna's model was developed at a fortunate time in many ways. The social climate of the nation was ideal with America coming through a depression and a world war from which it emerged as the leading power in the free world. Technology and communication as well as the economic conditions were also right. Hanna's model was soon adopted by many school systems and by textbook publishers. It is, to this day, the most common model used in elementary schools in the United States.

From the 1960s to the 1970s a spirit of reform gripped the social studies. It manifested itself in a series of well warranted criticisms of the expanding environment curriculum as it was by then represented in textbook series and school curricula across the country and in the development of new curricula, many of which were closely tied to the various social science disciplines. Critics pointed out that social studies teachers relied too heavily on textbooks and that there was too much memorization of facts. But there was major curricular criticism as well. Critics charged that the social studies lacked sufficient substantive content, that African Americans, Hispanics, women, and other groups were insufficiently represented; stereotypically represented or misrepresented; and that significant issues and content topics of controversy were avoided. Theories of reform efforts and projects that resulted from this criticism are sometimes referred to as "The New Social Studies." Spurred in part by federal funding and in part by the social consciousness and concern of the period, the lasting changes injected into the social studies by these reform efforts during this era included

- A greater sensitivity to the representation of various ethnic groups and women in social studies material.

- Focus on inquiry and values

- Greater global consciousness

- Focus on social sciences other than history and geography as sources of insight and methods of inquiry about the world

- Greater awareness of and ability to deal with controversy in the social studies classroom

- An emphasis on learning concepts and generalizations rather than isolated facts

More recent efforts to set direction for the social studies have reaffirmed the importance of history and geography while at the same time accepting a less structured and more incidental social studies content for the primary grades. Perhaps the most prestigious of the recent groups to examine the future of the social studies was the Curriculum Task Force of the National Commission on the Social Studies in the Schools. In its report,

Charting a Course: Social Studies for the 21st Century, the task force advocated a curriculum of stories about people accompanied by holiday study and following up time and place location information in reading stories, mathematics and other materials. The Task Force suggested that such a program was sufficient to ensure elementary understanding of world geography, the civic and political traditions of the United States, and human life in different continents and at different times in the past (Task Force of the National Commission on the Social Studies in the Schools 1989, 9). The Task Force envisioned three courses being taught in grades four, five, and six, which would include (in no specified order)(1) United States History, (2) World History, and (3) Geography.

INSTRUCTIONAL THEMES IN SOCIAL STUDIES EDUCATION

In the emerging 1990s and on into the twenty-first century, elementary school teachers with concern for the social studies will continue to search for meaningful frameworks that will help them structure social studies learning. One of the ideas that offers promise is using focus themes taken from the social science disciplines and representing their essential lines of inquiry. Following a kind of candlewick principle, these themes can run through topics of study and across grade levels drawing essential content and skill development to themselves. Thematic units are integrally related to literature-based whole-language programs and unify the content of the social studies with other curricular areas. In nongraded settings, thematic units can be part of an internal structure.

Following is a series of both typical and less usual examples of thematic unit topics at each grade level. The list is not presented as a sequential model curriculum and certainly will not precisely reflect any particular school or textbook curricular program. These unit topics are presented here simply to give an idea of what might be taught and to illustrate the notion of thematic threads.

WHAT IS THE PLACE OF THE SOCIAL SCIENCE DISCIPLINES?

Social studies is the name given to a broad curricular area taught in elementary schools. The focus of the social studies is on the child learning to understand, interpret, and live in his or her world and we have looked, in Chapter 1, at the basic goals of that broad area. Social studies is also an inclusive term that is used to describe courses in middle and secondary schools that focus specifically on history, geography, sociology, economics, psychology, government, and related subjects. Some people use the phrase the seamless web to describe the relationships among all of these subjects. They like to see the social studies as an interdisciplinary curricular area that

	Unit on Topics	Possible Theme(s)	Likely Central Discipline(s)
Kindergarten:	School social studies typically begins with topics related to home, family, and school. Emphasis is on the immediate environment, but there needs to be plenty of opportunity to look at the world beyond.		
	Who am I?	Identity/personality	Psychology
	Our families	Interdependence Sociology	
	Friends away from Home	Socialization	Sociology
	Rules we need	Responsibility/authority	Political science/ psychology
	Who makes the school work?	Authority/society	Sociology
	Being careful, going shopping	Consumption/resource distribution	Economics
	The world, the continents, the ocean	Location	Geography
First Grade:	Units on this level begin with the local area and associate it with the larger world. Often comparisons are made. Emphasis is on individuals.		
	The shopping mall	Consumption, exchange	Economics
	People we need	Interdependence	Sociology/Economics
	What happens in the Factory	Production	Economics
	Great men and women	Leadership, individual differences	History
	Families in India	Cultural diversity	Anthropology
Second Grade:	Contact, travel and relationships among neighborhoods are often emphasized.		
	Moving Around and Telling others	Transportation Communication	Geography/history
	Neighborhoods changing	Cause and effect	History
	Farms and cities	Resources/regions	Geography
	Fast foods	Exchange Economics	
	Suburbs	Adaptation/location	Geography
	Money and banks	Exchange	Economics

	Unit on Topics	Possible Theme(s)	Likely Central Discipline(s)
Third Grade:	The larger community is generally the focus with the intent of developing an understanding of the conceptual characteristics of a community, community differences, and community changes.		
	How the city changes	Adaptation, change	Political science/ geography
	Special cities	Physical differences	Geography
	Towns and cities in Early America	Historical change	History
	Feeding the people	Transportation, production, exchange	Economics
	People who made change	Historical judgment	History
Fourth Grade:	Environmental features of the earth are emphasized and regions of the United States are studied. How to go about adopting and adapting to the environment and the home state are sometimes part of the focus.		
	Living in the deserts of the world	Region/adaptation	Geography
	History all around us	Change	History
	Rain forests in Africa and South America	Location, physical features	Geography
	The Midwest	Regions	Geography
	Regions of the Unitod Statoc	Regions	Geography

	Unit on Topics	Possible Theme(s)	Likely Central Discipline(s)
Fifth Grade:	The history of America is studied at this level with emphasis on the United States or the United States and Canada, or the United States and South America.		
	New lands, new promises	Cause and effect location	History/geography
	Forging the nation	Historical judgment, authority, and responsibility	History/political science
	African Americans	Identification, change, equality	History
	Trappers, miners, and settlers - the American west	Historical progression, location	History/geography
	The end of compromise: the American Civil War	Change, causation, historical judgment	History/economics
	The rise of American industry and labor	Change, adaptation	History/economics
Sixth Grade:	The program at this level may include a study of Latin America and Canada or may emphasize Western civilization or the history of Europe and Asia.		
	Models of government: ancient Greece and Rome	Citizenship, authority	Political science/ history Change
	Castles, moats, and drawbridges	Adaptation and adoption, cause and effect	History
	New visions and dreams: Renaissance and Reformation	Change, cause and individual impact	History/geography

	Unit on Topics	Possible Theme(s)	Likely Central Discipline(s)
Seventh Grade:	The home state is often studied at this level. Another common topic of study is world geography.		
	Our state and how it came to be	Physical features, historical judgment, location	Geography/history
	Africa: A continent of nations	Location, physical features	Geography
	The millions of Chinese	Historical causation	History/geography
	The Nations of the third world	Scarcity, distribution of resources	Geography
	World resources and their distribution	Distribution of resources	Geography/economics
	Looking to the future	Predictions	History/geography
Eighth Grade:	The return to a focus on the United States and its heritage is common at this level, with a chronological approach.		
	A virgin land	Adaptation, cooperation	History/geography
	Building a new nation	Cause and effect, conformity, authority	History/political science
	Those who made the new nation	Historical judgment	History
	New lands for the new nation	Change	History/geography
	The unrepairable rift: Civil War and Reconstruction	Cause and effect, conflict	History/geography
	Industry and power	Production	History/economics
	A world power	Influences, power	History/political science
	Into the age of technology	Power, change	History/economics

draws its content from what scholars in a variety of disciplines know about the social world.

The disciplines themselves would more correctly be called social sciences, and each of them offers different content emphases and different methods of inquiry than the others. The study of scholars in each of the social sciences has produced a vast number of concepts, generalizations, and facts. When social scientists start counting off the social sciences, different numbers are likely to be given. That is partly because there are some disciplines that some people accept as social sciences and that other people see as humanities or even natural sciences. Philosophy and religion are examples of disciplines sometimes thought of as humanities. There is also disagreement because each social science keeps dividing as specializations develop. The social sciences are sort of schismatic. As a specialization gathers more scholars and knowledge, its perspective and methods of scholarship change too. Over time, it becomes as different from its parent discipline as that discipline is from every other one. Some people want to continue to see archeology as a part of anthropology and some even still wish to include anthropology as a branch of sociology.

For our purpose, let us admit to eight social sciences, while recognizing that someone else might have a different list. The eight we will look at are, in alphabetic order: Anthropology, Economics, Geography, History, Political Science, Psychology, Religious Studies, and Sociology. We will look at each of them in turn, basically to refresh our memories and clarify our thinking about the chief concerns of these disciplines and the essential roles each plays in elementary social studies. Though we introduced them initially alphabetically, we will begin our descriptions with history and geography, often seen as the root disciplines of elementary social studies. Then we will move to the other six. While we need to keep in mind that each of the social sciences utilizes concepts from all of the other disciplines, we also need to recognize that each discipline has unique contributions.

History

History is the study of the past, or at least the surviving record of the past. Generally, we limit our study to the human past, but that in itself is very broad. It includes the arts and literature, politics, government, religion, science, and invention. There is a history of scholarship, of military events, and of economic, cultural, and social phenomena. History examines, in fact, the whole spectrum of humans in interaction with one another and with the earth.

The problem of history, at once terrible and wonderful, is the record of the past itself. It is always most incomplete, full of bias and very distorted. This problem has produced two schools of thought regarding historical inquiry. On the one hand, narrative historians, sometimes called humanist historians, suggest that the inadequacies of the record and the complexity of the past defy any attempt to make generalizations. They conceive the historian's job as one of basically describing the past more accurately, insightfully, and fully. Scientific historians, on the other hand, attempt to use scientific methods, often with quantitative data.

The historian studies documents and records of all sorts from personal letters and diaries to business and legal papers such as inventories, wills, and bills of sale, to public records such as newspapers and government papers. Historians also study and compare the physical remains of the past from buildings, roads, and walls to the smallest of objects either preserved through time in someone's safekeeping or found in such places as ruins and tombs. Historians also look at such things as paintings, recordings, photographs, and, for most recent times, video recordings. Finally, historians use people as a resource through approaches like interviews and observations.

Elementary social studies programs are usually developed with the learning of historical facts as one of their purposes. Some critics of the social studies feel that this should be an even stronger emphasis. Involving children in the narrative or the story and drama of history and in the quest for historical knowledge is essential if history is to be learned effectively. Historical fascination is the key to historical learning.

History deals with questions through which a picture is reconstructed of how events actually occurred, why they occurred, and how they impacted on subsequent events. Teachers can stimulate a genuine interest in what life was like in the past. When children are led to examining history as a series of mysteries and problems, they can be naturally led to look at some of the primary resources that historians use. Because of the breadth of history, compilations and lists of historical concepts and generalizations seem to go on and on. It is really exciting, though, to watch what happens when children have experienced a few "Aha!" moments when they discover something about the past that they find fascinating. Once they begin expecting and seeking this, concepts like historical change, cultural bias, civilization, colonization, and cause and effect begin to be perfectly logical to them and to come with the learning.

Geography

Geography is often seen as just maps and globes. Certainly these are among the major tools of geographers and a particular branch of geography, cartography, is devoted to the science of mapping. The field of geography, though, is far broader, encompassing the study of the earth's surface and how that relates to human beings. Geographers are interested in how humans adapt to various living conditions and how humans alter the geography. Physical geographers tend to focus on the earth's natural features (topography, landforms, climate, bodies of water, vegetation, animal life, etc.). Cultural geographers are concerned with people and with the factors that influence their location as well as how humans use and impact resources.

Basic to geographic understanding is some knowledge of where places are located in the world. This area has caused some major concern in recent years. Many feel that children and their teachers as well lack very basic information about their world. This seems very sad when you consider what fascination maps can have for children. With the great variety of colorful, interesting, and attractive maps available to use with children today, there is little excuse for not drawing children into hours of map study. In a world where people have become much more mobile and where people are drawn closer by communication and transportation revolutions, it seems fairly clear that children need more place location knowledge than ever before.

Geographic knowledge is basic to understanding and knowing about the world and its people, and geographically related problems are among the most important ones facing the world today. Children in elementary school are aware of many of these problems and need to be informed and knowledgeable about their impact on their world. Children often have only heard enough to frighten them about geographically related problems ranging from overpopulation to pollution, from the depletion of the ozone to the destruction of the rain forests, from the rapid consumption of fossil fuels to world famines and droughts.

Geographic knowledge is so vast that it is altogether essential that some major categories be used to help us determine just what we should expect children to learn. As defined by the Joint Committee on Geographic Education of the National Council for Geographic Education and the Association of American Geographers, geographic education is focused on five themes.

1. Location: Position on the earth's surface

2. Place: The characteristics that distinguish and define each place

3. Relationships within places: advantages and disadvantages for human settlement

4. Movement: Interacting of humans

5. Regions: Areas that display unity in terms of selected criteria

The questions that geographers ask deal with where people live and why. They are interested in the factors that make the earth habitable. They are also concerned with how variations in geographic factors influence economic development, culture, and sociopolitical organization.

Geography is naturally enchanting to children. They are easily drawn into a study of other settings and other people. The variety and quantity of visual materials of all types is almost unbelievable. The fact that everything has geographic setting and the realization that we understand events and people's actions better when we know more about that geographic setting make the study of geography important for every subject children study throughout life. Flora and fauna or minerals and rocks they study in the sciences, stories and poems they read in literature, and the people and events they study in the past all relate to numerous geographic factors.

Anthropology

Anthropology is the study of culture, especially human culture. *Culture* may be defined in many ways, but it generally consists of a system of beliefs and values, behavior patterns, and customs that is shared by a society of people. A sense of sharing and of oneness with others in this society is often part of what defines and distinguishes particular cultures. Scholars in the field generally like to think of their approach as holistic because they are interested in everything there is to know about a culture. Anthropologists study everything from ancient ruins and human remains to existing cultures. There are numerous and varied specializations within the field, including archeology and ethnography. Because cultural change is a major concern of anthropologists, technological development within a culture has immense importance in many of these specializations.

Anthropologists are always looking for cultural universals. They want to know what defines a culture and what makes it fit together. Anthropologists look carefully at a process they called *enculturation*, which has to do with how young people learn about their own culture, and the influences that cultures have on one another, especially those that result in acculturation or the cultural exchange that occurs when there is long-term contact. Like geographers, they are concerned with the natural environment. However, anthropologists have a different perspective; their concerns being mostly with how culture is influenced by environment and what part culture plays in how humans adapt.

A problem that continually faces anthropologists has to do with their perspective. They want to immerse themselves thoroughly within a culture, often becoming very personally involved. From this experience, they expect to gather immense amounts of data about that culture for further study. There are real questions about whether anthropologists can be objective scholars under such conditions. There is also the continual concern over how much anthropologists will be influencing a less technologically advanced culture even as they study it.

The concept of culture is an essential one for elementary school social studies. There is real concern that children become less ethnocentric and that they learn more about other cultures. Not only are major ideas and facts taken from anthropology, an important part of interdisciplinary programs, but the focus of many primary units is on comparing cultures. The social studies have also found that some of the investigative techniques of anthropologists, chiefly archeological site excavation and interviewing and observation, are highly adaptable for use with elementary and middle school children.

Economics

Economics deals with resources and with the production, exchange, and consumption of goods and services. Economics is perhaps the most problem centered of the social sciences, since its basic concept is scarcity. The resources are scarce and are always likely to be exceeded by human needs and wants.

Economists try to analyze the use of and demand for various resources in order to make recommendations about the problems that relate to scarcity.

Economics is the most mathematical and quantitative of the social sciences. Economists continually try to predict the future and to recommend courses of action that will create a more fortunate situation in the future. Therefore, they are continually trying to find ways to look at quantities produced, exchanged, and consumed. Because in societies where there is specialization, some medium of exchange (money) is going to exist, economics is also concerned with money and other forms of capital and with related areas such as banking, taxation, and investment.

The real importance of economics to elementary children is that throughout life children will be playing roles of worker (producer of goods or services), consumer (user of goods and services), and citizen (part of a society that operates under some economic system). They need to learn a number of economic consumer skills and develop economic values that can be embedded in the social studies. These have to do with such diverse areas of their lives as handling money, banking, budgeting, buying and selling goods and services, and choosing a way of making a living. They also will need to learn to deal with how scarcity relates to and impacts on their own lives. There is also some important economic content for children both as future citizens and as students studying other countries. In both roles, children need at least some understanding of how the economy operates and how this affects people's lives.

Political Science

Political science is the study of government and of all that is associated with the governing process. It deals with human behavior throughout the entire political system and includes the study of the legislative, the judicial, and the executive process. Political scientists study governmental organizations, political parties, pressure groups, voting and elections, and other related parts of the process. They also study different types of government and different types of performance by those involved in governing.

It is easy to think of political science as merely descriptive, trying to give an accurate and complete picture of the way that the political process works both generally and at particular points in time. Certainly, the basic tools of the political scientists are analyses of documents, court cases and governmental acts, and media coverage of political events. But political scientists are also attempting to be predictive, based on the notion that when conditions are similar, it is likely that outcomes and results will tend to repeat.

In the elementary school, children are in the process of becoming aware of the forms and functions of government. Their political awareness is often closely linked to their geographical and historical understanding. Research seems to support the notion that children are "politicalized" by the age of 12. Throughout the elementary grades, they are developing numerous political concepts, including right and wrong, justice, authority, power, security, and politics. They become aware of their own exposure to vast barrages of propaganda.

Political science is the source of a great deal of useful information and concepts in the process of learning about government. Since political science is largely based on questioning the process, in looking analytically at every event, the methods of the discipline are also useful at the elementary level.

Psychology

Psychology is the study of the behavior and thinking of individuals, especially humans. One branch of psychology, social psychology, is even devoted to behavior in groups. Psychologists study development across the entire life span. They are interested in a number of factors that relate to the social studies, including individuality and self-concept, motivation and attitudes, learning and cognition, human personalities, and behavior of individuals in groups.

Psychology provides us insights into social behavior in the classroom and into several elements related to learning. As elementary children learn about other people and other times, they need to understand why people behave as they do. They also need to understand something about the kinds of action taken by different types of leaders.

Religious Studies

Religious studies examines the systems of beliefs and the various practices associated with the various faiths of the world. It is an extremely broad field. Scholarship in religious studies reaches from large formal religions such as Buddhism, Islam, Christianity, Hinduism, and Judaism, to small, relatively obscure cults. Likewise, the spectrum goes from ancient religions that have not been practiced for centuries to modern religions with both ancient and recent origins. Religious study scholars also have great interest in political philosophies that contain substantively religious ideas and have important ramifications that impact on religious practices. Confucianism and communism are examples of such.

The importance of religious studies to elementary social studies relates to the importance of religious beliefs in people's lives. As children study other times and other places, they need some understanding of the religious context. Geography and history are at least partly attributable to religious factors.

It may also become important for children to understand that religious views may impact on some of the activities of the classroom as well. They need to understand the difference between studying religious views and advocating them. There may be families represented in the class with religious beliefs that will not allow the children to participate in some school activities. In the last half century, a related issue has been the place of religious beliefs in the schools. Several questions have been raised about traditional school practices that are related to religious beliefs. These questions have brought about a number of constitutional controversies involving infringement on freedom of religion and the concept of separation of church and state.

Sociology

Sociology is the study of how people act in groups. Sociologists are interested in different kinds of groups, both formal and informal, and in how these groups operate and interact with other groups. They are interested in individuals only with regard to the roles they have within groups. They are very much aware of the influence that societal values and norms have on an individual. An essential assumption of sociology is that individuals need groups in order to survive.

Sociologists study many groups that are very important to elementary age children. They examine the family, the classroom, the school, the community, and numerous types of organizations within the community. Sociology's important contributions to elementary social studies have to do with what the discipline tells us about group behavior. Sociologists offer perspectives about how people act in different institutional and community settings. Sociologists also examine how changes in the institutions occur. They look at social order and influence and authority within groups. They examine the different roles people play and social relationships. They study the impact of technological change on social institutions.

LOOKING BACK

The social studies program is constantly changing because of the variety of influences and pressures for change. The elementary curriculum for over a half century, though, has in some way related to the concept of expanding the world of the child. The most significant changes over the past two decades has been an increasing emphasis on multiculturalism, a move toward thematic topics, and a concern for the importance of children's literature in social studies instruction.

Social science disciplines have had a continued and important role as the source of content of the social sciences. Each of the social sciences, history, geography, anthropology, sociology, economics, political science, psychology, and religious studies, offers a body of knowledge, a unique perspective about the world, and a method of inquiry from which students can learn.

SELF-TEST

1. What factors contribute to controversy over what is taught in the social studies?

2. How does the Expanding Environments curriculum relate to the curriculum of contemporary social studies programs?

3. What is the difference between the terms the social sciences and the social studies?

4. Why have social studies programs tended to focus on history and geography?

5. How has geography in elementary school gone beyond the image of studying maps and globes?

6. How does anthropology relate to and differ from geography?

7. Why is economics important to elementary children?

8. Why do children need to be politically aware?

9. Does the study of religions conflict with the American constitutional concept of separation of church and state?

REFERENCES

Hanna, P.R. (1957) Generalizations and universal values: their implications for the social studies program. in *Social studies in the elementary school: fifty sixth yearbook of the national society for the study of education.* Chicago: University of Chicago Press, (pp.27-47).

Hanna, P.R. (1963). The social studies program in the elementary school in the twentieth century. in Sowards, G.W.(ed.), *The Social Studies.* Glenview, Ill.: Scott Foresman.

Jarolimek, J. J.(1981). The social studies: an overview. In Mehlinger, H.D. and Davis, O. L. (eds.) *The Social Studies: Eightieth Yearbook of the National Society for the Study of Education.* Chicago: University of Chicago Press (pp. 3-18).

Superka, D.P.,Hawke, S.and Morrisett, I. (1980). The current and future status of social studies. *Social Education*. 44 (October), 362-369.

Task Force of the National Commission on the Social Studies in the Schools. (1989). *Charting a course: social studies for the 21st Century*. Washington, D.C.: The National Commission on the Social Studies in the Schools.

SUGGESTED READING

Knight, P. (1989). Research on teaching and learning in history- a perspective from afar. *Social Education*, 53 (September) 306-309.

Massialis, Byron. (1992). The new social studies—retrospect and prospect. *The Social Studies*, 83 (May/June) 125-128.

NCSS (1991). Position statement: social studies in the middle school. *Social Education*, 55 (September,) 287-293.

4 Textbook Units and Their Uses

LOOKING AHEAD

Whenever educators and researchers have examined the teaching of the social studies in the past several decades, they have inevitably come to the conclusion that social studies curriculm is generally textbook driven and that the teachers responsible for teaching the social studies depend text-books. This may be especially true of beginning teachers who need the se-curity and the help afforded by such an authority as a textbook affords. This dependence is a point of concern and the focus of a lot of criticism.

The principal concern of the critics is that textbook teaching is likely to be the very opposite of a problems approach. It will not be creative, exciting, or in any way motivating, and it will not focus on thinking skills and inquiry.

The critics are not unsympathetic to the teacher; they just feel that text-book centered instruction gives up too much.

The good news is, of course, that this need not be so. There are ways that the teacher can fall back on the obvious advantages offered by text-books as resources, yet bring exciting problem centered approaches to the classroom. In this chapter, we will focus on using the textbook as a tool rather than letting the textbook be both the curriculum and the teaching approach. What makes this focus even more important is that the basic ideas presented here actually go far beyond the textbook. They apply to any resource that the student is going to need to read. Because the social studies is an information centered-curriculum area, notions about how to enhance students' abilities to use print materials can be extremely useful.

CAN YOU? DO YOU?

Can you

- Identify the specific reading abilities students need in the social studies?
- Tell how we can use textbooks with students who cannot read?

Do you

- Know several ways to teach new concepts and new vocabulary?

- Know some ways to actually shorten what students have to read?

- Know why it is important for students to understand the organization of reading material?

TEXTBOOK UNITS

Textbook programs dominate elementary and middle school classrooms (Ball and Feiman-Nemser 1988). You may remember the discussion in Chapter 2 which pointed out that using textbooks does not eliminate the need for preparation but does reduce the amount of preparation and does, to some extent, take the responsibility for making decisions about what children ought to learn out of the teacher's hands.

Textbook units offer some important instructional advantages. For teachers who use such units, there is a common reading material containing the same information for all students. This is of tremendous advantage, for it makes it possible to give single assignments and to unify instruction. Another important positive about this type of teaching is the security of knowing that those who have prepared the material have knowledge and expertise in the field, have done a good deal of research into content, and have given thorough professional attention to the preparation of the text. There is added teacher peace of mind in knowing that modern technology has made it possible to keep the reading level of textual material more precisely at the intended grade level than at any point in educational history.

Textbook centered units emphasize, usually above all else, is getting information from print, most specifically from the textbook. Assignments involving reading pages, portions of chapters, and entire chapters in order to answer sets of questions or do other types of written exercises are most common.

MAXIMIZING EFFECTIVE TEXTBOOK LEARNING

Reading is an interactive process. It cannot take place unless meaning is involved. Although the best of scholars in the field of learning do not understand the reading process, educators like to think that effective reading involves coupling decoding and comprehension skills with background knowledge and an awareness of the interrelationships of elements in the text (Vacca and Vacca, 1993. pp. 15–20). The questions in using textbooks in the social studies are the following: How can we make textbook assignments have the most meaning and usefulness to the greatest number of students? How can we aid students in relating background and in seeing the interrelationships of parts of the text?

A fundamental issue is making anything students do with the textbook meaningful, important, and purposeful. This was brought home to me very powerfully by a visit to an intermediate classroom a few years ago. I have tried to preserve faithfully the details of a short exchange between the teacher and the class.

After placing me in an advantageous spot to observe her social studies lesson, the teacher opened by saying, "Let's turn to page ___ in our social studies book." (She named it, but out of respect to the publishers and authors, I will not.) At this point, an audible groan rippled through the classroom.

The high twangy voice of a girl in one of the favored seats near the front piped up at this point, "We've already read that!" Her tone was one of complaint.

The whole thing was starting to embarrass the teacher. (Remember, I was there as an invited guest, sitting in the back of the room.) Turning to the girl sternly, she replied with a forced brightness, "Not orally! I want you to read that without missing any words."

Unfortunately, the incident is not that different from what seems to go on in a lot of classrooms. In fact the major criticism of textbook teaching is not so much an attack on the textbooks as on teachers who seem to make text assignments that just do not have any real meaning or purpose. Research seems to indicate that though teaching in content areas such as the social studies is textbook centered, reading to learn strategies is not an important component of teaching (Smith and Feathers 1983, Ratekin et.al. 1985). Assignments are given and perhaps checked and counted. But doing the assignment really does not matter because it does not relate to evaluation or even to other class activities.

If textbook units are to be used effectively, students are going to have to view work as something more than a series of things to complete and teachers need to see curriculum as more than a number of pages to cover (McCutcheon 1981). But this is going to be important with any social studies approach in which students are using textbooks or other print materials to get information or ideas. Let us look, then, at what teachers need to do to use textbooks and similar reading materials effectively.

- Give specific purposeful assignments. Not only does the teacher need to have clear and important purposes for having students read material, the students need to understand what these purposes are. Talking with students about what they are reading for should be as important as telling them what to read. It also means that the teacher will need to have a fair degree of certainty that the students can actually accomplish those purposes.

- Stimulate interest in doing the reading. Fortunately, teachers have several ways available to arouse interest, most of them involve creating curiosity. The teacher can, for instance, ask questions that can be answered by the reading material, point out curious and interesting illustrations that are explained or further described in the text, start and leave incomplete stories that are finished in the assigned reading: or give thumbnail sketches of people, places, or events in the text.

• Make sure that students have the skills needed to do the assignment. Many reading skills are needed in the social studies. A partial list of these appears below. If the teacher does not know the mastery level of a needed skill, it is a good idea to provide at least a review demonstration and monitored practice before the students do the assignment.

• Provide supervision, monitoring, and help where needed.

Monitoring is important for a number of reasons. First, it is an effective form of teaching and at least in some instances allows the teacher to keep students from deep learning of incorrect ways of doing assignments. Second, it helps teachers spot cases of "frustration" easily so that directions can be clarified or help given to students who do not understand assignments. Such help, particularly the right kind of help, is not always available to a child outside the classroom. Third, monitoring gives the teacher feedback about the effectiveness of the preteaching, the clarity of the assignment, and the ability of the students.

• Follow up on reading assignments. If students are required to read and do tasks associated with reading, it should be because this will help them learn important things. What they learn needs to be applied and used in ways that make learning from print important.

READING ABILITIES AND SKILLS NEEDED IN THE SOCIAL STUDIES

A number of identifiable reading activities and skills are important if students are going to get meaning from textbooks and other reading materials. Following is a list of those activities and the skills involved.

1. Recognize the organization of reading materials.

   • Use bold faced headings as cues to content.

   • Recognize topic sentences and using these in skimming. and scanning.

   • Identify main idea(s).

   • Find supporting ideas.

   • Learn vocabulary and concept meaning.

   • Recognize and using context definitions and identifications.

- Use glossaries and outside resources to find the meaning of vocabulary.
- Use structural analysis and context clues to obtain vocabulary meaning.

2. Bring meaning to reading.

- Relate what is read to personal experiences, observations, and past learning.
- Relate new material to previous studies.
- Recognize and following relationships in text (e.g., sequence, chronology).
- Relate what is read to particular problems and purposes brought to reading.

3. Reading for a purpose.

- Understand questions and problems in order to be able to recognize appropriate solutions.
- Skim for overall meaning.
- Scan for specific information, answers to questions, and do on.
- Use the table of contents and index to find specific information.
- Obtain information from maps.
- Interpret charts and graphs.

4. Read critically

- Recognize author bias.
- Recognize discrepancies, contradictions, and missing information.
- Identif relationships among elements (e.g., cause and effect).
- Distinguishing opinion from fact, description from interpretation, and so on.

READING PROBLEMS AND HOW TO DEAL WITH THEM

There are a variety of strategies and techniques for helping students who have problems reading textual and reference material. Some are simple and direct, while othere are complex. What you want as a teacher is for students to be able to get maximum use of printed social studies material of all types. I would like to suggest a kind of grand, four- step strategy.

1. Preteach difficult vocabulary prior to reading.

2. Reduce the length of independent reading tasks.

3. Provide specific clear purposes for reading.

4. Develop predictive skills so that students use features of text (such as pictures and bold faced headings), features of tasks (such as key in question words) to anticipate more accurately.

By specifying a series of steps I do not mean to imply a locked-in sequence. The precise order of the steps as well as the decision to include any one of these specific steps may be varied greatly according to teaching style and other individual and classroom factors. More importantly, I do not want to convey the impression that these steps can only be carried out in one way. The steps suggest general approaches not specific techniques. Some notion of the range of possibilities is indicated in the examples that are given in the following sections describing each step.

Strategies for Developing Vocabulary

The single most important factor in reading comprehension is vocabulary meaning (Davis 1968). Every student develops and extends four basic vocabularies throughout his or her education: reading, listening, speaking and writing. For most students, substantial listening and speaking vocabularies exist when they enter school. They attach a set of meanings to many words they hear and use a large number of words in speaking. Most of the materials designed specifically for early reading instruction are limited to include only those words that the child is likely to know. Because the listening vocabulary far excludes all other vocabularies throughout the elementary years this is not a particularly limiting factor. Most of the words they encounter in reading are words they have heard and for which they have conceptualized meanings.

But because the social studies deals with other cultures and times it is vocabulary rich. Many words are introduced for which the student has few related experiences or concepts. Proper nouns, particularly names of people, places, and events, are abundant. Many complex abstract concepts are also given word labels in the social studies. In fact, the most important new words that children encounter in social studies reading materials are terms which are entirely new to them, terms that are not in their speaking or listening vocabularies. Teachers are responsibe for providing enabling experiences and building necessary concepts and vocabulary. New vocabulary to be understood by the child must be fitted into perceptions and experiences that form the child's existing view of the world (Smith 1975). New concepts then become part of the child's world view only when they can be related to that view as it already exists.

If children are to be successful in understanding or making sense of social studies reading tasks, they should be helped to thinking about new words before reading. Preteaching of essential new words and the concepts they represent prior to any reading task will save both teacher and student frustration. Many types of activities and techniques can be used for developing vocabulary meaning prior to reading. A few ideas are suggested and described.

Teacher Explanation of Meaning

Often the most efficient way of introducing vocabulary words is for the teacher simply to explain the meanings of crucial terms prior to reading. If several terms are involved, a chalkboard or duplicated list or one provided in the text should be followed. In any event, the contextual importance of the terms for the particular reading assignment needs to be described and the word needs to be seen in written form by the students. Though it is the *quickest* way to introduce vocabulary, it can also be the least effective. Students will sometimes feel no need to listen, particularly if the routine of the explanations becomes too tedious and regular. When the teacher uses this approach, presentations need to be varied, exciting, full of reinforcement, and interspersed with other approaches to vocabulary development. At its simplest, the teacher explanation involves pointing out to the students where the text uses and defines particular terms. Teacher definitions might include a handout or chalkboard or poster list of simple definitions of key terms. The teacher may point out pictures, maps, and charts that illustrate the concepts involved in particular terms and bring objects with which students might have term-related multisensory experiences.

Classifying Experiences

Using classifying charts helps students see how terms fit into various systems of concepts. Charting is an effective way to help children categorize and see relationships among words and terms. Though such charts are more often used in reviewing after reading, they can also be ways of helping children build a conceptual framework for new words. For example, the terms *bayou* and *canal* might be understood better if shown on one or both of the following charts.

Other classifying experiences may simply involve the students in sorting and prioritizing terms and words or a series of questions that bring out previous associations in pupil's minds which will enable them to classify the terms.

Extended Teacher Definitions

If a few words or terms are central to understanding total reading selections then the teacher may need to give a more extended definition including illustrations. For example, the terms *pioneer* and *frontier* are abstractions that are crucial to understanding entire areas of study. The teacher may

Chart 1

Term/Features	Natural	Man-Made	Examples	Related Geographic Features
bayou shallow, sometimes navigable			Louisiana River	Low-lying marsh land, usually river or river related
canal Shallow but navigable,			Erie Canal	Construction usually for transportation in conjunction with a large body of water locks to change water level

Chart 2

Waterways	Land Forms	Types of Vegetation
bayou	isthmus	deciduous trees
canal	delta	savannah

want to go to elaborate lengths to develop these understandings, including reading contemporary descriptions of features of pioneer life, showing audiovisual materials, and providing a wide range of experiences prior to reading. An extended discussion to reach a group consensus about definition would be still another way to introduce terms. The following questions might serve as a guide to develop a consensus definition of the abstract term *democracy*.

- What are your first thoughts about the meaning of *democracy*? (This might start a round of association play.)

- What are the features or characteristics of a democracy? (Prepare a list on the board.)

- Do *all* leaders in this country (depending on pupil knowledge, you might ask about particular contemporary or historical individuals and their differences) have the same concept of democracy?

- Does democracy mean equal opportunity? Participation in government? Equal wealth? Freedom (what freedom)? Equality?

- If a country has democratic ideals does this mean it will have democratic practices?

Teacher Provided Experiences

Some terms may be better understood if the teacher can provide real or vicarious experiences to illustrate the concepts involved. Names of articles of clothing or utensils from a culture, for example, may be better understood if the children see the objects and try to use or wear them. Foods that can be tasted may leave a more lasting impression.

Where real experiences are impossible, vicarious experiences may also be useful in developing concepts. These experiences may include hearing or reading fictional stories, seeing and hearing audiovisual presentations, and other activities where the child can identify with the people involved.

Students' Researched Definitions and Meanings
of Words, Names and Terms

Finding meanings for new words can be an exciting new adventure for children or it can be routine, unpopular, busy work. The number of words must be limited with special thought to age and ability so that the task does not become drudgery. Student involvement and participation in the discovery of new definitions will slow the instructional process, but will ensure a greater understanding. The techniques are numerous and only a few can be described here.

- The word experts: Each student is responsible for just one word, or, at most, two that appear in a unit to be studied. The job of the *expert* is to become so knowledgeable about that word that if any question about its meaning is raised, he or she will feel comfortable in attempting to answer.

- Picture definitions: The students are responsible for the meaning of a term or word in visual form. Posters, collages, and rebuses are among the many possible forms these defining visuals may take. Collages may be especially useful in depicting abstract concepts such as democracy, as well as developing a concept of a particular person, their character traits and accomplishments.

- Sound pictures: A few particular social studies terms lend themselves to sound pictures as a way of vocabulary introduction. In some cases, a student may have to take a tape recorder to the best place to collect the sound picture. For example, the call of a muezzin or the singing of a cantor might be ways of gaining concepts of what these individuals do in a study of religion. A foreign language or dialect, a musical instrument, a type of song or dance melody, and other similar concept words can be defined through experiencing the sound.

- Word look-outs: Each student is responsible for one or two words and their meanings. Over a period of several days' class activities, every word will come into discussion. When an individual's word comes up that person is responsible for noticing, defining, and writing the word on the chalkboard or on a classification chart.

- Contextual locating: Many terms are defined either directly or indirectly by the reading context. As a skimming exercise, have students look for and read definitions of words and terms as the text defines them.

- Creating context: Often the best way to learn what a word means is to use it. In this technique, students are demonstrating that they know the meaning of a word by inventing a context where the word can be used properly. The particular context required of the student may vary greatly -a story, a descriptive paragraph, a single sentence, a poem, a poster or cartoon caption, a bumper sticker, a picture title, a type of poem. These and many others can be creative applications of words through written contexts. Following are examples of a Diamond poem for the word *scimitar* and a descriptive paragraph for the word *senator*.

Scimitar

Keen

Curved blade

Defense of Islam

Saracen

Sword

No matter how big your state is or how many people it has there are always two *Senators*. *Senators* are elected every six years. There are fewer *Senators* than there are Representatives.

Ways of Reducing the Amount of Reading in the Social Studies

Reading is the means not the end of dealing with social studies materials. Understanding and being able to understand the idea content of materials is the goal. Therefore, more comprehension can be achieved by cutting the number of actual pages of reading. For some children, a reading assingnment of two pages of print versus one of twenty pages of reading may mean the difference between their being willing to read the material or unwilling to readi it.

One of the most creative ways a teacher can help a child with reading difficulty in the social studies is to control the amount of material that the student has to read. The trick is to find ways of focusing the individual student's reading effort on the particular information that he or she absolutely needs to know. Because social studies materials are most often written at or above grade level reading ability, reducing reading may be helpful for many students. Following are several ways of reducing the reading load:

- Use student written summaries instead of the text.

- Use teacher-written summaries instead of the text.

- Use textbook cut-ups.

- Try textbook high-lighting.

- Experiment with question write-ins.

- Cooperate with class divide-ups.

Using Student-Written Summaries

One way to reduce reading is to collect, over a period of several years, student-written summaries of chapters or sections of printed material. These can be put in binders or folders with illustrations and then used as reading material for students unable to read the text or the resources. The time needed to collect good summaries puts the beginning teacher at a disadvantage. A teacher may have to have several classes before a sufficient number of good summaries can be assembled. Cooperation from a teacher and class in a high grade may be one way of overcoming this difficulty temporarily. Good student written summaries have several advantages.

- They are usually closer to the language that students speak and hear daily both in sentence structure and vocabulary than are printed materials.

- They reflect digested rather than raw content. That is, they include the message that one child has received from print.

- They are usually brief and to the point, leaving out many things a teacher would include.

Before student summaries are used as a substitute for textual materials, the teacher must do some careful editing. This can be very time consuming. The following example was done by a sixth grade student. The teacher read and corrected the paper and, after a conference, the student rewrote it. A few minor corrections were still needed and these could be made on the copy that was to be used. In fact, it may be some advantage psychologically to the student experiencing reading difficulty to see that the material he or she reads has errors. This may help the child's self-confidence and willingness to try to write themselves. This summary is a child's view of an entire chapter of a social studies textbook.

Example of a Student Summary *

The first industry to grow in the United States was the textile industry. This happened after Samuel Slater brought the idea of cotton spinning machines to the United States and Francis Lowell

---

*Summary of Chapter 13, "An Industrial Nation,"— *The United States Yesterday and Today.* (1990) Morristown, N.J.: Silver Burdette, pp. 280–297.

built machines for making cotton cloth. Eli Whitney came up with the idea of mass production and interchangeable parts.

After the Civil War, more money went into industries and many industries grew. Andrew Carnegie built the steel industry into an empire. When he was 66, he sold all his companies and retired. Other industries that grew were the banking industry and the oil industry. Industries got so big that they became monopolies. There were also new farm machines and scientific developments during the industrial revolution. One famous scientist was George Washington Carver. People moved off the farms and into the cities. Many people also immigrated from other countries to the United States. In the cities, people began having problems because of houses with poor safety and sanitation.

Teacher Summaries

Well-prepared teacher summaries of printed materials also take a great deal of time to produce. However, they may be written when the teachers *have* more time available than they do in the classroom. I have written them in the summer, on airplanes, in hospital waiting rooms and in other locations when I just *needed* something to occupy my mind. Such summaries are especially useful because they may be written to include all specific facts and ideas that the teacher especially wants children to know. They can be written to fit the test or evaluation if necessary. Vocabulary can be specifically controlled and limited. The teacher should have a clearer and more complete understanding of the conceptual content of the material than do children and be able to give the purposes and themes more emphasis. Teachers are also less likely to make spelling and grammatical errors than are children. Clear references to pictures, diagrams, and other features of the text can be inserted.

Because of the time that summaries require the teacher usually should not try to write summaries for all readings the first year. In a few years, though, a substantial number can be collected. Such summaries may be duplicated and used with an entire class, with groups of students, or with individual children with special reading problems.

Following is a teacher's summary of the same selection covered by the student write-up. Similarities and differences in style and completeness can be noted but the one crucial quality of shortening the material read is the same. Thus, both make good substitute reading materials.

Example of a Teacher Summary

This chapter deals with the Industrial Revolution in the United States. This "revolution" began in the first half of the 18th century

---

*Summary of Chapter 13, "An Industrial Nation," *The United States Yesterday and Today* (1990). Morristown, N.J.: Silver Burdette, pp. 280–297.

with the textile industry in New England. Two men made this happen—Samuel Slater and Francis Lowell. Slater was an Englishman who built the first cotton spinning machines. Lowell built factories with weaving machines that made cotton cloth. The Industrial Revolution was also aided by Eli Whitney, the inventor of the cotton gin, who introduced the ideas of mass production and machines with interchangeable parts.

After the Civil War, the development of a national market due to transportation developments made more money available for industry. Among the great industrialists were Andrew Carnegie who built a huge steel making industry and J.P. Morgan, who built a large banking industry and later bought Carnegie's steel empire. Another leader was John D. Rockefeller who founded Standard Oil. This was one of the businesses that grew so large that it could put competition out of business. The government became so concerned about such businesses that it tried to regulate them through a law called the Sherman Antitrust Act (1890).

New farm machines and scientific developments revolutionized farming and caused many people to move to the cities where jobs were available in factories. Large numbers of immigrants also came from Europe and Asia to the cities. Cities grew so quickly that they developed problems due to crowded areas and poorly built buildings. Sanitation and safety in tenement (apartment) buildings was very bad.

Attempts to deal with the problems were called reforms. Limits were set on immigration. Laws were passed to improve housing and sanitation. Settlement houses were founded to provide services. One of the reformers was Jane Addams who founded a settlement called Hull House in Chicago.

Textbook Cut-ups

Textbook cut-ups requires that the teacher have a free rein with the printed materials. It also demands extra copies of materials and a ruthlessness in destroying books and similar materials that repels many teachers automatically. It may be an especially good way of salvaging texts no longer in use.

Two copies of each page to be used may be needed for every cut-up version unless the material is printed on only one side or careful editing is done. The teacher cuts out only the most important sentences, pictures and other things appearing on the pages and glues or pastes them in order on a clean sheet. A textbook chapter can usually be reduced to a few pages. The print authority is preserved as assurance to the child that he or she is reading a real book. But the overpowering and discouraging number of pages that may keep many children from ever attempting to really *do* an assignment is present.

Textbook Highlighting

A felt-tip highlighter or underliner is needed for the old college student trick. Go through the chapter before the student does and highlight the parts to which he or she really needs to pay attention to. Warn the student about what is important and what is not instead of letting the child figure it out. Make sure the child knows what has been done and why before he or she reads the material.

Write-Ins

Writing in the text is something that students have done and which teachers have discouraged. This technique causes a breaking of the taboo. It is a technique that is easier if only a few problem readers are involved where the teacher aids them by marking up their texts.

The teacher draws attention to major points and to questions answered by writing notes in the text. If textbook questions are used, they may even be cut out and taped directly next to the answer. Arrows can be drawn to maps, pictures and charts from the descriptive references to these in context.

Class Divide-ups

Instead of having every child read every part of the text assign only portions of the text to each child for reading. All can still have the benefit of the information in the entire reading. Each child might be assigned half the chapter and have a partner assigned the other half. The partners then have to prepare one another with the important and useful information in the other half. Another way to work this is to have various groups each assigned sections. After reading the section, the group meets to decide what they need to teach the class from their section and *how* this can be done most effectively. Until the children become good at this, it will be necessary and helpful for the teacher to sit in on the meeting of every group to provide guidance.

Aiding Predictions

Effective previewing or surveying of reading material:

- Provides purposes for reading in the form of expectations.

- Heightens anticipation and interest.

- Helps determine in what way materials relate to particular interests, questions, hypotheses, and so on.

- Provides advance organizers for thinking about what is read.

- Aids in predicting.

According to Smith (1975), greater accuracy in prediction is highly important to reading comprehension. That is, if the individual has a better idea about the nature of the reading content *before* reading, he or she will understand it better. Study skills development key in on such predictive skills. Herber (1970), for example, has described a technique called SQ3R. SQ3R. is a 5 step procedure consisting of steps labeled:

Survey

Question

Read

Recite

Review

Of these steps, surveying or previewing the materials seems to be most important because effective surveying helps all other phases. If the student can predict, he or she can follow the direction of the writer and anticipate his or her thoughts.

A number of teaching techniques, including the following, can help students predict more accurately the content of reading materials.

- Point out the headings and boldface type so the students recognize them as organizers.

- Have students discuss speculations from titles and headings about what content is logical.

- Point out pictures before reading and discuss them. From the pictures and the captions, intelligent guesses are possible about the accompanying written material.

- Point out specific references in the text to maps and illustrations so the students will know to look for these during reading. For example, the text might refer to stone ruins which an illustration will show.

- Provide an outline or introduction overview and discuss it. A simple outline for the selection involved in the student and teacher summaries used previously might be

  I.   The Textile Industry grows in the United States

  II.   Transportation aids the growth of industry after Civil War.

  III. Machinery revolutionizes farming.

Purposeful Reading

If asked, "Why are you reading this?" most students in social studies classes respond with a shrug of the shoulders or, at best, answer, "Because the teacher told me to." The most effective readers are very aware of their purposes for reading and areas to find very specific types of information. This alertness to purposes allows students to cover printed material more rapidly, use context and format clues in locating information, access and use such features as index and table of contents, and even determine appropriateness or inappropriateness of the material. Reading to achieve specific purposes aids in developing predictive skills described earlier.

To help poorer readers use their social studies textbooks and other reading materials with a better sense of purpose, social studies teachers need to set purposes for such students that are specific and clear, guide them so that they read to understand those purposes, and follow through to emphasize the importance of the purposes.

The major learning students need for some purposeful reading is that the objective of reading in social studies is not simply to read the material. In fact, reading is incidental and only a tool by which the student gains the necessary information. Some very common procedures of social studies textbooks focus on providing purpose for reading regardless of whether the teacher is aware of this purpose.

These procedures include

- Providing guide questions before reading which identify specific types of information and understandings the student is to gain.

- Providing study questions that ask the student to identify the ways an author thinks and to go beyond the author's thoughts. For example, after reading material on historical periods, questions might be asked to get the student to explain how people in those eras might think about the way we live in the present.

- Alerting students prior to reading to follow-up tasks that will employ particular knowledge and concepts. For example, in the chapter on the industrial change in America, students might be asked to build a model of a farm before the change another to show how farming had been revolutionized.

When tasks related to *reading* are given to students, the purposes need to be made clear. It should not be assumed that students understand why they are reading or know what to look for.

Practice exercises such as skimming and summarizing for particular facts, details, or headings can help students become more aware of the importance of purposes in guiding how and what they read.

TEACHING STUDENTS HOW TO READ QUESTIONS AND TASK STATEMENTS

Many students have difficulty in reading social studies materials simply because they do not make effective use of question clues that could help them be more purposeful in their reading and more accurate and correct in the way they respond. Teachers can incorporate direct teaching about question clues into social studies or reading study skills instruction. One of the most fundamental skills in dealing with questions has to do with getting an immediate idea of what a question is asking and being able to relate that to the reading material. One of the ways that effective readers do this is by being sensitive to the nature of question words and to the nature of the answers these words demand.

Question words such as who, what, where and when call for particular kinds of answers.One does not have to have any knowledge at all of the reading material itself to know that the answer to "Who was the English king who was a leader in the Third Crusade?" will *not* be, "The Long Bow," "The Battle of Agencourt," or "The Holy Roman Empire." The question word *Who* dictates a particular kind of answer including the name or description of a person or group of persons. Any question, in fact, offers cues to the length and nature of acceptable answers by the question words that appear in it. Many students intuitively learn this as they develop their skills in reading and thesocial studies. For some, though, it is crucial that the teachers develop their sensitivity to the influence of key words on question meaning.

Even alerting students to organizational features of textbooks related to questions may be useful to them. For example, students should realize that answers to lists of questions in the text are usually found in the same sequence that they are asked. As simple and logical as this may seem, there are many students with reading difficulty who may need to be reminded often.

Another feature that students should recognize is to question reversal and parallel structure. These both refer to questions that are written in exactly the same language as the text but with change in sentence order. A question such as, "What was the ruler of Ancient Egypt called?" will probably be answered in the text with a statement such as, "The ruler of Ancient Egypt was called the Pharaoh."

Teachers of the social studies constantly grapple with problems students have in grasping and retaining content through reading. The teacher needs to remember that the social studies objective is not to have children read so much as it is to have them learn to use reading as one way to master concepts, learn facts, and obtain information relative to problem solutions. If this is kept in mind, a more purposeful and effective strategy can be developed.

LOOKING BACK

The social studies textbook is often the major teaching tool in the social studies. In order to teach effectively from a textbook or any reading material, the material has to be meaningful and purposeful to students. Teachers need to give purposeful assignments, stimulate interest, make sure that students have the skills needed to do the required reading, provide proper and sufficient supervision and monitoring for reading tasks, and follow-up effectively.

When students have problems reading content material, there are several strategies that teachers can use. Among the most important of these is preteaching vocabulary, reducing the actual length of reading assignments, providing sufficient and clear purposes for reading, and developing predictive skills.

SELF-TEST

1. Why is making anything students do with the textbook meaningful, important, and purposeful the fundamental issue of this chapter?

2. Name several things that teachers can do to make the use of textbooks more effective.

3. Describe several ways of teaching concepts and vocabulary to children.

4. What is SQ3R?

5. What is meant by the term *purposeful reading* and why is the concept important?

REFERENCES

Ball, D.L. and Feiman-Nemser, S. (1988). Using textbooks and teachers' guides: a dilemma for beginning teachers and teacher educators. *Curriculum Inquiry*, 18 (Wingter), 401-423.

Davis,F.B. (1968). Research in comprehension in reading. *Reading Research Quarterly*. 3 (Summer) 449-545.

Herber, H.L. (1978). *Teaching reading in content areas.*(2nd ed.). Englewood Cliffs, N.J.: Prentice Hall.

McCutcheon, G. (1981). Elementary social studies teachers' planning for social studies and other subjects. *Theory and Research in Social Education*, 9 (Winter), 45-66.

Ratekin, N. et al. (1985). Why teachers resist content reading instruction. *Journal of Reading*, 28 (Fall), 432-437.

Smith, F.A. (1975). *Comprehension and learning: a conceptual framework for teachers.* New York: Holt, Rinehart, and Winston.

Smith, F.R., and Feathers, K.M. (1983). Teacher and student perception of content area reading. *Journal of Reading*, (Fall), 348-354.

Vacca,R.T., and Vacca, J.L. (1993) *Content area reading* (4th ed.). New York: Harper-Collins.

SUGGESTED READING

Smith, B.A., and Larkin, A.G. (1990). Should place vocabulary be central to primary social studies. *The Social Studies*, 81 (September/October), 221-226.

Vocke, D.E., and Hahn, A. (1989). What does reading research say to social studies seachers? *Social Education.* 53 (September), 323-326.

5 Organizing to Teach, Assess, and Evaluate in the Social Studies

LOOKING AHEAD

Evaluation is an important and ongoing part of the educational process in the social studies. It has high visibility because of the importance that educators, students, and the public attach to test scores and grades. But this emphasis poses a danger because the curriculum that we teach becomes driven by feedback and measurement. It should be the other way around. The evaluation should reflect what teachers and schools are trying to accomplish.

This chapter focuses on the tools of evaluation. We want to stress not only that the evaluation process should reflect the aims and the objectives of the social studies program, but that in a problems approach, the tools themselves should be consistent with problems orientation. Even the evaluation experience should involve children and should develop their ability to solve problems.

CAN YOU? DO YOU?

Can you

- Tell why grades and test scores are so emphasized in schools?
- Tell how teachers go about determining grades?
- Explain what holistic evaluation is?

Do you

- Know why evaluation is always comparative?
- Know how evaluation should be different in the problems approach?
- Know the weaknesses and strengths of objective and subjective tests?

WHAT IS EVALUATION ALL ABOUT IN THE SOCIAL STUDIES?

Teachers and students have a tendency to equate evaluation with grades. This is like thinking of art as color or even as a paintbrush. Grades are only one of the tools of evaluation. They are indicators of student progress and learning, the degree of teaching success, and areas of strength and weakness, so too are diagnostic and achievement tests, teacher observations, and student work of a variety of types. It is extremely important that teachers do not lose sight of the fact that the true purpose of evaluation in the social studies, as in any other area of instruction, should be to help children learn better.

Evaluation and test scores take on special importance to teachers, students, and parents. The significance attached to these measures far exceeds the mere notion that evaluation uses grades and tests as tools. What makes grades and tests so important is that they are the major feedback to the students, parents, and others; they are concrete and a matter of permanent record; and they seem to be based on solid performance data. It is easy to lose sight of the fact that feedback is only a small part of the reason for student assessment. Other important things we are trying to do are related to finding out how well we taught, how well the student learned and can perform, and what still needs attention.

Even grades and test scores themselves have more than one basis of comparison. Though all measurement of student assessment involves comparison of student performance, different points of comparison are used. The student may be compared to some criteria of success, to some standard, to classmates, to a national average, or to his or her own past performance or perceived potential. Normative evaluation, for example, is the basis of most standardized tests and is used to compare the performance of one person or group to average performance in either an age or grade group among all people taking the test. In criterion based evaluation, the concern is about the extent to that an individual is able to meet indicators of success which relate to particular characteristics. Levels of performance are set in advance on the basis of some preconceived notions of what constitutes *mastery*, for example.

In instructional planning, these preset criteria are called *objectives*. Objectives describe the specific knowledge or skills that are expected to result from the teaching/learning activities. Objectives, or learning outcomes (another term that is sometimes used with almost the same meaning), usually are more clearly defined if they name behavior that might be an indicator that the objective has been achieved. Evaluation in teaching is usually most effective if we base it on objectives or desired learning outcomes that we can then use as indicators of the degree of success we have had in teaching. Mastery learning programs are based on the notion that instruction about any basic learning needs to continue until that standard has been achieved.

In the social studies, we have been struggling for a long time with some particular evaluation dilemmas that educators in other curricular areas may be just now starting to see. One of these dilemmas has to do with the overall evaluation process, but most especially with that part that has to do with giving grades. Social studies learning outcomes involve the acquisition of knowledge; the development of skills, the variables of interpersonal relationships, very complex and often subtle changes in personal values, philosophies, and beliefs; and others that relate to performance and to development of products that are often intricate and elaborate. For some of these outcomes, it is very easy to design ways of evaluating that can be easily measured. For what may be considered the most important learning outcomes, though, measurement and evaluation are much more difficult and subjective.

EVALUATION AND THE PROBLEMS APPROACH

That a teacher takes the problems approach to the social studies does not necessarily mean that all of the traditional evaluation tools will be abandoned. Grading systems and the testing program are almost certainly going to be controlled at a high administrative level. In addition, the traditions of feedback are deeply entrenched and of even more importance in an age of family crises, societal unrest, and more common recourse to litigation.

What it does mean is that the evaluation focus of the teacher is going to be different and the criteria for evaluation are going to be altered. Success in the traditional classroom was based on the ability to remember specified information and the mastery of particular technical skills. In the classroom that uses a problems approach, each problem may demand different information and skills. The ability to obtain information and to learn skills is most important. Learning to learn, becoming an independent learner are stressed. The foci of evaluation are expanded to include such factors as the ability to identify and define problems, flexibility to handle new situations, ability to apply knowledge in different settings, and openness to many ideas and solutions. The real concern is the ability of students to handle with problems.

While in traditional social studies instruction the emphasis in evaluation is on what is learned, what was called inquiry- based social studies, which dominated the 1970s and early 1980s, moved that emphasis toward the process of learning or how we learn. The problems approach stresses an even more holistic view of evaluation, focusing on the ability to find and use knowledge in dealing with problems. It takes into account that evaluation of a child may reflect a number of factors including academic ability, verbal skills, creativity and problem solving skills, personality, work habits, home environment, personal history, effort, and ability to deal with people.

The tools used in evaluation and even for grading, or at least the way that these tools are used differs in the problems approach. Some indication of that difference is shown in the following table of some of the evaluation tools. Please note that the table should be seen as a way of depicting the differences in perception and emphasis rather than as based on research data.

GUIDELINES FOR EVALUATION

Evaluation may require many different types of instruments and forms in the social studies, including quizzes, tests, examinations, observations, oral examinations, interviews and conferences, check-lists, holistic evaluation of projects and papers, self-evaluations, portfolios, and a host of others. Even if we limit our concern to just grading and other forms of feedback, the complexity of the evaluation process is sometimes overwhelming. It might be illustrated by taking a look at a typical six week grading period. An intermediate level (fourth to sixth grade) social studies teacher, even one of the fairly traditional kind, might have the following variety of information on which he or she would like to base grades:

- Scores/grades on one or two unit tests and perhaps a quiz or two

- Records of homework and/or seat work completed

- Evaluations of map work of three or four kinds that the student have done

- Recorded grades from several pieces of evaluated written work (Stories, poems, essays, reports, outlines, questions answered.)

- A holistic evaluation of a group project involving working together to produce a group report and some display (diorama, mural, table scene.)

- Grades for an individual research project given both in writing and orally

- Observations of participation in class activities and discussion

- Notations on volunteer projects including some very elaborate ones showing a great deal of energy and interest

- Student self-evaluation and peer evaluation of projects

Evaluation Tools	Traditional Teaching	Problems Approach
Daily assignments	2, 3	1
Short quizzes, review	2, 3	1
Short quizzes, problems	1	2
Objective tests, recall	2, 3	1
Objective tests, application	2, 3	2
Essay tests, informational	2	1
Essay tests, problems	1	1
Individual		
Projects	1, 2	2, 3
Reports, written	1, 2	2, 3
Reports, oral	1	1, 3
Group/collaborative		
Projects	1, 2	2, 3
Reports, written	1, 2	2, 3
Reports, oral	1	1, 3
Teacher observation	1	2, 3
Self assessment	0, 1	1, 2, 3
Journals	0, 1	1, 2, 3
Stories and other writing	0, 1	1, 2, 3
Games and active discussion	0, 1	1, 2, 3
Problem solving activities	0, 1	1, 2, 3
Dramatic activities	0, 1	1, 2, 3
Participation in community		
service projects	0	1, 2, 3
Personal portfolios	0	2, 3

Indicators

0 – Not Used

1 – Used Sparingly/Occasionally

2 – Used Frequently

3 – Of Critical Importance in Evaluation

The problem that this teacher has is more than one of determining the various numbers to plug in or coming up with a formula that weights the various activities. Some of the activities on the list may be evaluated in such a way as to yield very definitive and objective grades. Others, though, may have been evaluated in very subjective ways, even if check lists were used. For others, there may be only check marks denoting completion. Then, too, there is the problem of deciding relative value or percentage of grade for different tasks and performances.

The point is that evaluation, even the simple part of it we call grading, is never easy and never without flaws. All grades are truly arbitrary and, therefore, debatable. There are, though, some things to keep in mind that might help you be a better evaluator. These guidelines for evaluation include the following:

1. Both the form and the substance of any evaluation should be based mostly on teaching objectives. Only if we think through in advance what we want to accomplish and what is an effective way of showing this can we establish an acceptable approach to evaluation.

2. We need to evaluate what is taught, which should reflect what we want as learning outcomes.

3. We need to focus evaluation on what is important rather than on what is easy to measure or assess.

4. Ongoing evaluation is preferred over endpoint or final evaluation, so incorporate evaluation into regular activity.

5. Evaluation of teaching should be based on what students learn rather than on what they know and can do; therefore, evaluation should begin before the teaching.

6. Students need to have a clear notion of the purposes of any evaluation and the reasons for the evaluation.

7. Students need to perceive the evaluation as fair and honest, not tricky or directed at catching" them.

8. The evaluation procedure should be built around the notion of finding ways of improving instruction.

9. Effective evaluation gets the student involved in self- evaluation, thinking about how he or she can do better, and taking responsibility for his or her own learning.

10. A teacher should always remember that evaluation is at its best a subjective and risky affair
    A. Anyone *can* be wrong about a grade or any kind of assessment and everyone *is* sometimes wrong.
    B. Anyone can be incorrect about information.

    C.   Anyone can misjudge a student or a student product.

    D.   Anyone can be wrong about what they should be evaluating and teaching.

    E.   Everyone will be guilty of all of the above on a regular basis.

Many of the techniques and tools of evaluation are well known because we have experienced them as students ourselves. Nonetheless, it is important to reflect on these measures and indicators as they relate to purposeful evaluation as well as a fair approach to grading.

EVALUATING THROUGH TESTS AND QUIZZES

The very first thing many people think of when the subject of evaluation is mentioned is tests and quizzes. Tests always involve performance, and we use them because they are the quickest way available of finding out what people (or animals or even inanimate things, for that matter) know or can do. Nationally normed standardized tests, though not as well known in social studies as in reading and mathematics, are given system wide and state wide because they have been viewed as a way of comparing and evaluating students as to their mastery of information and skills. Though many responsible educators are dissatisfied with these tests and the way the data from them are used, there has been a movement toward national testing programs.

In the social studies, the most widely used forms of tests are written ones that involve answering questions or performing specified tasks. Generally, we label those tests that involve little or no judgment in grading as *objective measures*. Included in this group are true-false tests, multiple-choice tests, labeling of diagrams and maps, matching, and some short-answer and fill-in-the-blank tests. Most of these tests can also be called High-Cue tests because they contain a lot of clues and may even supply the correct answer (e.g., matching). The kind of thinking that is required may involve recognizing rather than remembering information.

The advantages of objective type measures mostly relate to the unchanging quality of the test items. The correct answers are thought to be verifiable and absolute. Except when the teacher makes a detectable and documentable error, there is little or no danger of misinterpreting or wrongly grading an answer. In addition, such questions can cover the material to be tested by sampling what is important in a very equitable way based on pre-established criteria, and performance data can be gathered to establish the value of individual items. Once such tests are established, the teacher or anyone else can correct them fairly quickly.

However, there are many criticisms of objective tests. Some of these lead to the conclusion that they are really not objective at all. Many such criticisms have to do with test-item construction. Here are some of the typical criticisms.

- Insufficient information is given to call for one specific answer (multiple choice stems and completion or fill-in-the-blank: e.g., All of the ____ were ____.).

- Items are written deliberately to be tricky or misleading (e.g., True-False: Cortez conquered the Incas in Mexico.).

- Test items tend to concentrate on the less important and even trivial aspects of a topic of study (e.g., Short answer: How many Pilgrims survived the first winter in Plymouth?).

- Test items require the students to share an opinion. (e.g., True-False: The greatest woman of the nineteenth century was Florence Nightingale.).

- Questions are often long, wordy, and confusing.

- More than one alternative is plausible as an answer.

- It is difficult to write objective items that involve creativity, evaluation, and application, and few objective tests include such items.

- Such tests work to the advantage of lucky guessers and chance plays too large a role.

Those tests which require value judgments in evaluation are described as *subjective measures*. Subjective measures include nearly all types of essay and problem-solving work where the process is as important as the answer and where thought and creativity are often part of the judgment. These can be called *Low-Cue test items* because they depend almost wholly on the ability of students to remember information relative to the question and use it. Little or no information is actually supplied.

Subjective tests are supported by some people because they are believed to require students to think and to structure their thinking, recalling the appropriate information. They also allow different students to use different arguments and information. There are as many common criticisms of essay tests as of objective measures. Critics claim the following:

- There is no fair and consistent way of grading an essay test.

- Students who do not write well do not do well on essays.

- Many students are able to be too creative in their answers.

- The kind of thinking required in essay tests is beyond the ability of most students, so the measures are unfair indicators of what they know.

- Essay tests can only sample a smaller amount of the material covered, not all of the objectives.

- Essay tests take much more time to grade and must be graded by someone who both knows the material and knows how it has been taught.

One of the answers to many of these criticisms seems to be an approach to grading essay work called *holistic evaluation*. In this approach, the preparation procedure includes supplying students with thorough descriptions of various performance levels for essays. These descriptions range from descriptions of characteristics of poor answers on up to the attributes of superior essays. These criterion-based descriptions become the basis for the grading, which, in essence, is the process of categorizing essays into particular levels.

Holistic evaluation has been a way of responding to legitimate recognition of a testing problem. It is a good way to show that simply by knowing the pitfalls of any form of test or test question, makes it possible to avoid or at least reduce the dangers. The form of test or quiz and the kind of test questions that a teacher uses should be a matter of sense and judgment. Some tests provide information specifically to help planning and teaching (formative evaluation); some are merely diagnostic; and others are intended to be final, exit evaluations (summative). Any *good* test for the social studies, whether it includes subjective or objective questions or both and regardless of its intended use, is going to do the following:

- Measure what it is supposed to measure (prerequisite knowledge, what is important, what has been taught and learned, etc.)

- Require the thinking skills that the teacher wants the students to use

- Allow the teacher to evaluate how well the objectives have been achieved

- Be an additional learning experience for children.

- Be constructed and evaluated with fairness

- Be carefully and clearly worded and understandable to the students

- Not be a test on which children fail because of the lack of reading ability

- Be constructed so that the students can be expected to complete it in the time allowed

- Relate to all objectives in an equitable way

- Be of a length and type that is appropriate to the students, the material covered, and the way the material was covered.

Developing a test or quiz and even deciding to use one that has been prepared to go with a text or other educational material should be a thoughtful and purposeful procedure. The first consideration should be the purpose that the test or quiz is going to serve. A number of additional thought-steps are needed, which might include the following:

1. Think about your specific purposes in the evaluation, what you are trying to find out about what the students have learned or what they can do with that knowledge.

2. Consider how much time you want the test or quiz to take, accounting for attention span, ability level, the breadth and depth you want in the evaluation, and the importance attached to the particular evaluation.

3. Decide what kind(s) of activities or behaviors you want the test or quiz to include.

4. Develop a plan for dividing the test or quiz into its component parts. (This may take such forms as outlines, sets of objective statements, and organizational plans allocating percentages.)

5. Prepare the individual items.

6. Carefully check the items for content, wording, clarity, readability, and so on.

7. Have someone else read the items to see if they understand them as you intended them and if they see any ambiguity, possibility of multiple interpretations, trickiness, and so on.

8. If possible, have someone do the test to see how that person interprets it and answers the questions and how long it takes to complete. (As a rule of thumb, multiply adult time by three to get an estimate of child completion time.)

9. Observe students as they take the test to note ease or frustration, commonly experienced difficulties and individual problems, and differences in rate of completion.

10. When grading tests become aware of instances where student answers consistently vary from what you believe is the correct answer.

PROBLEMS IN EVALUATING PROJECTS AND REPORTS

Projects are extremely difficult to evaluate. They often involve art ability or other abilities outside of those which are directly related to social studies learning and thinking, sometimes reflect parent help and/or differences in financial and other resources; and, even for a similar assignment, vary immensely in type, complexity, and learning value. When projects are done by groups, various members may make vastly different contributions. All of this is almost an essential part of the nature of this type of activity, so, too, is the fact that project work, at its best, involves a tremendous amount of thought and effort in conceptualization which may not be reflected to the evaluator in the finished product. At the same time, some project work may be strictly copy work, reflecting almost no thought or originality, which the teacher never detects. Flashy and impressive projects may, in the final analysis, reflect little learning or teaching; unimpressive projects, on the other hand, may be the result of much more time and thought. Even so, it is within the very qualities that make projects difficult to evaluate that the true value of project work is found. Projects involve students; they make them think and apply what they learn; they require conceptualizing, problem solving and solution finding; they provoke research and questioning; they necessitate planning and organization; and, in the case of group projects, they involve group interaction skills and teach some valuable lessons about how other people operate and think.

Reports, whether oral or written, present similar evaluation difficulties. They involve language abilities of different types and the student's self-confidence and ability to communicate to and/or in front of people may influence how good the report seems as much or more than the actual thought and work involved. Availability of resources may also be a factor as may the nature and form of the assignment. A well structured report assignment, for example, should produce better results.

Projects and reports may be evaluated in a number of ways. The most common of these are any number of types of subjective evaluation with or without comment, check list evaluation, analytical evaluation, peer evaluation, and self-evaluation.

SUBJECTIVE EVALUATION

Subjective evaluation is probably the most common approach in schools. It is authoritarian in style and relies almost entirely on the teacher's professional judgment. The reasoning is that the teacher observes a project or report through its development, has an intimate knowledge of individual children, and has had a great number of past experiences with student projects and reports. Subjective evaluation assumes the authority of the teacher and his or her right to be the judge. Students are discouraged from questioning any grade or judgment from the very beginning. At least an unconscious reason for this discouragement is that the criteria for judgments is not easily verbalized and is not very consistent. In fact, a teacher or a child could bring almost any factor into a justification argument. It is very difficult to give instructive and useful diagnostic feedback in this approach. When instructional suggestions and comments are made, they tend to be interpreted by the student as the teacher's rationale for the grade given. This may not actually be true.

Mechanical flaws (or the absence of such flaws) and appearances sometimes influence teachers judgment of substance and ideas in this approach without their being aware of the fact. Often ideal models are used to show students in advance what a good report or project looks like. This may or may not have positive effects. On the other hand, seeing the models may reduce creativity in some cases or even cause student frustration at not feeling able to complete equivalent work. On the other hand, models may provide students with clarification about expectations.

CHECK LIST EVALUATION

Using check lists to evaluate produces an evaluation that, at least in appearances, is more criterion based. The checklists may identify the features that the project or report is to include and the characteristics that the teacher expects in a report or project. When checklists are given to students in advance they help the student in clarifying teacher expectations and give them some sense of security about how they can be successful in meeting these expectations and getting a good grade. Such thinking may produce some very regimented work, though, and cause students to work too much on meeting the criteria and too little on creative problem solving.

Following is one example of a checklist that might be used with an upper grade reporting activity. The items on the checklist might be treated with a simple check mark indicating acceptability or might be rated in some way showing how well each criterion has been met. The report

- ___ Has a clear, creative, descriptive title.
- ___ Attempts to solve a problem or answer a question.
- ___ Deals with an important topic.
- ___ Is well organized with at least three subtopics.
- ___ Has a list of references (in correct form).
- ___ Shows that the references have been used.
- ___ Covers the topic completely.
- ___ Is presented in an interesting way.
- ___ Shows that the writer or presenter is knowledgeable about the topic.
- ___ Uses visual material (pictures, charts, maps, etc.).
- ___ Shows concern for mechanics (grammar, punctuation, and spelling).
- ___ Has a good summary and conclusion.

ANALYTICAL EVALUATION

Analytical evaluation is based on careful examination of student behaviors or products in the light of clearly identified criteria. This approach may take several forms. When projects or reports are evaluated analytically, the teacher usually examines them very carefully and gives a detailed reaction. Sometimes this is a preliminary evaluation after which the students have the opportunity to revise, change and improve. This view treats the work that has been done as a phase in the process of learning how to do this type of project. It is a draft. Whether the analysis is merely a step in the process or comes as a final feedback session, it can take one of two basic forms. One approach is for the teacher to begin with no criteria, basically letting the work itself dictate how it is analyzed. The idea is to give feedback of strengths and weaknesses that will allow students to improve. Another analytical approach involves the examination of a report or project to see how well it meets a number of standards. Comments would then be made relative to each of these standards. For example, the following categories might be the basis for evaluation of a project:

- Topic (What thought is evidenced in the selection of the basic idea?)

- Approach (How unique and interesting was the approach used?)

- Effort (Does the project show industry and care?)

- Purpose (Is the project purposeful and instructive?)

- Visual quality (Does the project attract attention and interest?)

- Mechanics and content (How well does the project reflect research and knowledge and is it done with a care for correctness?)

PEER EVALUATION AND SELF-EVALUATION

Peer evaluation and self-evaluation by the students are really the aim of all evaluation. At their best, they show that the student has learned to judge a report or project, to know what it ought to contain and what distinguishes high quality performance, and to think critically about a product. There is more than one reason why such evaluation does not meet this ideal. The immaturity and self-interest of children are, of course contributing factors. But an even more important factor may be that teachers often fail to teach students how to make such judgments, fail to carefully structure the way that self-evaluation and peer evaluation are to be done, and neglect the kind of follow up that such activity requires. The result is that self-evaluation and peer evaluation are often very superficial activities lacking in any real learning value.

TEACHER OBSERVATIONS AND ANECDOTAL RECORDS

Teachers have very little time to take notes on children. What is more, descriptions of such observations do not easily translate into a form that can be considered in grading. In spite of these arguments, teacher observation is an invaluable tool in evaluation. One of the reasons is that the development of the child is full of subtleties and nuance. Teachers need to be reminded that the essence of an individual is not really something that can be quantified.

The best teachers of the social studies are those who are most reflective. The records of day-to-day actions of children often give such teachers the very best substance on that to reflect. In addition to the paper trail of children, these records are of two broad types: criterion based quantitative observations which usually take such forms as checklists; and qualitative observations that take the form of narrative descriptions. If either type is used it needs to be done in a systematic regular way, and it needs to be kept up over a longer period of time. Because this record keeping cannot be done when teachers are presenting to the class, the logical times for such record keeping are when children are engaged in activities that require little teacher supervision and at times during and at the end of the school day when children are not present.

What becomes obvious with only a little knowledge of the techniques of teacher observation is that checklist techniques are a shortcut to developing systematic records of how children are behaving and progressing. They give the teacher a record that helps him or her make sense of the class, and they do so with very little time spent outside class beyond determining and setting up what qualities the teacher is going to look for. Checklist evaluation also relates well to determining the actual accomplishment of at least certain kinds of objectives.

Checklists may take a number of forms. One of the most common is a list of very specific competencies or knowledge (e.g., knows the cardinal directions). When a child masters an item on the list his or her name is checked. A check list might be set up to keep systematic track of group activity as well. The following list might be one that the teacher might carry about the room during independent group work activity.

Date_____

Name	Works without conflict	Gets on task	Problem solves	Shows leadership	Behavior is appropriate
Group 1					
Billy					
Maria					
Heather					
Eric					
Group 2					
Jason					
Freddy					
Michael					
Starla					

As much as checklists are a time-saving form of evaluation, anecdotal teacher observation records are time demanding. Anecdotal material may reflect specific observations during the day. It is narrative in form and describes actual behavior. Such comments may not need to be lengthy or provide a lot of detail, but they do need to be complete. The teacher may or may not want to create categories for such notes prior to observation. Some may be behavioral, for example, "When John lost his place in line at lunch he shoved several children and made threatening remarks." Others may reflect participation, for example, "Caroline raised her hand for several questions in discussion. On two occasions that I called on her she answered completely."

Such notations of observations mean little unless they show a pattern. The patterns emerge when dated observation notes are kept for longer periods of time. Until recently teachers could not verify conclusions from such observations unless an outsider observed the classroom over a period of time. Technology is quickly giving us another tool for observation, one through which teachers can verify or disprove their impressions of students. More and more teachers are doing at least some videotaping of regular classes, not just special lessons. With the focus of such taping away from the teacher and on the students we have an additional tool for looking at patterns of behavior.

The time required by anecdotal-observation approaches to evaluation almost demands that such observation be focused on particular problems or particular children. The data can be very helpful in instances where faculty are going to meet and discuss a particular child or where reference material is being gathered to recommend special attention for a child. The type of information may also help a teacher deal with a particular classroom management problem. However, the approach takes a great deal of time which may be beyond that available in many classrooms.

STUDENT SELF-EVALUATION AND PORTFOLIO ASSESSMENT

One concern about evaluation of children that will influence social studies as well as other areas of the curriculum is that the means of evaluation that we have been using are not doing the job. There is growing faith in the belief that no test is going to be adequate because the quality of learning does not lend itself to being quantified. There has also been concern that students have only a receptive and even passive role in the evaluation process. At most, they take part in a limited number of in-class experiences where they have graded their own work or that of other students. Students are given few, if any' experiences where they have the opportunity or the need to examine their own thinking and work reflectively and diagnostically.

The movement that has concentrated its attention on assessing the quality of learning is called *authentic assessment*. Educators involved in this effort are looking more to methods of evaluation, which get at performance and at what children can do, particularly what they can do over more extensive periods of time.

One of the major changes advocated in authentic assessment is a new reliance on individual portfolios or collections of student work assembled over time. The student takes an active and important role in the development and organization of the portfolio. He or she usually helps decide what goes into it. The student may also be responsible for organizing and record keeping with regard to the contents of the portfolio. Some emphasis may be given to student initiative in conferences with the teacher. The individual items in the portfolio become the basis for student-teacher conferences and the base of comparison for future work. The student learning to gather and organize the material is not only more active in his or her own evaluation but is learning a skill that will be of benefit in the world of work. For assessment purposes the portfolio may be limited to a certain number of pieces and these may have to be of particular types (e.g., book reports, essays, answers to comprehension questions, poems, stories, maps, pictures, problem solving activities, and group reports).

LOOKING BACK

Evaluation is an important and complex part of the social studies. Assessment tools allow teachers to examine their own effectiveness as well as the learning of their students. Sound evaluation begins by comparing what has been learned to what the teacher intended to teach. In other words, achievement is measured against objectives.

Teachers assess this learning through student behaviors and student products. They need to be constantly aware of the need to focus on what is important, not just what is easy to measure. The most traditional assessment tools are tests, quizzes, and papers, but evaluation based on these tools alone does not give a true or authentic picture of student capability. Other student activities, some much more difficult to assess, are as important or more important than tests and written papers. Teachers may attempt more complete assessment by using observational tools including check lists and by recording students in action.

SELF-TEST

1. What is the "basis of comparison" in evaluation?

2. Explain why both the method and the content of evaluation should be based on the teaching objectives.

3. Identify the criticisms of both objective and subjective tests.

4. What are the traits of a good test?

5. What are the steps in building a test?

6. What do you think is meant by the term *authentic assessment*?

SUGGESTED READING

NCSS. (1991). Position statement: testing and evaluation of social studies students. *Social Education*. 55(September), 284-285.

Wood, J., Miederhoff, J.W., and Ulschmid, B. (1989). Adapting test construction for mainstreamed students. *Social Education*. 53 (January), 46-49.

6 Reading and Writing to Learn Social Studies

LOOKING AHEAD

Information skills are the base of the monument we call the social studies. Obtaining, processing, and using information are necessary for problem solving and decision making. The answers to questions either consist of information or depend on the information available and how it is interpreted and used. That means that children's ability to deal with information is one of the most important skill areas for teachers of the social studies.

Most of the ways that information is obtained, including those involving computer technology, require some kind of reading. Likewise, the most varied and systematic uses of information involve writing in some form. This chapter deals with the development of those information skills most essential in the social studies. It focuses on some of the types of materials and writing assignments that teachers traditionally have found to be useful. At the same time, the chapter takes a look at ways of dealing with the pitfalls and problems that teachers and students encounter in these reading and writing activities.

CAN YOU? DO YOU?

Can you

- Name the four basic purposes for reading and writing assignments in the social studies?

- Think of ways to use fiction books in the social studies?

Do you

- Know what children dislike most about using references?

- Know how to break children out of the "copy from an encyclopedia" rut?

- Know how to make social studies book reports interesting?
- Know how **to help children learn to organize their writing?**

EFFECTIVE READING AND WRITING ASSIGNMENTS IN THE SOCIAL STUDIES

Reading and writing are closely related activities in the social studies. Not only are students expected to get information through reading, many kinds of social studies activities require writing to show or use that learning has occurred. Reading and writing activities are most often used as independent seat work or as home work assignments. Lee and Pruett (1979) have suggested that such assignments are used for one or more of four basic purposes

1. *Practice:* This is the most common type of assignment and the simplest. It is given in order for students to master specific skills or learn specific information. Practice exercises need to be limited to material presented in class.

2. *Preparation:* Such assignments are given to help students get in the most benefit possible from subsequent lessons.

3. *Extension:* These are usually application assignments given to see if students can transfer a skill or a concept to some new situation. They require more abstract thinking than practice assignments.

4. *Creativity:* Such assignments require students to pull together many skills and concepts to produce a new response. Creative assignments often take more time to complete, ranging from several days to several weeks.

USE OF REFERENCE READING AND CHILDREN'S LITERATURE: PROVIDING FOR INDIVIDUAL DIFFERENCES

If we really give serious thought to individual differences and the social studies, we must pay some attention to reference materials and children's literature. The social studies is information based, meaning that any inquiry in the social studies area requires that data and facts as well as interpretation be found. In order to find information, children need to know how to use reference materials. We also want children to learn to take delight and have their curiosity stimulated in a good browse through a variety of reference materials.

Children's literature is as much a source of impression and story as anything else. Books paint a mood and catch the feeling of the times. They tell personal and detailed information about people's lives and they form an image that we either like or do not, relate to or do not. Good story tellers give us a sense of "being there." This is equally true for those who are mischievously humorous and anecdotal such as Jean Fritz (*Why Don't You Get a Horse, Sam Adams?*), those who are outrageously imaginative such as Robert Lawson (*Ben and Me*), and those who are intent and serious such as Elizabeth Spear (*The Witch of Blackbird Pond*) or Esther Forbes (*Johnny Tremain*).

Well-selected books at appropriate levels of difficulty can excite an interest in history and in other cultures; provide information and concepts about events, historical and contemporary people, and the way people have lived or do live; create vivid mental images of life in other times and other places; and help readers deal with and solve their own problems. Children's literature is sometimes the best and may often be the only available source that can tell us about the emotional climate and the inner motivation of people in other times and places.

DICTIONARIES, GLOSSARIES, AND INDEXES

We often consider sources such as dictionaries, glossaries and indexes as shortcuts to understanding and finding information. This is not the feeling most children have. We often take children to these sources dragging and kicking all the way. They simply hate it. Nothing could be greater drudgery, no task more tedious.

The trick is to make it easy, competitive, and fun. I like to tempt children by showing them what they *do not* have to do to look things up. One thing that they *do not* have to do is be able to spell words accurately. Another thing they *do not* have to do is read every word or even most of the words. Beyond just knowing alphabetic order, three skills do have to be mastered to use these kinds of resources: (1) When searching for a topic, they have to be able to think of alternative words to look up if their first guesses are wrong; (2) they have to be able to think of likely spellings for words; and (3) they have to be able to scan or go down a page quickly to find one word.

The shortcut feeling can be enhanced in the social studies by making dictionary, glossary, and index work collaborative. The teacher can help younger children build a class dictionary for any unit of work. The children can also build their own card files of personally owned words. (*Owned words* are those that they can consistently recognize and are therefore among their own personal sight words). Older children can keep either a personal or a group notebook dictionary with each topic studied. Dictionary and index work can also be turned into competitive, speed and accuracy games too.

ENCYCLOPEDIAS, ATLASES, AND ALMANACS

Children need to learn when and how to use specialized reference materials. The first problem is always to identify where to look. The type of reference chosen may depend on the amount and kind of information needed as well as how quickly it is needed. Structured exercises with encyclopedias, atlases, and almanacs will help children learn the contents, organization, and style of different types of references. Following is an example of an encyclopedia scavenge. I have the children work in pairs, each pair with a different volume. Each pair is in a race to complete all the items and to do so first.

1. Find an entry of at least two pages.

2. Find a country and tell its population, area, and one other fact.

3. Discover a biographical entry and tell two types of information it includes.

4. What is the shortest entry you can find?

5. What is the longest entry you can find?

6. Find a reference that sends you from one entry to others.

7. Make an educated guess about how many entries there are in your volume. (Tell what reasoning your guess is based on.)

8. Find an entry that is not a proper noun.

9. Identify three entries that deal with the same broad topic. (You do not have to limit your suggestions to your volume.)

10. Name the first and last entries.

BIOGRAPHIES AND OTHER NONFICTION

For more depth and information, students need to learn how to identify, use, and appreciate biographies and other nonfiction materials. There are increasing numbers of boldly exciting and informative nonfiction books written for children that deal with social studies topics. Many of these, especially the biographies, have real depth and feeling as well as interest-arousing information. Such books can be used in a lot of ways in addition to standard classroom browsing or interest tables and reporting activities. The following are among the criteria to consider when choosing nonfiction books for children

• The book should provide information that has a degree of difference and a lot of interest or it should put the information it presents together in a provocative way.

- The content should be accurate (as far as you can tell) and should reflect a level of completeness that is appropriate for both the book's purpose and the needs of the children.

- Non-fiction books should provide different and more personal points of view than textbooks.

- The book should have some emotional impact.

- The books should be usable by the children as a research source.

- There should be a high level of interest and appeal and the reading level should be appropriate for the intended use by children.

Primaries may find simply written, colorfully illustrated books like those in the *Where We Live Series* (Steck-Vaughn) or the *Count Your Way Series* (Carolrhoda) to be good read-aloud experiences. There are also some very good event books such as *The Glorious Flight* (Provenson and Provenson) that children delight in hearing and in seeing the illustrations.

Biographies at the primary level have to be full of anecdotes and stories. Some of the best ones have eye-catching illustrations and many have humor that this age group can understand. S.N. Monjo's *The One Bad Thing about Father* or Doug Quackenbush's biographies are examples of the kind of book that works well at this level. Teacher costuming and reading or telling the story aloud the role of a friend of the subject creates an atmosphere that make the character more real and believable with children through the middle grades. Children will also benefit from drawing a picture of the character they have read about and then telling about their picture.

Photographs and other illustrations in a number of books make them ideal for thumbing through with a "what's that?" attitude with small groups. The Silver Burdett series, *The Human Story,* is typical of large, heavily illustrated books developed especially for upper-grade children, which are ideally suited for this purpose. The same kind of curiosity browse can be done with younger children using books such as Peter Spier's *People* or Virginia McLean's *Chasing the Moon over China.*

Some books like the *Turning Points of History* series from Silver Burdett or Aliki's *A Medieval Feast* or *Mummies Made in Egypt,* are almost ideally suited as manuals for laying out historic events geographically and walking through them in a step by step pantomime. These books or others such as Macauley's *Castle* or *Cathedral* can inspire the young "architectural artists" in a class to drawing and model building.

In the upper grades, it is important to choose biographies which show the real and human side of their subjects. Books such as Jean Fritz' *Where Do You Think You're Going, Columbus?* present historical figures in an interesting way with their human problems and weaknesses. An idea worth trying with biographies is based on the concept of meeting of minds. Instead of giving a book report, the students take the role of the title character. Then in small groups they talk about issues and questions in role. The biographied characters need not be contemporaries. In fact, it adds an element of interest if they are not. What would Alexander the Great say to Napoleon or to Susan B. Anthony? Other biography book-report alternatives for the upper grades are the quiz show and the news magazine show. Both are based on television models and involve the children taking the character roles. Examples of quiz-show models include a "Who is the mystery guest?" panel show or "Who is the best _____? (based on 2 or more people who have read about the same figure, each playing that person). News-show formats can vary from interviews to "You are there" spots with the character being his or her own reporter.

FICTION AND POETRY

The things that are different about the social studies in the Land Where There Are No Children's Trade Books are:

- Children sleep in school a lot more because they use nothing but textbooks and that makes it very boring.

- No child at all can read the textbooks because reading is so uninteresting that no child bothers to learn how to read.

- Living in a free country means a lot less because children do not read about the experiences of others and, therefore, are limited only to what they have experienced themselves.

- Conversation is a lot duller because children do not have good books to talk about.

- Every child has more trouble solving problems because no one has read about heroes and heroines in books solving problems in different ways.

- Fewer moral lessons are taught because there are no stories with morals from which children can learn.

- There are no such things as "wild things," "hephalumps," unicorns, or other fantasy creatures because fantasy itself does not exist.

- A hero is *really* nothing but a sandwich.

- There are no happy endings and not much comedy.

- People are all much duller in Social Studies in the Land Where There Are No Children's Trade Books.

Fiction almost always deals with people. Even when the characters in a story are animals, it is the human qualities of the personality and problems of these creatures that are most important. Poetry is the most economic, intense, and focused form of verbal communication. The basic job of poetry is to express personal feelings and thoughts either in song or story form. What this means, in effect, is that the content of all fiction and poetry can be called social studies.

It is important to realize the value of literature and make use of it. Fictional writing for children is most often more appealing to them than nonfiction. Good stories are simply more interesting and readable than textbooks, for which the job of covering specific content is going to control the writing. The art and imagination of the storyteller creates characters and plots that are consistently exciting and appealing to the emotions. The facts are not always so interesting. Many children who will give only minimum effort to textbooks and other nonfiction, are avid fiction readers. They can often be guided to a lot of history, geography, and other social studies content through fiction. In fact, there are many people who grow up to love the social studies who have their first interest stimulated by fiction.

Obviously, any number of criteria can be developed and considered in guiding children to good fictional books and stories as well as poems. To my way of thinking, though, a book should be given if it can be said to meet some, but not necessarily all, of the following conditions:

- It tells a good story well.

- It develops strong, real characters and confronts them with important and believable problems.

- It contributes something to the child's knowledge and understanding of the world (other people, other places, other times, the self).

- It presents strong and believable viewpoints.

- It provokes the reader to think and feel about some human problem or situation.

- It helps the child develop personal values.

- It helps the child deal with his or her own problems.

There are many types of fictional books that relate to the social studies. Though far from complete, the list given here provides a fair sampling of the varieties of story types that can be used as part of the social studies program.

Fiction

Folk Tales

Fairy tales and myths

Fables and moral tales (Aesop's Fables)

Legends and hero stories (Robin Hood, King Arthur, William Tell)

Tall tales

Historical novels that focus on particular events

Historical novels that focus on living in particular times

Biographical novels with real and important individuals as their subjects

Biographical novels written about real, but relatively unknown historical figures

Novels in different geographic settings

Fantasies

Books dealing with personal survival

Books dealing with the problems of family living

Books in which characters are faced with socially significant problems

Books that deal with contemporary social problems

Books that center on social relationships (including some mysteries)

Books that present characters who have admirable and desirable qualities

Poetry

Poems that tell the story of real or legendary events

Poems that deal with historically significant individuals

Poems written by historically important people

Poetry that id a folk art form of a particular culture

Problem poetry

Self-description poems

Poems which express emotions

Poems about human activity (work, recreation, etc.)

Lullabies

Work songs

Ballads

Love songs

Holiday and calendar-related poetry

Geography and weather poems

Fictional books and stories such as the ones listed here are full of social studies content. Some excellent teachers make it a practice to find time to read at least a portion of some really powerful and interesting books with solid social content aloud every day. One reason for doing this is that the children really enjoy it. In addition to the motivational value, reading aloud to children is good modeling; children see the teacher who they admire and look up to reading. Research and common sense tell us that children can often listen with understanding, memory, and appreciation to books and stories that are too difficult for them to read themselves.

Fictional books and stories as well as poems are usually full of drama and can be turned into skits, role plays, pantomimes, and other acting-out experiences. Some poetry lends itself to choral reading and independent read-aloud activity.

Fictional books also may be a really superior alternative to topical assignments for children to practice reporting skills. Oral reporting in the social studies often turns into futile and meaningless drudgery as children read-aloud and with great difficulty papers copied verbatim from encyclopedias. We will talk more about reporting skills later in this chapter. But here are ten ideas that, with a little thought and planning, a teacher might use to get children to do some different and interesting fiction book reports.

TEN WAYS TO DO BOOK REPORTS "THE SOCIAL STUDIES WAY"

Fictional books and stories are all full of social studies content. They have geographic settings and often present vivid and interesting pictures of cultures. Fiction also has a time reference, and many books present historical events and times. Fictional books vary as to the accuracy and the fullness of detailed content, but all involve human characters with human values, emotions, and desires.

1. Economic book reports: For a story or book, draw two circle graphs. On one, show the expenditures of the main character. On the other, show that character's income. The circles should be segmented estimating the percentage of the total budget the character would have had to pay on today's market for the goods and services received in the story and the sources of income.

2. Archaeology book reports: Create a shoe box dig for a book or story. Having read the story, try to imagine that archaeologists are digging into the site of the main story events hundreds of years after the story happened. In the shoe box, create in miniature the artifacts they might find at the site.

3. Story museum reports: Create a miniature museum exhibit commemorating the events depicted in the story. This can be done as a diorama or through a series of drawings.

4. Comic book reports: Create a comic book for the book or story using cartoon drawings to show the story events.

5. Shoe box story parade: Read a fictional book about a historic event or a biography of a historical character. Create a float out of a shoe box showing the most significant or memorable scene from a book or story. When everyone in the class has done a different float, they can be formed into a parade with each person serving as commentator as his or her float passes by.

6. Book trials: After a significant number have read the same book or story, stage a mock trial of one of the story characters or a trial of the author(s) for "corrupting the youth." Assign the roles of attorneys, defendants, witnesses and jurors.

7. Historical creation book reports: Create documentary evidence that traces the history of a book.

8. Story geography: Map a book or story showing the location of the episodes and events described. Then give a map talk taking the major character(s) through these events step by step.

9. Sociometrics of books: Develop diagrams showing the relationships of people in a book. Small circles represent individuals, dotted lines show kinship ties, and solid lines with arrows stand for positive feelings of like or love. The oral report consists of explaining the diagram.

10. Publicity and review reports: Do a promotion for a book as it might be sold in a television commercial or develop a review that might be given on a television review program if the book were a movie.

WHOLE LANGUAGE AND THE SOCIAL STUDIES

Language learning dominates the elementary school. Teaching language skills, especially reading, has always been considered the first task and primary responsibility of the elementary teacher. Leaders and thinkers in language arts education have become increasingly concerned with the whole child and the whole curriculum in recent years. The term *whole language* has emerged to describe this emphasis. People who subscribe to the notion of whole language emphasize the importance of involving children in using language as a way of meeting their own needs. Children develop their language, in this approach, as an integrated part of learning. Above all, children's literature is central as the tool of whole language programs.

What this means, in effect, is a growing unity of purpose between the social studies and language arts. The curricular concerns of these two areas of the curriculum are now very similar and the focus of each area more closely tied to the other. Both are concerned with the whole child and with his or her total development. The difference between the two has to do with the learning outcomes that these two areas are most interested in, and even in this it is more a matter of degree. Though somewhat oversimplified, one way to say it is that social studies is more interested in the substance and content, the information about the world and the life values. The major thrust of language arts is the language and thinking ability needed to deal with this social context.

ORGANIZING TO WRITE:
NOTE TAKING, QUESTION ANSWERING AND OUTLINING

Reading and writing activities or assignments in the social studies may take several forms. Follow-up of a class or group reading assignment might include having students do any of the following activities:

- Answer questions

- Write a summary

- Write a solution to a problem using information from the reading material.

- Write a reaction or response.

- Write an evaluation or critique.

- Make up a story involving the time or place described.

- Write a description.

- Write book reports on single books read independently (e.g., biographies, books about events, "You are there" type books, viewpoint books, etc.).

- Write summaries of articles in magazines and newspapers.

- Make written plans for a project or activity.

- Take notes or answer a set of preassigned questions about an experience such as a field trip, a visiting speaker, a movie or videotape, and so on.

- Write letters requesting information or materials.

- Write letters of appreciation.

- Imitate literature types from other cultures or times (e.g., Japanese Haiku poetry, tall tales, ballad type songs, etc.).

- Write stories about other times and other places using the sum of knowledge gained in reading and listening.

- Do in-role writing activities in which the student pretends to be in another culture, place, time, or position.

- Do map-making, map-labeling and chart-making types of activities.

- Write dramas and skits related to unit topics being studied.

- Write narrative reports of library research on a topic using one or multiple resources - an experiment conducted, a series of observations, an interview or conversation.

- Prepare posters, time lines, maps, charts, etc. for display or for oral reports, demonstrations, etc.

- Make notes for oral reports.

- Develop essays or themes.

- Make up rules, generalizations, hypotheses, cause and effect statements, etc.

- Answer test questions completing sentences, writing entire sentences, writing paragraphs, and writing complete essays under test conditions.

The major problems with reading and writing assignments in the social studies have to do with how well the teacher prepares the students for the assignment and the readiness of the students. The base skills for many if not all of these writing jobs are note taking, writing answers to questions, and outlining. All three involve the ability to see what is most important and what is relevant for particular purposes. For children to learn these skills, they have to, first, be able to see the essential purpose of each; second, be able to pick out central messages both as they listen and as they read; and, third, scan for messages related to particular criteria.

For note taking, writing answers to questions, and outlining, as with other skills, following a gradual and systematic teaching procedure can save a lot of anguish and frustration. The procedure must be a simple one. You just have to go step by step, so that you teach the children how to take notes, answer questions or outline, and not just assign them the job of doing it. There are two related tricks to learn if you are going to be a success. One is learning where your students are and what they can do. This relates to monitoring or watching to see how they are doing, and pacing. You simply have to work at a rate that will not lose students and yet keep a pace that is fast enough to keep students from getting bored. The other trick is to keep the possibility of excitement and interest alive. Note taking, question asking and answering, and outlining can be boring, especially if the students do not understand the assignment or if the content you work with is dry material. I think that part of the mastery of this trick is to work with fun stuff to learn the skill. Outline the sports section of the newspaper or a Shel Silverstein poem, for example, or take notes on a comic book or a travel brochure. The other part is to be *absolutely sure* that students do understand what it is they are supposed to do. One procedure to try is the following:

1. Define the skill that you want the children to have and analyze the steps they will have to go through in performing that skill.

2. Find out what the children can do by giving them a very simple and short supervised task involving the skill.

3. Model the skill, using a question-and-answer format to get the children to look at what you are doing analytically.

4. Repeat the model, going step by step with new content allowing the children to do the work as a class. Monitor to make sure that they are all with you.

5. Supply exercises in which part, but not all of the structure is in place.

6. Gradually withdraw the structure until the children can perform without it.

That procedure sounds simple, but teachers do not follow it. Research indicates that teachers rarely make certain that students understand the questions in textbook assignments (Anderson 1984) and that there are often major comprehension problems inherent in the questions themselves (Cooper 1986, Schneider and Brown 1980). The questions may be unclear in their wording. Students may lack the background knowledge needed to understand them or may be unable to see just what it is that questions are seeking.

In spite of these problems, research supports postreading questions as contributing to learning (Walberg 1986). This would seem to indicate that if teachers would be more careful about assignments and about preparing students for them, such assignments could be beneficial.

Sometimes you really have to plan to keep an assignment within reach for a particular group of students. By "within reach" I mean that the assignment is one that these students can do in what is *for them* a reasonable amount of time. One approach that has been very successful is cooperative learning, which involves students in a helping relationship with one another. Other approaches that seem to be successful suggest that reducing assignment length (the number of questions to be answered) while providing more guidance and feedback, is beneficial (Slavin 1987, Loring 1975). Mechanisms for doing this include dividing work among students, segmenting assignments, and identifying assignment mentors (Turner 1989).

Following are a few guidelines (adapted from Turner 1989) which may make textbook question assignments more meaningful:

- Assign questions only after reading them carefully.

- Give clear, complete directions both in writing and orally, taking time to explain and answer questions.

- Call attention to special problems and trouble spots students are likely to encounter.

- Point out where questions call for the student to evaluate, be creative, or give interpretation.

- Teach the students about question words and that questions in texts are answered in the order that they are asked.

- Follow up completed assignments by going over them in a meaningful way.

DEVELOPING RESEARCH AND REPORTING SKILLS

Students are often asked to make reports in the social studies. Such activity may serve one or more of several purposes

- Writing both necessitates and helps thinking. By asking students to do reports we are giving them valuable practice in thinking skills (Turner 1989).

- Writing is developed by practice. By involving students in writing activities, we help them develop their writing skills (Lundsteen 1976).

- Reporting activities allow students to pursue individual interests and work at their own levels.

- Giving a report gives a student a sense of authority. He or she becomes an expert and gains ownership of a unique and special knowledge.

- Reporting can help a student develop and improve self-expression.

- Presenting a report can be an application of the entire spectrum of language skills.

- Reports can give oral and visual display of writing and/or speaking.

- Reporting can be structured to foster social interaction.

- Reports provide checkpoints where student learning is observable and in a form where such learning can be evaluated.

Reports can be written, oral, or both. The first reporting activities are informal but prepared kindergarten and first-grade experiences like show and tell. Writing an experience story as a class in early school experiences is also a preparation for reporting, especially if one child reads the entire story back after the class has composed it. Reading, writing, and oral language skills are combined into reporting. Among the most common problems associated with reporting assignments are wholesale copying from reference books, students' lack of comprehension of their own reports, stumbling and stiff presentation of oral reports lacking in meaningfulness or purpose, and inattention of students to one another's reports. It is easy to see that all of these problems are somewhat related. Fortunately, they are also avoidable.

None of the problems associated with student reports is attributable to the nature of reporting itself. They seem to be more related to the lack of thought by teachers relating to the clarity of reporting assignments and the readiness of students for particular types of reporting assignments. Problems also come due to the failure of teachers to teach children how to write reports and to lead them through the steps of preparing the report.

Let us first look at the assignment stage. Reporting assignments may be set in several contexts: (1) as assignments everyone does (everyone reports on the same thing), (2) as parts of sets of assignments from which everyone chooses (students may choose among two or more projects), (3) as a form of recognition or distinction to better students (reporting activity is done only by students that the teacher sees as capable and likely to put forth the effort), (4) as volunteer activities that are encouraged and rewarded (extra credit and praise). None of these forms is inherently better or worse than any of the others. What is important is that the students know and understand which set(s) of rules is operating. A logical rule of thumb seems to be to keep the system simple, especially with younger students.

There are a number of types of reporting assignments. Earliest reporting activity in elementary school begins with sharing or show-and-tell activities and with language-experience approaches. Sharing activities are important because they develop children's ability to talk in front of an audience and can help them learn to distinguish important and appropriate things from those that have less significance and relevance. Language-experience approaches, which are a form of teacher led corporate reporting, have similar value and teach children sequencing and ordering skills as well.

One type of individual reporting that can begin very early is experiential reporting. "What I Did/Learned/etc. on My Summer Vacation," the most trite example of this kind of report gives this type of assignment a bad name. At its best, an experience report is a positive learning experience. It involves having students give true accounts of events that have reality to them. There is a natural narrative and sequence and an opportunity to learn the importance of supporting detail, note cause and effect relationships, and draw conclusions.

The same can be said for observational reports which are accounts of events witnessed and sometimes staged and orchestrated by the student. Observational reports can be made about movies, television programs, dramas, field trips, and other events witnessed by the students both as individuals and as groups. They may even be done collaboratively (see Chapter 4).

Both direct and phone interviews can be the basis of interesting reports. Children need to be given a structure of questions to ask in the interview. This can be provided by the teacher or developed in a guided class discussion. Audio or video recordings of the interview can be useful both in report write ups and in segments as part of oral reports.

Reports may also take the form of demonstrations. Children can show either directly or by simulation how something was or is done in a culture. They may also use drama as the vehicle for the report. (More ideas related to this will be presented in Chapter 10).

A real danger in reporting is that of mindless, copied reports. This danger can be averted by clear directions that specify how the report is to be organized.

Whatever form of reporting or writing students may be asked to do, success rather than failure can be expected if the teacher follows certain principles.

1. Assignments should be stimulating, interesting, and challenging to students.

2. Writing assignments ought to be clear. Teachers need to provide both a written description and an oral explanation of the assignment and then see feedback about how well students understand it. Teacher failure to determine student understanding of assignments is rated in the research as a major problem.

3. Assignment length and complexity need to be within the capabilities of the students. This can be achieved by

   A. Limiting the length of the assignment.

   B. Segmenting the assignment into logical steps or components.

4. Provide a structure for the report. Among the many structuring devices that might be used are outlines, sets of questions, dramatic devices (e.g., job applications for biographical reports on historic characters), a list of key points, or chronologies.

5. Successful and satisfactory writing assignments result from embedding the teaching of necessary directions and skills development into the writing assignment process.

   A. Such assignments specify and direct length by specifically defining length (number of words or sentences or pages) or space provided.

   B. Such assignments embed the teaching of such skills as summarizing, paraphrasing, skimming and scanning into the development of the assignment.

   C. Such assignments provide a structure of steps to follow in doing the assignment.

   D. Such assignments specify and provide the resources to be used and direct students on how to use them. (School librarians are often very helpful. Use them, but be sure resources are available.)

WRITING CREATIVELY

Writing can actually make the social studies more fun. The variety of creative-writing tasks that can relate to any social studies topic is really limited only by the teacher's imagination. Any idea used ought to be mentally tested with three questions before it is tried. (1) Is doing this task really going to serve some purpose related to understanding what is being studied? (2) Can the students do this task and do it in a reasonable amount of time? (3) How is this task going to affect or relate to the other activities that we are doing?

A number of beneficial writing activities can be described as in-role writing. In-role writing means that the writer is pretending to be someone else as he or she writes. One kind of in-role writing involves trying to go through some authentic writing exercise from a particular time period, such as writing letters, wills, and epitaphs for famous and nonfamous historical characters. Another type of in-role activity involves imagining how a historical character might deal with some of the paper work we deal with today. For example, how would that character fill out a job application or some questionnaire. Students can also write in-role autobiographies and poems.

Another type of creative writing with several twists is imitating a writing form of a particular culture. Children studying Japan can, of course, write Haiku poems. The study of Germany and France invites fairy tales, the American West suggests tall tales, ancient Greece and Rome might produce myths and fables, and the New England colonies bring sampler messages and Horn Book type sayings and stories. Based on this very small number of examples it is easy to see that reading a story or poem that comes from any culture creates a model for meaningful creative writing.

A third type of writing that holds exciting promise is problem- solving stories. Usually the teacher provides a story starter which is a problem scenario. The children then have to write a story in which the central characters try to solve the problem. For example, I gave a fifth grade class a scenario about two children from the North who found themselves deep in the heart of the Confederacy at the outbreak of the Civil War. They had to write a story in which the children figured out how to find their way back. If you have trouble thinking of them, problem scenarios can be easily adapted from the plots of books and movies because they all begin with a problem.

One activity that I find particularly useful, though, utilizes simple stories that children make up about fictional children that they imagine in the cultural setting they are studying. With older children, I sometimes set this up as a long-term project. I try to get them involved to the extent that they feel that they are actually doing research in order to write the story. It gives them what amounts to a real scholar's purpose for studying.

MATHEMATICS AND THE SOCIAL STUDIES:
CHARTS, GRAPHS AND MAPS, AND STATISTICS AND DATA BANKS

Mathematics goes to work in the social studies. There are many ways in which measurement and calculation enable social scientists to see and to show social relationships. It is important to get children to begin using the mathematical tools. The place to begin is with everyday things that can be part of children's lives. The experience can begin as a class activity and then slowly move to group and individual practice. Charts and graphs can be used to show, for example

- Each child's attendance
- Completed work
- Teacher conferences
- Children's independent reading
- Class opinions
- How related ideas are alike and different
- Days remaining until some special event
- Competition among groups
- Numbers of different kinds of objects
- Work completed

Mathematics is also an important part of map skill. Practice in measuring distances on maps is a critical part of learning about scale and about place relationship. With intermediate grades, you can have children create their own ruler from a piece of string and then make a game out of measuring distances. Making grids to draw smaller and larger maps can also help children with measurement skills. Younger children can begin with a map divided into four numbered quadrants and locate places by quadrant.

Computers in schools are making it possible for children of a range of ages to work with a lot of data. Data banks refer to large amounts of information that is stored for analysis. More often today when we talk about data banks we refer to information collected for computer use. In the social studies we are often looking to analyze the information to see what has happened to the subjects of the data or to make comparisons and discover patterns. A data base containing information on cities, for example, would allow us to compare the cities, to look at locations, and to look for common patterns of city development. In the future, students will need to be able to look at numbers and do the computer manipulations needed to work with such data bases.

LOOKING BACK

The social studies is knowledge based and that knowledge is most readily communicated through print. That means, of course, that reading and writing are critical skills areas in the social studies. Teachers give reading and writing assignments for the purposes of reviewing information, preparing for new studies, extending what goes on in the classroom, and to develop creativity Children need to learn to use a variety of resources including children's literature and several types of reference material

The whole language movement, with its emphasis on children's literature, is an indicator that there is a growing unity of purpose between the social studies and the language arts. Yet another such indicator is the increasing importance of a greater variety of types of writing assignments in the social studies. Social studies teachers are turning more to imaginative writing.

Research skills remain, though, as an area of critical concern. Educators know that writing skills grow through practice and that writing is linked to the development of thinking skills. They also know that even mathematical learning can be used by students in student research in the social studies. It is especially important that teachers move beyond those report assignments which required little thought other than that needed for copying and rote reading. Carefully structured writing assignments and follow-up can lead to more meaningful writing.

SELF-TEST

1. What are the four basic purposes for which reading and writing assignments are used in independent seat work?

2. What are the qualities that you need to look for in a nonfiction as well as a fiction book?

3. What are some different kinds of fictional material that can be used in the social studies?

4. How does the social studies relate to whole language?

5. What are the purposes of learning research and reporting skills?

6. What are some guidelines to make textbook questions more meaningful?

7. Why do teachers have students write reports and give them orally?

8. What place does mathematics have in the social studies?

REFERENCES: PROFESSIONAL MATERIALS

Anderson, L.W. (1984). What teachers don't do and why. *Education Report 27, no.3*. December.

Cooper, D. (1986). *Improving reading comprehension*. Boston: Houghton Mifflin.

Lee, J.F. and Pruett, K.W. (1979). Homework assignments: classroom games or teaching tools? *Clearing House*, 53 (September).31-35.

Loring, R.A. (1975). *Relative effects of massed and distributed scheduling of homework assignments on eighth grade mathematics students*. Doctoral Dissertation Abstracts International. Ohio State University.

Schneider, D.O. and Brown, M.M. (1980). Helping students study and understand their social studies textbooks. In Patten, W.E. (ed.). *Improving the use of social studies textbooks*.

Bulletin 63. Washington D.C.: The National Council for the Social Studies.

Slavin, R. (1987). Cooperative learning: where behavioral and humanistic approaches to classroom motivation meet. *The Elementary School Journal*, 88 (September), 29-36.

Turner, T. N. (1989). Using textbook questions intelligently. *Social Education*, 53 (January), 58-60.

Walberg, H. (1986). Synthesis of research in teaching. In Wittrock, M. (ed.), *Handbook of educational research: a project of the American Educational Research Association*. (3rd ed.) New York: Macmillan, 1986.

REFERENCES: CHILDREN'S LITERATURE

Aliki. (1983). *A medieval feast*. New York: Crowell.

Aliki. (1979). *Mummies, made in Egypt*. New York: Crowell.

Forbes, Esther. (1943). *Johnny Tremain*. Boston: Houghton Mifflin.

Fritz, J. (1980). *Where do you think you're going, Columbus?* New York: Putnam.

Fritz, J. (1974). *Why don't you get a horse, Sam Adams?* New York: Coward, McCann, Geoghegan.

Haskins, Jim. (1987).*Count your way series*. Minneapolis: Carolrhoda, Inc.

Human story, The. (1987). Morristown, N.J.: Silver Burdette.

Lawson, R. (1939). *Ben and me*. Boston: Little, Brown.

Macaulay, D. (1977). *Castle-the story of its construction*. Boston: Houghton Mifflin.

Macaulay, D. (1973). *Cathedral*. Boston: Houghton Mifflin.

McLean, V. *Chasing the moon to China*. New York: Redbird,1987.

Monjo, S.N. (1970). *The one bad thing about father*. New York: Harper and Row.

Provenson, A. and Provenson, M. (1983). *The glorious flight*.New York: The Viking Press.

Spear, E. (1958). *The Witch of Blackbird Pond*. Boston: Houghton Mifflin.

Spier, P. (1979). *People*. New York: Doubleday.

Turning points of history series.(1989). Morristown, N.J: Silver Burdett.

Where we live series. (1990). Austin, Texas: Steck-Vaughn.

SUGGESTED READING

James, Michael, and Zarillo, James.(1989). Teaching history with children's literature. *The Social Studies*, 80 (July/August), 153-158.

McGowan, T., Guzzetti, B., and Kowalinski, B. (1992). Using literature studies to promote elementary social studies learning. *Social Studies and the Young Learner*, 5 (September/October), 10-13.

7 Study Skills: The Edge Is the Urge

LOOKING AHEAD

Information is only important if it can be put to use. Children feel this as much as adults, and they often feel that they are asked to learn information for which they have no use at all. What may be more important is that children do not always learn in school the skills they need to use information.

In any problems approach, information is constantly being used to solve problems. The focus of this chapter is on those skills that are needed to make the best use possible of information in every problems context. The chapter begins with general information skills and then moves on to two specific areas that have special importance to the social studies, map skills and time skills.

CAN YOU? DO YOU?

Can you

- Identify several ways to make children curious?
- Understand why map and globe skills are so difficult for children?

Do you

- Ever get the "Columbus urge"?
- Know that there are several kinds of memory?
- Know what a mnemonic device is?
- Know how children develop time and space concepts?

BUILDING THE DESIRE TO MASTER STUDY SKILLS

In elementary and middle school, children have to master some very complex and difficult information-processing skills very quickly. It is a big job and it is not easy. What makes it even more difficult is that children have to deal with all of this during a period when they undergo tremendous physical change and face a number of stressful social changes. Add to this the fact that a majority of children face stressful home situations. Many are latchkey children; ever larger percentages are from single parent homes; many face physically or mentally abusive situations; and many are in homes where unemployment, insufficient family income, or other economic problems are major.

There is an expression, "an urge gives you an edge." What it means is that the desire or wanting to do something well is a distinct advantage in actually doing it well. The best opportunities that teachers have to help children get such an edge is when they are trying to teach them to put information to use. Using information is, after all, the heart of a problems approach. When students learn that knowing information and how to get it is useful in solving real problems, it gives the information purpose. They learn because they need to know and want to learn, not because the teacher wants them to know. That "edge" is important, too, because learning to use information is not easy. What is more, children have to deal with information that comes from several different types of sources. There seems to be an almost endless variety of print materials that contain all kinds of information. Not the most exciting of these or the easiest to handle is the textbook. More exciting, but sometimes requiring more interpretation is information that comes from audiovisual materials, from artifacts and other objects, from people, and from computerized resources. Reading, observation, and listening skills as well as technical ones are needed as the basis for study.

First and foremost, children need to be able to know where and how to find the information they need. As an accompanying processing skill, they have to be able to decide if information is true and accurate, relevant, important, and useful. Finally, they have to be able to remember, use, and present the information.

FINDING INFORMATION

When it comes to locating information, there is one thing that teachers can help children acquire which is more important than everything else. Yes, locating information does require that children learn about different kinds of resources and the type of information they contain. Mastery of accessing skills is needed too, using various types of indexes and tables of contents (often called *menus* in computer programs). Children need to be taught skimming and scanning skills. But those skills will come with time and effort. What children most need is what I call the Columbus urge. The Columbus urge is that irresistible desire to explore, to find out. Trite as the expression may sound, it is the thrill of discovering and the sheer satisfaction of knowing that you know that makes real self-starting students. If children can acquire this one quality, they will be driven to learn all of the necessary skills that it takes to acquire information.

The Columbus urge can be encouraged if not created. There are several teaching elements that are necessary, including the teacher modeling an excitement about learning. It is also necessary that the classroom be a busy, exciting, stimulating place where provocative questions are constantly being asked and where tidbits of curious information of interest are constantly being unearthed. You do not want to get too gimmicky, but here are a few ideas to develop the Columbus urge.

- Regularly give children things to find out that really catch their interest and stir their curiosity. (Hints: You are going to have to find out about *their* culture and what interests them. You are likely to find that things like "firsts," "longests," "shortests," and "mosts" work consistently.)

- Leave questions dangling and unanswered and challenge them to find out.

- Model the excitement of researching and finding out.

- Make a fuss about student discoveries.

- Challenge the children to come up with questions and curiosities for you and for their classmates.

- Obtain and have where children can see and use as many interesting information sources as possible.

- Give children lots of opportunities to find information and then use it.

- Remember that "knowers" love to show off, so don't just let them; encourage them and even plan opportunities for them to do it.

- As a time filler, play the "I know something" game. In it the children try to discover what it is that the teacher, or someone else, knows. The children have to be trained to know that their first job is always to find out *where* the information can be found. (Is it in the dictionary? an atlas?)

- Have constantly changing displays and bulletin boards where students encounter people, actions, and things that are different and that create curiosity.

DECISION MAKING WITH INFORMATION

I like to give children lots of practice activities in this area. Most school materials just do not have enough examples. However, one of the most prevailing problems of both real life and student life is deciding what is *most* relevant, important, and useful. To give children the idea, I sometimes start with things in the popular culture where they know the differences and I do not. How do you tell Smurfs apart or distinguish Leonardo from Raphael? Playing stupid helps here, so I ask them about attributes of the characters that I know are not relevant but are nonetheless traits of the characters. *All* Smurfs are blue and little. *All* turtles have shells. These are characteristics all right, but they do not help us tell the characters apart. With younger children who are very ego centered, I may even go to the children themselves. "Let's see why I like Bryan." "Is it because he's wearing a blue shirt?" You can easily see where this questioning would go. The important thing is that through it the children are learning that what may be important and relevant to one question, has no merit or use with another.

We also do a lot of listing of traits. For example, if we are studying a country, a city, a state, or a geographic area, I like to make a list of the characteristics of the area with the children. I often do this as part of a "Would you like to live there?" activity. That way, we can have two columns, one of traits that make a difference and one of traits that do not. We can do a similar listing with historical people or current candidates for political office. We are just deciding different things, whether they did their jobs well, whether they are suited for office, and so on.

Once they have the idea I move to some type of game activities. One of the favorites across grade levels I call mysteries. These are multiclue riddle activities and they can even be done in groups cooperatively. The number of clues and the difficulty I fit to the class. The idea is to reveal a series of clues one at a time, beginning with the hard clues and going to easier ones. In some of these games, some clues may be irrelevant or unimportant.

Sorting activities also help children learn to distinguish relevance. One that I think works very well is called a *card sort*. The activity begins with a deck of cards with facts or single words written on them. Have labeled category boxes and sort the cards into these. After you have done this a few times as a group discussion activity, it may be assigned with multiple decks as a cooperative group activity as well. After the groups finish, they can explain their logic. It is good to include cards that do not fit any category in the deck.

REMEMBERING INFORMATION

In the social studies, students are required to remember information for three reasons. They have to understand and remember some things for a very brief time, just long enough to work through a single lesson or class. Other information they are going to have to retain for a while longer, perhaps a few days, in order to do particular assignments. Finally, there is information that teachers want them to remember over a long period of time. These three are referred to in various ways, but for our purposes let us refer to them as *working memory, long-term memory, and cumulative memory*. What we expect children to put in cumulative memory is usually related to what has been called *cultural literacy*. This term has gotten a lot of attention in education in recent years and is often used to describe what an "educated person" should know.

It is important to realize that all three types of memory are important. One of the teacher's jobs in the social studies is to help children learn how to decide what is important to remember and to distinguish whether information is needed for working-memory, long-term memory, or cultural literacy.

Part of the secret of getting students to remember information and ideas is to present it to them in memorable ways. That means it has to be interesting, even exciting if possible. That is why children can tell all about a movie they have seen at the mall but remember nothing they read in a dull textbook. What they remember is not just dependent on children doing what they enjoy or want to do. Sometimes remembering is work and requires a determined effort. There are several ways that teachers can help their students learn and remember information.

- Work on a can-do attitude. This requires both encouragement and task control to keep the amount of information at a level that students can handle. Students need to feel confident that they can remember. (If they feel they cannot memorize something, it will give them one more hurdle to overcome.)

- Understanding precedes remembering. Yes, nonsense words can be memorized, but generally anyone is more likely to remember what they understand than what they do not understand.

- Talk with students about what they already know. If students can relate or associate information to their own experiences, it will make it easier for them to remember.

- Organize the information for them in a way that makes sense. Isolated pieces of information are often more difficult to remember than information that has patterns and structures that relate individual facts.

- Provide mnemonic devices for sets of information. Memory-jogging associations that are catchy and full of images really do work.

- Make memorizing work as much fun as possible.

When it comes to reviewing for the purpose of remembering information of all types, the approach most often used is drill. But, watch out! Drill can be meaningless, boring, and totally useless as a learning activity. If children are tuning out mentally, they are not learning. This means that *You have to make it enjoyable*. If drill is the method, it needs to be structured carefully so that it also makes the fact that the children are supposed to learn mean something. A good drill is going to help the learner put the information into logical and meaningful structures. It will put the stuff together in a way that makes sense and seems useful. Equally important, the drill has to be one that the child will participate in fully. If children find the drill uncomfortable or boring, they will start tuning out, daydreaming, or thinking of other things. So, any and all gimmicks and games are welcome.

Generally, memories with positive happy associations are more vivid and lasting than those with negative associations. Experiencing information with as many senses as possible repeatedly usually helps us remember.

One of the best ways to make drill enjoyable is to turn it into a game, but not all drill games work. The game has to be one that the children will enjoy and also one that covers the necessary information repeatedly. The best drill games are those that keep the majority of the children mentally engaged most of the time. Because more senses are involved, I like games that give the information in writing as well as orally. I also prefer small-group games with the children controlling the pacing, but this is not going to work for all teachers and classes.

Many commercial board games and card games as well as television game shows and sports activities are adaptable to fact-learning activities. Games do not have to ask questions about the facts. They simply have to get the children to see, say, and hear the information repeatedly. "Monopoly" or "Candyland" types of games can be adapted so that the various board spaces and playing pieces are labeled to represent historic or geographic facts related to a topic being studied will enable children to encounter these words and images over and over. Similarly, many common games played with cards can be fact learning games with specially made cards.

TEACHING ABOUT MAPS AND GLOBES

An important skill taught in the social studies is how to use maps and globes. This skill is based on an extensive knowledge base of concepts and information about the location, size, and names of various places as well as an understanding of the structure, function, and terminology of different types of maps and globes. Maps and globes, in turn, provide important information that can help students learn more about their world.

Instructional Guidelines for Using Maps and Globes

We want to make children feel comfortable with maps and globes and to fascinate them with the kinds of information that they can find on them. We also want children to gain an understanding that different kinds of maps and globes can be used for different purposes. By the time they have reached the intermediate grades, if not before, children should be able to use maps and globes to answer questions and solve problems.

We can define a *globe* as a three-dimensional representation of the earth's surface or the surface of another astronomical body. A <u>map</u>, on the other hand, is a two-dimensional representation of an area. Because maps are flat, maps showing very large area, such as the earth's surface, are going to be distorted from reality in some way.

It is important to choose maps and globes for classroom use wisely and carefully. To begin with, teachers need to keep in mind that the best map or globe for a particular lesson will depend on several factors, including

- The conditions under which it is going to be used

- The number of children who will be looking at it (e.g., whole class, small group, individual)

- The ability, background, and skill levels of the students

- The purpose(s) for which it is going to be used for (i.e., the type of information that the map will need to show)

- The types of tasks that children are going to have to complete

In purchasing and collecting classroom maps and globes over time, teachers need to think about a number of things, especially the following:

- Relative cost

- Accuracy

- Readability

- Durability

- "Busy-ness" (For young children especially, maps need to contain minimal information.)

- "Mark-ability" (Maps on which you can write, draw, and erase are very useful in the classroom.)

- Store-ability. (Teachers have limited space.)

- Usability (Maps must be useful for a variety of teaching purposes.

Maps and Globes in the Primary Grades

One of the first geographic concepts that young children need to learn is what a map is. They can do this by working with very simple maps showing areas they can actually see. A map of the classroom or the scene shown in a sand table, or a map showing the location of items in a desk drawer are examples of places to map.

Along with the concept *of* map, children need to get some concepts *about* maps. They need to learn that objects on a map have a directional relation to one another and that we have to turn a map a certain way if we are to follow it. They also need to learn that maps use symbols and that maps simplify and summarize a lot of information. They can learn all of this and more by making and then following maps of the school or playground or of places they visit on field trips. These experiences early on will also help them learn that maps show very real places and will teach them the importance of accurate depiction of relative size on a map.

Following are a few ideas for consideration that might help primary children learn more effectively from and about maps:

- Try to use maps in a horizontal rather than a vertical position with young children because that is the way they see the world.

- Develop a habit of orienting a map (relating it directionally to the real world) whenever one is used with children.

- Give children a lot of experiences with maps of places they can see, places they have actually been, and places they will and can visit.

- Provide a lot of experiences with maps of smaller areas (e.g., neighborhoods, recreational places such as parks and zoos, and rooms in buildings).

- Give young children plenty of multisensory, manipulative experiences with maps (working with jigsaw puzzle maps, map outline and route tracing, feeling high and low places in relief maps, etc.) and, when manipulatives are used, opportunity toorally affirm things like place names and names of geographic features.

- Guard against misconceptions that are created by flat maps by regularly relating places on these maps to globes.

- Whenever place names are mentioned in reading stories, in class discussions, and so on, it only takes a minute to show them on maps and globes.

- Acquaint children with a variety of types of simple colorful maps, including pictographic maps, to make them aware of the map legends and symbols and to teach them that different maps show different types of information.

- Teach about scale, map distances, and direction experientially and at a developmental simple-to-complex pace.

- On a regular basis, have specific attainable but challenging objectives that relate to what children should learn about place location and geographic and map concept terminology.

Maps and Globes in the Intermediate Grades

Older children should be able to work with maps and globes containing differing amounts of information with increasing independence. As they spend more time learning about different cultures and regions, more and more information is presented to children in map form. By the time they have completed the elementary grades, children should be able to read, use, and make maps and globes in a way that shows mastery of the four basic map skills: (1.) reading direction, (2.) reading distance, (3.) understanding map legends, and (4.) orienting the map to the real world. They should be able to recognize and understand the purposes of the basic types of world-map projections and different thematic maps (rainfall, vegetation, product, etc.). Students at this level need to understand a number of terms related to maps and landforms.

Teachers at the intermediate grade level need to do map work carefully and often to develop map skills. Many of the guidelines that were suggested for younger children apply as well to the older ones.

- Never assume previous knowledge and skill in using maps without verifying that children really do possess that knowledge or skill.

- Teachers who have high levels of enthusiasm and high expectations about how much children will grow in their knowledge about maps and globes seem to be more successful.

- Ask questions in discussion and writing that require students to get information from maps and globes.

- Whenever topical references are made to places, take the time to have students locate them on the globe and on one or more maps.

- Have several easy-to-play map location and jigsaw-map assembly games and activities available in the classroom and encourage their use during free time of any sort.

- Set up map interest centers and map curiosity bulletin boards loaded with interesting maps and map. activities.

- Have plenty of activities such as treasure hunts and scavenger hunts, and mapping of field trips. that involve *using* or following maps as a means of reaching particular objectives.

Maps Are to Use

One of the reasons that children have trouble learning map skills is that the majority of map work they do in school is too often just a series of questions and tasks for which the children see no purpose. They really need to be exposed to maps in ways that seem meaningful and purposeful to them.

It seems amazing that we teach map skills without having students really use maps in the ways that adults do. Adults find they *need to use* maps. They really need them, and use them for a variety of reasons: to find out where they are going or how to get there; to find alternate routes when there is some problem with the original; to help them decide about a new job; to locate a friend or relative; to find their way around some place they are visiting; to make business decisions that require a knowledge of distance and routes; to consider distance to supplies, equipment or marketing; to determine the weather's effect on their travel; and to determine meeting places, etc. In short, adults use maps to plan, to understand, to solve problems, and to dream about their world. Unfortunately, the teaching of map skills to children contains too little of this. Map skills are taught in a way that says to students that maps are to look at; to answer questions from worksheets; and sometimes to color, draw, on or mark. Children fail to discover that maps are useful items and that they can help in real-life activities.

This appears to cause any number of problems relating to sequential development of skills and concepts. One of these problems is that students tend to see map work as lacking in purpose. A second is that they never really learn to use maps to find specific information or to follow routes.

Following are 10½ (two of the activities are strikingly similar) map-*using* activities in which children can participate and from which they can learn how maps can be used. Map-using activities is a descriptive title for this type of exercise. It includes any method by which students experience relating maps to physical space or in relating maps to problems involving that space. To be effective, such activities should be perceived by students as having sensible purposes and should involve short term, specific tasks that are tightly structured.

l. Map-reading scavenger hunt

The scavenger hunt taxes the students' abilities to follow directions given on a map or in a set of written directions accompanying a map. It is an adaptation of the gaming sport of orienteering. Groups of students are asked to find a treasure by following a precise routine in the shortest possible time.

Each group is equipped with a compass, a meter stick (think metric), and a set of directions or a map showing them their route to and location of one portion of their own team's treasure map. Each groups' route is different from those of all the others. The teacher will need to prepare in advance a treasure map or set of directions for each team. The treasure maps or directions are each cut or torn into sections and each section put into a separate capped plastic bottle or a can with a tight sealing lid. This enables the teacher to place the containers in advance without worry about weather damage. Of course, they cannot be set out too far ahead of time. Chance discovery and removal can happen too easily. The cans or bottles of all teams should be indistinguishable from one another. However, the maps inside might be color coded by team so as to be recognizable when discovered. The containers are then hidden in a pattern shown on the map or described in the directions. The sets of directions are written so that the discovery of one container gives a new set of directions leading to another. A team may, by following its own map, discover all of its own map pieces or directions. The activity should be monitored and any group that opens another team's container simply because it is discovered and not by following the map should be penalized by adding time (say, l minute). Teams are staggered in starting, but turns are recorded. The team completing the map in the shortest time wins.

2. Site stakeout

For site stakeouts students are divided into groups of six to ten. If possible, work with one group at a time and keep accurate record of the time it takes that group to complete the task and any errors corrected or help needed. Each group is assigned a different site. Sites may be such things as castles, forts, museums, public buildings (e.g., city hall, the school, jail or prison), typical small frontier towns, factories, or colonial farms. Groups are given drawings showing their own site in detail. Other information about activities on the site are also provided. The group's job is to "stake" its own site by outlining the perimeter and interior features as accurately as possible. Each group uses string and small wooden or plastic stakes (clothespins work well, too). Stakes are driven into the ground and string stretched between the stakes. The groups show such things as dimensions, relative size, and so on. All parts of the site are labeled corresponding to diagram labels. Upon completion, the staked out sites are evaluated in accuracy, timeelapsed in the stakeout, and the amount of adult assistance required.

3. Orienteering scavenge

For the orienteering scavenge some advance work will need to be done. Cooperation is needed among several people in the school and community. It is also recommended that an adult volunteer be recruited to accompany each team of children. The initial task is to identify places in the community, students' homes, places of business, offices, and so on, simply on the basis of the willingness of people in these places to participate in helping the students learn. A map of the community is drawn indicating by a number each of the places where a cooperating person is to be found. No names of people or place titles are listed on the map.

Each team is given a copy of the map and an order in which they are to visit each place. The order is indicated only by the number. (The order of the places is different for all teams.) Teams are sent out at 5-minute intervals. Their job is to use the map to find, in *proper order*, the places listed on their directions. At each stop, the team records the name of the person or the location and the time of arrival. The teams must get a verifying signature from the cooperating person at the site. (They may wear badges or caps if there are several people about). The objective for each group is to finish all scheduled stops in the *correct order* on a timed schedule (or in the shortest possible time).

4. Fantasy school map

The fantasy school map activity is designed to help children understand the concepts of miniaturization or symbolism as they apply to maps. It is a map-making activity in which students try to translate a part of the world onto a map. Imagination and policing are needed, but it can be well worth the effort in terms of practical learning. The amount of space used may vary. A large area, such as cafeteria, gymnasium, or playground is best. Students imagine that the area used for the map is a part of some larger, distant geographic area. For example, it might be seen as an area of the gold fields of California, a township in the Northwest Territory, an area of land being opened for homesteading, a feudal manor, a Roman military encampment, or a contemporary community in any country.

It should be pointed out that the size of the actual area being imagined would be much larger than the actual space used. The first job of the group of children is to arrange and label the features of the area. Existing furnishings should be incorporated. A chair may be used to symbolize a building, a bookcase may be a mesa, and so on. But added features may be created simply by labeling sheets of paper. The students then map the area they have laid out.

5. Best route

Best route involves studies in using maps to determine the best way to get from one place to another. For this activity students are put into small groups. Each group has a map of the local community around the school and a list of jobs to do. The tasks may simply be finding specific purchasable items (students need not buy, only locate where items may be purchased) or finding the best prices or set of items to deliver. But jobs could also include involvement in volunteer citizenship activities at several locations, community improvement or helping elderly or disabled individuals in which students actually do the work.

Each group is to determine the most efficient route for performing the tasks and the time it will take to complete those tasks. Groups go *together* and will need to use the map. They must anticipate delaying factors (such as hills or unmarked construction sites, heavily trafficked roads where crossing may be difficult or even incur backtracking) and keep in mind such effort and time influencing such factors as distances to carry heavy loads. A route plan and estimated time for each stop have to be submitted before the trip is taken. Afterwards, students can discuss alternative, better routes and factors influencing how well their plans worked.

6. Memory map-drawing

Have students draw, from memory, maps of places they have visited such as the zoo, a park, a theme amusement park, a historical site, and so on. If possible obtain an official map or promotion map of that site for comparison.

7. Map labeling

Provide students with an unlabeled map of a familiar area and have them fill in the labels. The location may be one seen and traveled regularly, such as some part of a local neighborhood or one visited one or more times. If the latter is used, informing students before the actual trip can improve observation.

8. Where does it come from?

Divide students into groups. Each group is given a world map and a list of ten products, ten animals, or ten plants. Using reference books, the group must determine locations where the items on their list may be found. They then must chart the shortest possible route for obtaining them.

9. Shortest Route to the Habitat

Give the students a list of ten animals and ask them to pretend that they have been commissioned to return each animal to its natural environment. Have students discover the shortest distance that these animals may be taken by plane to a safe habitat which is similar to the one in which they are naturally found. The catch is that they cannot carry animals beyond a specified total weight *or* animals that are natural enemies on the same trip. The list of animals should include some relatively heavy ones, some that are prey, and some that are predators.

10. Mapping a School Activity

Have students make and use a school and school grounds map to set up plans for a school activity. These might be a school carnival (with specific locations for all attractions), a walking field trip (with specific places of interest noted), a class party, parents' night, or open house.

10½. Story Maps

Have students do story-maps as book reports. A *story-map* charts the geographic areas used as settings for the book. Inferences and direct statements of the author about relative distances, landmarks, and features are used by students; movements of protagonists and other characteristics can also be charted. Interior as well as exterior maps may be made. Fantasy and realistic stories set in fictitious places may be mapped almost as easily as those whose settings are real places.

A caution and guideline: Depending on school policy, these activities may be designed in such a way that they take students around the neighborhood for variety and interest. Local school policies, community cooperation, and the neighborhood will be determining factors in deciding if and how to use orientating approaches. Parent or other adult volunteers are essential precautions for many. However, simple adaptations may be all that is needed to use some such activities within school grounds. (By the way, did everyone figure out which activities made up the two "halves"?)

TIME CONCEPTS AND SKILLS

Children are very aware of time. Developing time concepts and skills not only helps them understand history, but it enables them to better understand the events in their own lives. Their awareness of time and time words should become more and more specific as they progress through the elementary grades.

Time understanding for children begins with a mixture of vague and precise time references in their lives and in the language around them that is most likely to be confusing. For example, when someone says "in a second" or "in a minute," they do not mean precisely 1 or 60 seconds. In fact, the reference, in a child's experience, might have meant several hours and is no more precise than the very uncertain "in a little while." Other seemingly precise time references also have had a wide range of meaning to children. Tomorrow may have been meant just that, or it may be a word used for when something was not going to happen for days if at all. Part of the job of the school is to help children clarify and distinguish both the vague references and the more precise ones.

Children's Understanding Of Time

The following description of each stage of children's understanding of time is based on Vukelich and Thornton (1990, 22-25).

Age (in Years)	Stage Description
3–5	Capable of sequencing daily events, can rank order family members by age
6–8	Develop the ability to use "historical numbers" to represent the past; can sometimes match dates with major events (e.g., Christmas is December 25)
9–11	Become capable of matching persons and events with textbook descriptions (e.g., colonial period)
12–14	Able to use time classifications with increasing ease (e.g., decade)

As children grow in their understanding of and ability to deal with time, they begin to have increasingly more precise reference points on the clock and the calendar. They begin to understand that one of the ways to understand time is to visualize time passage as space distance. Visualizations through a variety of types of time lines help children to better see events in relation to one another. In the process children begin to learn

- The multiple meanings of time and calendar words

- The precise meaning of time words used in the measurement of time (second, minute, hour, day, week, month, year, decade, century, millennium, etc.)

- How time is sometimes represented by distance (time lines including calendars and some clocks)

- Information about clocks

- Information about calendars

- Information about other types of time lines

- Event sequence

- Events in relation to one another

Children learn about time by developing meaningful reference points. The schedule for the school day is one of the major devices used to learn about clocks and acquire shorter time references. Scheduled events at school and outside of school as well as the so-called Holiday Curriculum are the major means through which children learn about the calendar. Multisensory experiences that add meaning to events and associate their occurrence with dates help children remember the time and place of the events.

A calendar is one of the earliest time lines that young children are exposed to in school. Kindergarten or early primary teachers, for example, often use the space above eye level on all four walls of the classroom to make an in-the-round pictorial calendar of the year. On it they show the seasons, the months and sometimes weeks, school starting and ending points, holiday reference points, and even class and personal events such as birthdays. Such a time line not only supports self concepts but also shows the difficult-to-comprehend cyclical nature of repeating time lines such as calendars and clocks.

Learning about the relationship of events and people through time lines continues with such activities as the following:

- Have children make a personal time line of their own lives.

- Have children line up according to birthday.

- Let each child do a stair step family time line tracing one strand of his or her forbearers.

                         _____Great-great grandmother

                    _____Great grandmother.

               _____Grandmother

          _____Mother

    _____Me

- Help students do human time-lines in which each individual represents events and historical people. Chalk marks or masking tape on the floor can show precisely measured distances to represent decades, centuries, etc. Costume creation and reporting-type activities can be added to make it even more fun.

Human time lines can be used to represent events relating to one another during a relatively brief period of time (e.g., events surrounding the break up of the Soviet Union), the time relations of different people or events (e.g., inventions that changed our lives), or the relationship of several important events over a broad span of history.

- Have children play a quiz game in which they get to add themselves to the human time line by answering a time-relationship question.

- Make clothesline time lines. Have the children add events as they are talked about, clipping the new events to the time line using a squeeze clothes pin.

- Have children make an objects time line lining up objects either in the order they were invented or the order they were obtained.

- Give children in groups of three or four a deck of cards each labeled as a different holiday. Have children experiment sorting and ordering the holidays in different ways, including chronological order.

ECONOMIC SKILLS

Economic skills that children begin to learn in elementary school have to do mostly with their roles as consumers. However, they also need to learn something about how producers and others operate. Among the areas of economics that children need to begin dealing with are the following:

- Money concepts

- Managing money and time

- Understanding needs and wants

- Concepts of value and price

- Comparative shopping

- Exchange

- Banking Skills

- Credit

There are, of course, hundreds of different activities that can be used to practice and learn about the economic world in which we live. In mathematics, money amounts and costs of goods and services can be used for very meaningful practice in calculation.

Situational scenarios and hypothetical problems related to economics can be used at almost any level. Even in kindergarten economic thinking is part of many of the locational centers that can be set up in the classroom: kitchen centers, post office centers, building construction centers, and so on. One interesting activity that children of all ages like is to trade things.

Trading games and activities can provide an experiential basis for discussion of relative merit and relative value. Lots of commercial games deal with budgeting and with using and conserving resources.

Activities that can build economic skills if carefully planned include the following:

- Planning dream vacations

- Buying, selling and trading games

- Practicing at exchanging play money

- Simulation and role play activities in which there is exchange of goods and services and of play money and checks

- Pricing practice using advertisements and catalogs

- Planning budgets (e.g., the class budgets field trips, activities at which food is served, etc.)

- Price following activities and games (e.g., stock market, home prices, automobile prices, etc.) over time

- Setting up in-school systems where purchases are made and rewards for work are given

- Pretending to exchange currencies of different countries

- Involving student hobbies in which value is built (e.g., collections)

LOOKING BACK

Well developed study skills give students a winning advantage, an edge, when it comes to any learning task. The most important study skills include knowing how to find necessary information, being able to make decisions about information, and being able to organize and remember information. Some study skills have special importance to the social studies because they relate especially to one or more of the social sciences. Teachers can help students learn map and globe skills more effectively if they expose children to many experiences with maps and map problems, use maps that are simple and purposeful, and teach about distance, direction, scale experiential and at a developmentally appropriate pace. Maps should be used purposely in the classroom with a variety of applied map reading activities. It should be stressed that maps can be fun and there should be an abundance of map games and other activities that the children enjoy doing. Time skills also require hands-on activities with concrete materials which will expand the awareness of time. Lots of experiences with calendars, clocks and a variety of other time lines is important.

This is a society in which the development of economic skills is essential to survival. Children need experiences in dealing with money and growing understanding of credit, banking, budgeting, and other economic planning.

SELF-TEST

1. What are some ways to create the Columbus urge in children?

2. Why is it sometimes said that the social studies is information based?

3. What are some things a teacher can do to help children learn essential information?

4. What is a mnemonic device?

5. What is the difference between a map and a globe?

6. What are some guidelines for using maps and globes in the primary grades?

7. Why is it important to teach maps in a way that involves maps as tools of problem solving?

8. What are some of the time concepts that children need to learn?

REFERENCES

Vukelich, R. and Thornton, S.J.(1990). Children's understanding of historical time: implications for instruction. *Childhood Education*, 67 (Fall), 22-25.

SUGGESTED READING

McClure, J. (1989). Practical map examinations for geography. *The Social Studies*, 80 (July/August), 159-162.

Muir, S.P., and Cheek, H.N. (1991). Assessing spatial development: implications for map skill instruction. *Social Education*, 55 (September), 316-319.

Rae, C. (1990). Before the outline-the writing wheel. *The Social Studies*, 81 (July/August), 178-180.

Turner, T. N. (1990). *Brainstorms*. Glenview. Ill.: Scott Foresman.

Young, T. and Schiene, V. (1992). Writing to learn in social studies. *Social Studies and the Young Learner*, 5 (September/October), 14-16.

8 Teaching Thinking Learning Skills

LOOKING AHEAD

At the heart of the problems approach to the social studies is a way of thinking about teaching that is quite different. A teacher who uses the problems approach effectively must believe that students' being able to think and learn for themselves is all important. That teacher ultimately is going to make him or herself obsolete. The reason is that the ultimate goal of teaching is for learners to become more and more independent. Independent learners not only know how to find information they need, they know when to search and what to search for. They also look at each situation and problem that they face through a different kind of mind-set or grid. That grid, obviously an important part of their world view, determines how they will address these situations and problems. If the development of independent learners is truly the goal of education, then it is more important to teach children how to think than it is to teach them what to think. The first step in teaching them how to think is helping them develop the right kind of mind set or grid.

Thinking skills have been an increasing concern in the social studies. In the last decade, a number of national committees have attempted to set direction for elementary school social studies into the twenty-first century. One of these, a NCSS Task Force on Scope and Sequence (1984) stated that, "Social studies programs have a responsibility to prepare young people to identify, understand, and work to solve problems that face our increasingly diverse nation and interdependent world" (p. 251). A later NCSS Task Force on Early Childhood/Elementary Social Studies focused on cooperative problem solving, claiming that basic skills in reading, writing, and computing were necessary but not sufficient if children are to survive in today's world. Critical thinking and the development of positive attitudes toward self and others were given priority status in this report (1989).

More recently, yet another task force was appointed, this one by the National Commission on the Social Studies. From the standpoint of backing, this was the most high-powered group yet. Funding came from the Carnegie Foundation, the Rockefeller Foundation, the MacArthur Foundation, and the National Geographic Society, and the Task Force had the sponsorship of the NCSS and the American Historical Association. Over two years in preparation, the Task Force's report, titled *Charting a Course: Social Studies for the 21st Century* (1989), formulated a set of curricular goals for students, which included development of perspectives on their own life experiences so they see themselves as part of the larger human adventure in time and place, and development of a critical understanding of the history, geography, economic, political, and social institutions, traditions, and values of the United States as expressed in both their unity and diversity, and development of critical attitudes and analytical perspectives appropriate to analysis of the human condition.

Presentation-style social studies is not likely to develop children's thinking skills. Such skills require that students be involved and participate in the learning process. This means that discussion, teacher questioning, and carefully constructed assignments are very important.

CAN YOU? DO YOU?

Can you

- Tell three ways that teachers teach children to think logically?
- Identify some functions of the mind that relate to critical thinking?
- Distinguish among several different kinds of problem-solving tasks?

Do you

- Know how teachers can help children to understand and remember information?
- Know what a story map is?

THE THINKING SKILLS OF OBSERVING, LISTENING, AND COMPREHENDING

The term *thinking skills* is almost always used in a very broad way, so it usually means many things. Generally, thinking skills refers to all of the mental processes that individuals use to obtain, make sense of, and retain information, as well as how they process and use that information as a basis for solving problems. Obviously, information is taken in by observing, listening, and reading. Obtaining information and ideas is a sensory process and all of the senses are used in information gathering. Because there is substantial evidence that for many children and adults learning is easier through one sense than the others, teachers need to utilize multisensory learning materials wherever possible. But it should be remembered that learning to listen and observe purposefully are trainable skills acquired through directed, disciplined practice. Therefore, teachers need to help children acquire these important skills in a systematic and developmental way.

Information and ideas can be acquired and remembered without being understood. For example, anyone can memorize a set of nonsense words. Many adults can still recite things like Lewis Carroll's poem, "The Jabberwocky," which they memorized as children. However, information is more easily acquired and certainly of more use to an individual if it is comprehended. One of the major factors in understanding is how information fits into what people already know. Individuals make sense of new information on the basis of how well they can relate it to previous experiences and ideas. Therefore, the way that new information is presented may be as important or even more important than the information itself.

A term used to describe relating new ideas to experiences is schema. Schemata (the plural) are the various ways we have ideas and knowledge grouped in our minds. In order for us to have understanding, we have to tie our observation to one or more of these schemata. To do this, we look for assumptions, create analogies, and generally relate information to ourselves.

Another factor in comprehension is something that is referred to in the literature as *metacognition*. Metacognition refers to an individual's awareness of his or her own thinking processes. The term has come to be used to describe a person's awareness and understanding of the organizational patterns of reading material as well as that of speakers. Research seems to support the notion that individuals who are able to form clear and accurate story maps of reading material as well as spoken material have a clearer overall understanding of that material.

This suggests several implications for teaching the social studies. One of these is that social studies teaching should have a stronger, more clearly defined and communicated sense of plot or story line. The story aspect of history and of any culture being studied needs to be emphasized. Failing to do so means, in effect, that students are going to operate with a foggy sense of what is going on; they simply are not going to understand as well.

Another implication has to do with providing story maps for students before they listen to, read or view material. In effect, this means that teachers need to provide both sensitive and clear overviews of oral presentations, audiovisual programs, and reading material before students are exposed to it. Then, too, pointed reflective review of material will also help students develop their metacognitive skills. This may, in part, be why the body of research and experience in teaching has already demonstrated that such reviews increase learning and retention in a clearly measurable way. Such reviews generally involve teacher questioning, so that students become intellectually involved and, therefore, active in forming clearer cognitive maps of material covered.

Generally, teachers can help children to understand and remember information by following a few simple principles.

- Associate the new information with experiences that the children have had in the past.

- Connect each piece of new information to other pieces of information using a pattern that children can follow. (Sensory or visualizable patterns are best.)

- Repeat the information and the patterns often.

- Provide a shared purpose or use for the learning.

- Give opportunities for practice with feedback.

LOGICAL THINKING AND ANALYZING SKILLS

As individuals start to observe, listen, and read with understanding, and especially as they begin to know some things about a topic, it becomes useful and necessary to put that information into logical structures. They begin to see and even look for relationships and patterns; to put information together and draw inferences and make judgments based on that information; to recognize importance, relevance, and usefulness of information; and to differentiate among partial, convincing, decisive, and conclusive evidence.

In the social studies, teachers can help children gain logical thinking and analyzing skills in at least three ways: by modeling, through discussion, and through guided practice with feedback. Purposeful guided tasks and teacher questions are important in all of these approaches. The following are among the logical thinking skills related to the social studies that students need to acquire, along with a brief description of a kind of activity that might be used to develop that skill:

Thinking Skill	*Typical Activity*
Interpreting or explaining	Paraphrasing, rephrasing
Relating information to self	Advanced organizers for reading assignments
Applying previous knowledge	Charting, drawing parallels
Identifying implicit assumptions	Discussion of motives Defining, classifying
Identifying key features and characteristics	Defining, describing, giving back ground

Summarizing and synthesizing	Writing summaries, reviewing, giving closure to lessons
Comparing and contrasting	Identifying attributes, pattern finding
Organizing information	Outlining
Classifying and categorizing	Charting, sorting
Inferencing and concluding	Cause and effect exercises, following clues, guessing games, problem solving
Determining accuracy, completeness, reliability	Cross checking, maps of errors, peer evaluation

CRITICAL AND CREATIVE THINKING

Someone has said that the chief dilemma of teaching is to show students where to look without telling them what to see. In that sense, helping students learn to think logically should lead to critical and creative thought processes. The teacher wants the student to be able to make wise decisions based on the information available. The teacher also wants the student to have the ability and the kind of mental set needed to come up with multiple and original ideas as solutions to problems.

Critical thinking is defined in various ways. Most definitions attempt to describe the thought processes involved in making some evaluation or judgment of an experience. If the evaluation is based on analysis, then critical thinking contains an element of logical reasoning. Critical thinking involves comparing a personal set of experiences and values to current experiences, newly encountered data, and decision and judgment demanding situations. We think critically whenever we try to reason out decisions or judgments.

Critical thinking relates to some very important functions of the mind.

- **The symbolic process**: We allow words, numbers, and other symbols to stand for ideas.

- **Visualization**: We make mental pictures that represent our perceptions

- **Characterization**: We notice the qualities of things and that which we notice,in turn, builds our perceptions of likes and differences.

- **Classification**: We sort things into classes, types, families, and so on.

- **Structure analysis**: We notice how things are made and break classes into component parts.

- **Operations analysis**: We notice how things happen, successive stages, and so on.

- **Paralleling**: We see how situations are alike.

Creative thinking, while it may involve an evaluative mind set, even more importantly means fluency and flexibility of thought, originality, and the ability to develop and elaborate in solving problems. Creative thinking is what we need when we try to find new and different ways of solving both new and old problems. Though it would be an oversimplification to say that creative thinking is problem solving, that ability is at least the focus of creative thinking. Creative thinking differs from most thought required in school chiefly because of its emphasis on alternative approaches and solutions and on multiple solutions.

PROBLEM SOLVING AND INQUIRY

Creative problem solving most often begins with a situation that demands a solution or a response and there is no already defined answer or process for arriving at an answer available. In other words, a problem is only a problem if the individual has to figure out what to do and how to do it. Problem solving can actually be defined in a number of ways. For our purposes in dealing with thinking skills developed through the social studies, we can deal with any of the following as a kind of thinking difficulty that presents a problem to be solved:

- Dealing with a situation

- Overcoming an obstacle

- Bringing about a desired effect

- Making something happen

It should be remembered, too, that problem solving as a way of thinking is one form of thinking where there is a defined objective. One of the orientations that is of utmost importance is simply being able to recognize and identify problems in a social situation.

Teaching children to become independent thinkers and problem solvers is not new. In many ancient civilizations, part of the training for young men who were to become military officers was the study the problem situations in past wars and battles. As early as the medieval universities, medicine and law was studied by debating and analyzing past cases. At the elementary level, a few innovative American schools in the early part of this century took a life centered problems approach as well.

Since the late 1960s, a learning to learn approach to teaching social studies called the inquiry method was widely advocated. Inquiry focused on the student, instead of the teacher, asking the questions. In one sense, the method was revolutionary . The teacher was no longer perceived as someone who asked all the questions and knew all the answers. Neither was the teacher to be a presenter of information. Instead,the student was to ask the questions and the teacher was to be a guide to help the student inquire to find answers.

Earliest inquiry teaching models used what has been called the scientific method. Most of us learned some version of this method in science sometime between seventh grade and high school. The scientific method is simply a sequence of the steps involved in any research. Following is one of the ways of describing the scientific method.

Sense the problem (beginning with a doubt or uncertainty)

Define the problem

Come up with some hypotheses (possible solutions to the problems)

Gather evidence

Draw conclusions

Based on the inquiry method, children can deal with problems in a variety of ways. The following are among the most successful of the inquiry strategies for dealing with a difficult problem that seems to defy solution

- Restate the problem. Simply putting a problem into different words may make it more understandable and, therefore, more solvable. It gives the problem solver fresh perspective

- Segment the problem. Dividing the problem in some way, whether into identifiable components or simply into smaller pieces is a most useful strategy. Divided, the problem can be attacked as a cooperative learning task by a group or can be dealt with one piece at a time.

- Try solving tangential problems. Look at the impact of the problem and identify side effects. Work on solving these relatively minor problems and they may provide a key to the central problem.

- Look for analogies to the problem and try solving these analogous problems. For example, if we said that our polluted rivers are similar to clogged arteries and then looked at the solutions doctors suggest for clogged arteries, it may help us identify remedies for the rivers.

- Reduce the problem. If we try to say the problem in as words and as simply as possible, then we may understand its essence more fully and be better able to solve it.

The best way to get children to become active problem solvers is to give them lots of problems to solve. These do not have to be, and probably should not be the brain-teaser type. Real life problems are more effective. The teacher needs to treat situations in the classroom as problem solving activities.

As a teacher, I have often given my students a set of guidelines like the following. When we encountered problems, it was often stimulating to their thinking to lead them through the list and ask students for their thoughts about the problem in relation to each of the guidelines. The fact that every guideline did not apply to every problem was an important point to make in the discussion.

1. The best way to get super ideas is to get *lots* of ideas and then throw away the ones that aren't so great.

2. Try to come up with elegant solutions by searching for ideas that are just a little better, not the most original thoughts ever.

3. Write down your ideas before you forget them (within 5 minutes).

4. Begin with the obvious and then look for more than one right answer.

5. Ask questions, even dumb questions.

6. Remember that nearly all words have several meanings.

7. Visualize the problem. See it backwards, forwards, inside out and all mixed up.

8. Look for the assumptions that you are likely to be making and then challenge them. Always challenge assumptions.

9. Ask how nature would solve the problem.

10. Identify the best solution and then adapt to the possible.

In these discussions I always attempted to tolerate and even encourage the offbeat and to keep the controls and the classroom atmosphere relaxed. I also tried to help children realize that the true secret of problem solving is perseverance.

PROBLEM GENERATION

The first step in problem solving is identifying problems. Children need to realize that you do not really have problems until you recognize them as such. That does not mean that the problems do not exist, what it does mean is that you do not start to think or act to solve them.

Among the ways that teachers can help children to be more aware of problems, more sensitive to their existence, and better able to clarify the nature of problems are problem generation activities. The simplest form of problem-generation exercise involves taking a topic and brainstorming the related problems involved; for example, rose growing, shopping at a mall, getting along with brothers and sisters, and school. Similar types of idea-generation tasks can be built around book, story, and historical characters; news events; social situations; and so on.

Such activities need to go beyond the initial generation of ideas. Children need practice in clarifying and refining their notions of problems. So restating, shortening, expanding, redirecting, and refining problem statements need to be part of learning the problem solving process. Sometimes it is good to work with totally funny and ridiculous questions; for example, children might try to identify what problems and changes life would hold if elephants could fly or if school hours were at night instead of during the day.

TYPES OF PROBLEM-SOLVING TASKS

Beyond helping children learn to recognize and verbalize problems, problem solving approaches should stress identifying different components of problems, identifying and using different approaches to problem solving, and recognizing and following a series of steps in order to solve a problem. Following are a few of the approaches that can be used as models for problem solving with children. Sample activities are given with each approach.

1. *Approaches that emphasize looking at all of the factors and issues involved in and related to a particular problem:* In these problem solving strategies the emphasis is on the nature of problems that have multiple possible answers. The approach is one which is effective for complex problems for which there is no perfect set of right answers. The actual number of possible answers will vary with such problems. However, the problem solvers' task includes defining criteria for examining the appropriateness of answers. The total answer set that the problem solvers identify can be judged in so far as it takes into account those criteria or factors. Examples of this approach follow.

- Pilgrims' Progress: If you were embarking with the early Puritans or Pilgrims who came to settle New England, what sort of supplies would you take with you? Make a list that includes necessities as well as other things you might like to have. Remember that this is the 1600s. Think about where you are going and where you are coming from.

- Measured room: Let us look around the room. What kind of things could we measure in here and why might we want to measure them?

- Invention brainstorm: Suppose we put the word *invention* in the middle of the paper. Now let us think of other words that represent related ideas; we will place these words all around the page and connect the ones that are related to one another with lines.

2. *Approaches which focus on setting priorities:* Prioritizing is a lifelong problem. There are always too few resources, time, money, or goods for the demands. Individuals, communities, and nations continually have to decide which needs and wants to meet first. Prioritizing problems in the social studies usually involve looking at lists of equipment or provisions as they relate to a particular problem or being faced with a series of problems in a given

situation and having to decide in what order these problems need to be solved based on immediacy, importance, or a combination of the two. Following is an example of a problem solving task of the second type.

- Ship wreck rescue: You are the commander of a sailing ship bringing new colonists and supplies to the New World in the seventeenth century. Your ship has been caught in a terrible storm as you approach the coast. You have been unable to keep the ship from going aground on the rocky shore. The storm still is raging all about and may at any moment either wash you out to sea or break the ship into pieces. The water rushing all around is only about six feet deep and you can see a solid beach perhaps a hundred yards away. Here are all the problems that you must handle. Number them according to the order in which you think they need to be handled. Suggest a solution for each.

  - ___ Sharp rocks can be seen dead ahead.

  - ___ There is a gaping hole in the hull and some water is rushing in.

  - ___ You fear that hostile natives may inhabit this area of the coast.

  - ___ The food supplies are in the hold, which is fast filling with water.

  - ___ The crew members are unhappy and are arguing among themselves.

  - ___ One of the ship's cannons has broken loose and is careening across the deck.

  - ___ A woman on board is about to give birth.

  - ___ A small fire has broken out in the ship's kitchen.

  - ___ One of the ship's masts has been broken by the storm and has fallen, pinning a crew member, perhaps breaking both of his legs.

  - ___ Some of the colonists are trying to break into the powder magazine containing all of the ship's weapons and gunpowder.

  - ___ A passenger is demanding that he and his scientific records be put ashore in the ship's boat.

  - ___ A crew member has somehow managed to get drunk and is singing in his hammock.

3. *Approaches that focus on examining differing, conflicting, and opposing points of view:* Understanding, accommodating, and relating to the ideas and opinions of others is a major problem of cooperation. It is also the foundation of understanding conflict of all kinds. Problem-solving exercises of this type involve the student in actively trying to identify the likely opinions of others. Examples of this type of exercise include the following:

- **The Telephone**: Think about how people in the nineteenth century felt about the invention of the telephone. Think about the impact that the first telephones might have had on different people's lives. By just after the turn of the century there were only a few hundred telephones even in the very largest cities. But even then, people were beginning to see the change that a telephone network was going to bring. Write down a few sentences each about the views of the people that follow. Then, we will assign roles in groups and discuss what our feelings would have been if we had lived at the turn of the century.

  Opinion of the owner of the telegraph company

  Opinion of a messenger boy

  Opinion of a New York businessman

  Opinion of a New York housewife

  Opinion of a conservative, country minister

- **Programming**: Pretend that you are the programming director for a major television network. You are considering the eight o'clock Monday night slot, where this program will be up against established shows that have had good ratings. You are considering a long-running comedy program that has been revamped after being canceled by another network (as the ratings reached an all-time low); a new comedy with a star who once had a hit drama series but may not have comedic ability; a show aimed at teen and young-adult viewers and starring several young, unknown actors; a news program presenting controversial issues and public opinion; and a hard-hitting action show with an up-and-coming African American star and lots of violence. What would be the views of

  The conservative network president?

  The president of a fast-food chain that is a big sponsor?

  The head of an organization of concerned parents

  A 16-year old boy

  A 12-year old girl

  4. *Approaches stressing alternative possibilities, choices, and solutions:* These approaches involve examining the available options in a given problem solution. The basic question is, "What is the impact of any particular option?" Often, these approaches begin with descriptions of hypothetical situations and ask students to examine the possibilities of a gamut of consequences or causes. Examples of such situation include the following:

- What would your role be if you were cast in a re-make of *Gone With the Wind*?

- If the school were to make thinking skills the central focus of the school, how would it change the materials used?

- If your school were located in the center of a major zoo, how would it change the curriculum?

5. *Approaches that focus on identifying aims, goals, and objectives:* The focus in this approach is on identifying the purposes other people might conceivably have as well as our own. The basic strategy is to examine stories and situations, looking at the people involved in them. In each case the key problem is to identify the major aims, goals, and purposes that the indiviual or group is pursuing in this situation. This kind of problem focus should help students become more purpose oriented and help them to know the reasons they are doing things.

Examples include tasks such as the following

- Identify the central aims, goals and objectives of each of the main characters in a children's book or story (e.g., *Treasure Island, The 7 Dancing Princesses*).

- What were the main goals and objectives of Peter the Great?

- What are the main goals of the principal, the school nurse, the guidance counselor, and the school custodian?

- What are the aims, goals, and purposes of a problem solving program?

6. *Approaches that put the emphases on identifying advantages, disadvantages, and unique and interesting features:*

In these approaches to problem solving, the problem is an assertion or an idea to be examined. The purpose in the problem solving process is for the students to be able to see all of the possible advantages and problems or disadvantages that the implementation of that assertion would bring. A secondary purpose is to have them analyze the unique and interesting features of this assertion. The teacher might want to begin by having students show agreement by hand signals or standing up. A few examples of such assertions are

- Students should volunteer when they know the answer.

- There should be a law that all containers and print materials be recyclable and that users recycle such containers.

- Abraham Lincoln should have issued the Emancipation Proclamation when the southern states seceded.

- People ought to be able to do whatever they want to with property that they own.

INCORPORATING THINKING AND LEARNING SKILLS INTO THE SOCIAL STUDIES

Decision making and problem solving together form the core reasons for the social studies. The major thrust of the social studies is to develop the ability of students to think and learn for themselves. If they can do that, then they are ready for any body of knowledge and facts about any social studies topic. If they cannot think, then each topic and each encounter with content requires the teacher to present and guide them through, and the student is always a dependent learner. People who need such guidance are not going to be the kind of citizens that democracy absolutely requires to survive.

LOOKING BACK

There is increasing concern over the development of thinking in the social studies. If the major goal of teaching is to help children to become independent learners, then there has to be a real emphasis on the development of the ability to think and to solve problems.

Obtaining, understanding, and remembering information are among the thinking skills that are important to social studies learning. Generally, children can learn to relate new information to previous knowledge, to identify the patterns and relationships of information and ideas, and to identify purposes for learning. They can be aided in learning to remember through planned repetitions of information accompanied by appropriate feedback. More advanced thinking sills such as logical thinking and the ability to analyze can be taught through modeling by the teacher, through carefully planned discussions and through guided practice.

Problem-solving skill is the most essential thinking ability in the social studies. Problem solving is an important part of the inquiry process. The use of alternative problem-solving strategies can be taught directly through structured activities. Among these strategies, the following are useful as models:

- Identifying all the factors related to the problem

- Prioritizing

- Looking for different points of view

- Looking for alternative solutions

- Examining and defining the real purposes and goals

- Examining the advantages, disadvantages and interesting features of proposed solutions

SELF-TEST

1. What does the term schema mean and how does it relate to thinking?

2. What is meant by the expression story map?

3. Can you identify and describe some different types of problem-solving tasks?

REFERENCES

NCSS Task Force on Early Childhood/ Elementary Social Studies. (1989). Social studies for early childhood and elementary school childrenpreparing for the 21st century. *Social Education*, 53 (January), 14-23.

Task Force of the National Commission on the Social Studies in the Schools. (1989). *Charting a course: social studies for the 21st century*. Washington, D.C.: The National Commission on the Social Studies in the Schools.

Task Force on Scope and Sequence. (1984). In search of a scope and sequence for social studies. *Social Education*, 48 (April), 249-262.

SUGGESTED READING

Eeds, M., and Wells, D. (1991). Talking, thinking and cooperative learning: lessons learned from listening to children talk about books. **Social Education**, 55 (February), 134-137.

Fair, J., and Kachaturoff, G. (1988). Teaching thinking: another try. *The Social Studies*, 79 (March/ April), 64-69.

O'Reilly, K. (1991). The Commission Report on critical thinking: a defense. *Social Education*, 55 (September, 1991) 298-300.

von Eschenbach, J., and Ragsdale, C. (1989). The integration of elementary social studies and mathematics through experiential learning. *The Social Studies*, 80 (November/December), 225-228.

9 Developing Attitudes, Values, and Appreciations

LOOKING AHEAD

The word *value* may be defined in various ways. Value is another word for *worth*. We use the word in referring to goods and services and the price set on them. We also use the word *value* when talking about what in life is important. Our values are the principles or standards of quality we use in making all our decisions. Our values shape our attitudes toward actions, people, and things. They also direct our aspirations and ambitions.

An understanding of the ways that personal values are in the process of being shaped during the elementary school years is essential in a problems approach. It is equally important to think about the roles of teachers and schools in the formation and development of those values. Most true problem solving involves some interplay of personal values at every stage. From defining the problem to gathering data to solution finding, the decisions that are made emanate from an individual's own views. Anything that a problem solver does is based on some assessment of whether that action seems right or wrong, good or bad, desirable or undesirable, sensible or senseless.

Some values and attitudes are also an important part of school success or failure. On the one hand, they have to do with whether students do their work and how well they do it, with how they behave, and with how they relate to other people. Teachers deal with these values constantly. They want students to feel positive toward school; to strive to do their best work; to have certain kinds of ambitions for themselves; to be fair and friendly in dealing with other students; and to be honest, industrious, loyal, and so on. On the other hand, there is a delicate balance between values and ways of teaching and dealing with values that are acceptable and appropriate and those that are not. In American public schools, for example, it is inappropriate to teach religious values or to advocate a religion; but religious values are not the only ones that are inappropriate. There is a point at which dealing with political situations or teaching about loving one's country becomes indoctrination. There is even a point when teaching what are thought of as *family values* may be in conflict with what is taught at home.

This chapter focuses on values and attitudes and the ways that teachers can deal positively with them in elementary school. It takes the position that a problems approach offers the most acceptable way of dealing with values issues because this approach enables the children to make their own decisions, but to do so on a solid basis.

CAN YOU? DO YOU?

Can you

- Describe your own values and tell how they were formed?
- Identify or describe some specific decision-making skills?
- Think of some activities in which children could have experiences in determining alternatives?

Do you

- Know what values should be taught to children and how we should teach them?
- Understand why it may be necessary to deal with values related to living in a pluralistic society in school?
- Understand different ways of teaching about values?

ANOTHER LOOK AT WORLD VIEWS

There is a symbiotic relationship between an individual's world view and his or her values, attitudes, and appreciations. Don't you just love that word-*symbiotic*? It comes from biology and it refers to a close relationship between two organisms that may or may not be mutually beneficial. In this case, the word *symbiotic* is a perfect description because values and world views are related, but they are not the same thing. The relationships that an individual has with other people and the individual role that one sees for him or herself is dependent on both values and world view.

Particularly during childhood, values and world view are forming and changing. Society, through the family and school as well as through other formal and informal social structures, helps shape and form the individual's world view and his or her interwoven values, attitudes, and appreciations.

Every society tries to shape the values of the young. Those who personally care about an individual child-and hopefully this includes parents, teachers, and a lot of others—want that child to grow up with the very best set of values possible. But not everyone agrees about just what that set is or about how it needs to be developed.

Parents have one view. Various social groups also attempt to exert an influence, largely a conserving one. Conserving influence in any culture are those which transmit, maintain, and preserve that culture as it is. Religious, political, and social groups exert this kind of pressure. The chief aim of many of these social groups is to get that child to accept and believe in the values upon which the groups themselves are based. Schools also exert influence and that influence not always unified (or positive).

DECISION MAKING SKILLS IN THE SOCIAL STUDIES

One of the people I respect most in the social studies is Shirley Engle, a lifelong student and teacher. He is probably best known as an advocate of the belief that *decision making is the heart of the social studies*. The essential nature of the subject requires judgment calls. Evaluation skills are needed throughout life not only by social scientists but also by students who do not pursue history, geography, or the other social sciences as careers. People constantly have to decide not only what is the right thing to do, but what is the best thing to do, what they want to do and what they have to do. Evaluation skills are always so difficult because of dilemma and conflicts and because there is often doubt about evaluational criteria and questions such as relevance, truth and accuracy, suitability, importance, utility, greatness, potential, goodness, beauty, quality, effort, or even quantity.

Evaluation is almost always based on values. We make judgments and decisions on the basis of our world views and what we hold to be important, sensible, good, and worthwhile. However, the essential evaluation skills that teachers need to develop in children build from awareness and reasoning (the essential thinking skills discussed in Chapter 8). The awareness skills are taught chiefly by giving children frequent opportunities to make evaluations, by questioning them, and by teaching them to question what they see and hear and the basis of the decisions they make. Awareness is also developed by pointing out the specific examples of evaluation decisions that are based on differing kinds of reasoning.

Awareness in decision making also relates to understanding the basis upon which one is making a decision. Children need to learn to recognize and judge when decision making is

- Evaluation that is based on a single criterion

- Assessment involving several criteria

- Heavily value based because only partial information is available

- Holistic judgment based on experience and objective assessment of the overall product

- Personal, based solely on what serves one's own ends, personal ambitions, or feelings and emotions

There are several points at which values come in to play in decision making. These points all require different skills. Among the skills involved are determining what alternatives are actually available (what the options actually are), making choices among the available alternatives (what course to pursue, what is the best fit, what offers the most advantages or fewest disadvantages, and what is most dangerous or most safe, making distinctions in dealing with evidence (distinguishing fact from speculation, conclusion from opinion, fantasy from reality, truth from falsehood, etc.), determining relevance, determining adequacy of evidence, projecting a trend, and making personal decisions or determination of ultimate courses to take (e.g., defining justice or morality in a particular situation). Teachers who are trying to help children become better problem solvers have many opportunities in the social studies to give children experiences and practice that develop evaluation skills. Following are examples in each of the skill areas:

Determining Alternatives

- On a map, have children determine alternative routes to a single location or alternative destinations.

- Have children hold class contests for such things as favorite historical character, favorite book, ideal vacation spot, best place to live, and so on. Have a nomination process and then choose advocates.

- Have children nominate possible sites for real and hypothetical projects, field trips, and so on.

- Even young children can suggest menus, ingredients, activities, etc, for social events and cultural celebrations.

- Do brainstorming activities where children have a specific number of responses to something (e.g., ten best reasons for doing your homework, ways to interpret music through movement, etc.).

- Include nominating (favorite, best, etc.) as a regular part of daily activities.

- As children read about people's actions, stop and ask what else these people could have done.

Choosing Among Alternatives

- Give children alternatives from which to choose as a regular activity. (These can be very real decisions that have impact on them and what they do.)

- Talk about the reasonableness of different explanations and theories. (The alternatives available to different people in history, the school, the home, etc., and their possible reasoning in making the decisions that they did.)

- Give three or four alternative titles for stories and let children choose among them and explain their reasoning.

- Let children vote for favorites among short series of stories, television shows, movies, and so on.

- In studying history and geography, give children brief real or made-up biography-character summaries of several different people. Then have them choose the best person for such things as an arctic expedition, a Safari, a rescue mission, a delegation to take a particular message to the President, and so on.

Distinguishing Fact from Speculation, Conclusion from Opinion, Fantasy from Reality, and Truth from Falsehood

- Give children a series of statements and let them try to identify which statements are fact and which are opinion.

- Give children a series of untrue statements about some topic they have been studying and have them tell why the statements are untrue.

- Have children identify fantastic elements in stories, television shows, movies, and so on.

- Bring in a magician who will talk about the ways that magicians fool people.

- Show a picture and let the children make a series of statements about the picture. As each statement is made, have the other children determine if the statement is actually true or if it is speculation, conclusion, or opinion.

Determining Relevance

- Give children a statement that makes an assertion or hypothesis. Then present them a series of other statements of fact and opinion. With each of these, have the children decide if the statement is relevant.

- Write a question on the board. Have children scan a paragraph and volunteer to read any statements that are relevant to the question.

- Give children a proverb, truism, or superstition. Follow it with a collection of action statements and facts. Let the children classify the actions and facts as relevant or not. (They should be able to reach the conclusion that a fact may be relevant and supportive without proving the original statement to be true.)

Determining the Adequacy of Evidence

- Give children a series of arguments or reasons and then ask them to judge if a case has been made.

- Give students a series of "If A and B, then C" statements. Have them determine which ones they accept and which ones they do not.

- Give children a series of assertions. Ask them to tell what it would take by way of evidence for them to accept the truth of each one.

- Tell students a preposterous story about a well-known historical person. Make it so farfetched that they cannot believe it. When they start expressing their disbelief, have them try to tell why they do not believe. (Two of my favorites are stories I weave around the characters of George Washington and Christopher Columbus. In the Washington story, I build a tale that it was not George Washington but an exact look-alike who turned up at Mt. Vernon who became the first president. With Columbus, I make the claim that it was really a woman masquerading as a man who made the voyages.)

Projecting a Trend

- Give students a series of events and have them predict the event(s) that will follow.

- Describe a series of events and have students give the trend a name.

- Have students do a relevance web showing the connections among events that make the series of events a trend.

Defining Justice for Particular Instances

- Read stories with a moral to children and let them verbalize their own views of what the moral is.

- Provide a series of open-ended scenarios and problems and ask the children to tell what they think would be the right thing to do in these situations.

- Read some examples of actions of courts and governments and ask the children to decide if the action taken was fair.

WHAT VALUES DO WE WANT TO TEACH?

The place of values in the classroom is controversial. Whether teachers should teach values is not really the point. Nearly everyone concedes that teachers have to deal with values. Opinions differ, though, about what values should be taught and how we should teach them. Teaching a particular religious or political viewpoint, how to vote in an election, or what constitutes acceptable reading or entertainment are certainly questionable. There are, however, at least three areas where it seems important that the schools take an active and effective role in developing children's beliefs. These are:

- Values related to living in a democracy
- Values implicit within a multicultural society
- Values that relate to school success and to the functional classroom

Values Related to Living in a Democracy

Many educators believe that social studies education is really defined as citizenship education. That is, they believe that the main purpose of the social studies is to teach children or at least to help them to be good citizens. But when educators start to define and describe exactly how that is done, disagreement almost immediately follows. What values should be developed in children about their country, their state, their community, and their group, and how they should feel toward them? Such questions, while easy to answer under some forms of government, are controversial in a democracy. The way that we teach such values is also of concern to many. Emotional charges of indoctrination are levied quickly and words such as *nationalism* are intoned with positive and negative meanings.

Despite such a broad spectrum of viewpoints, there do seem to be at least six areas of values where teachers need to work in order for the democracy to continue to exist.

- The need for participation
- The worth of and rights of the individual
- The rule of the majority and the rights of the minority
- Personal responsibility
- Respect for law and authority
- Equality and justice

Teachers can work on these in a number of ways. One of the important things they do is to help children become more aware of what has happened in the past and what is happening now related to their own country and others. Knowledge of how and why governments have developed and the events leading up to the present is essential for understanding the present and for preparing for the future. Simply looking at the founding of the country and its history is, of course, an obvious educational tradition where this was and is supposed to occur. Perhaps the most important and necessary approaches for education in a democracy are those that make the classroom a place where the children are given responsibility, make decisions, and develop their own views. Teachers can hold mock elections and mock trials and they can use opinionaires and polls in the classroom. They can set up classroom governments, and look at questions of rights and responsibility in current events. Even so simple a thing as playing games and sports can become occasion to talk about the importance of rules, personal responsibility, and concern for the rights of others. Things that teachers do to help individuals gain acceptance, success, and confidence are all an important part of citizenship education in a democracy.

Values Implicit within a Multicultural Society

One of the terms that has received a lot of attention in recent years is *multicultural education*. Multicultural education is a definitive attempt to make students more aware of the distinguishing differences and unifying similarities among various cultures and ethnic groups in the world. It is not simply education of a particular nature designed for minority groups. Part of its outcome should be helping students to value themselves and others. Multicultural education is directly tied to our democratic values, the principle of equality, the pluralistic nature of our society, and the concept of the global village. Multicultural education is aimed at the eradication of racism, classism, discrimination, sexism, prejudice, and ethnocentrism.

There are many reasons for moving to greater emphasis on multicultural education in the social studies. Among them are the following ideas:

- We live in a pluralistic society.

- We live in a global village.

- Almost without exception, cultural groups have a history of prejudice and discrimination.

- There is a natural tendency among human beings to distrust people who are different and to hold them at arm's length.

- It is generally believed that the more people know about another culture, the more positive they will feel about it.

- Women, a number of ethnic groups and racial groups, and numerous cultures have been largely ignored or misrepresented in curriculum materials in the past.

Multicultural education works on several basic assumptions and beliefs. For example, there are some generally held beliefs about the nature of various cultural, ethnic, and racial groups in the world. One of them is that members of every cultural and ethnic group have been and are productive and resourceful and, therefore, have made substantial contributions to world civilization. Another is that no sex and no race or cultural or ethnic group is innately superior or inferior to any other. Such assumptions become important teachings in multicultural education as do assumptions about people. The latter include the belief that historic injustices and discrimination are not reasons for present personal guilt or retribution and neither are they cause for the continuation of prejudice into the future. An important realization that is part of this assumption system is that everyone has prejudices and biases.

Finally, multicultural education is based on some major educational assumptions. The chief among these is that ethnocentrism, racism, and provincialism are going to continue to exist without multicultural education.

These beliefs have led to the development of a variety of goals. Typical of such goals is the following set.

Students will develop

- Understanding of cultural diversity within our society and diversity within culture groups.

- The ability to communicate with other culture groups both to resolve conflict and to improve relationships.

- Attitudes, values, and behavior that are supportive of ethnic and cultural diversity.

- Pride in their cultural heritage.

- Knowledge, appreciation, and understanding of other cultures both in this country and throughout the world.

- A sense of the history of both their own culture and those of others.

The most significant tool of multicultural education is knowledge. Knowing about one's own and other cultures, viewing others through undistorted pictures of their strengths and accomplishments is essential to appreciation. Naturally, it follows that increased positive, mutually beneficial contact with people of other groups (e.g., other cultures, races, religions, sex) is going to promote mutual understanding and appreciation.

Values that Relate to School Success and to the Functional Classroom

Values relating to being good students are important not only for the immediate present and future but for the more distant future of adulthood. The success of the school experience is based on the student's doing his or her own work, giving his or her best effort, staying on task, completing work and doing it on time, getting along with people, always trying, always participating, not bothering others, obeying the rules, doing what the teacher says, and other related behaviors. These, in turn, are based on values such as: (work) integrity and honesty, the work ethic (the view that success ought to come from work and indeed will result if you work hard), the high value of achievement, the importance of honest effort, the importance of (and belief in) the essential code of fairness, justice and equality governing individuals, and (to an acceptable extent) societal behavior, concern for others, and complying with and having respect for authority.

The fact is that schools function on such values. The classroom can only "work" if most of these values are, at least in some measure, broadly accepted. The same is true of most work-places and of the entire society. A teacher has to have control and be the authority. The school must be a place to work and grow in ability to do work.

Essentially these values are taught in a number of ways, not the least of which is seen in traditional expectations which children bring to the first day of school. Children come to school expecting to have to behave in certain ways and with a set of pre-formed notions about what teachers are and how they are supposed to be treated. Schools continue this development through the personal classroom expectations of teachers, through the development of patterns and habits of behavior through constant and consistent practice, through setting and making clear sets of school and classroom rules, through involving children in the rule-making and decision-making process, and through the development in the students themselves of a rationale for order and good work that continues throughout the school years.

HOW DO WE DEVELOP VALUES?

Those who attempt to develop values and beliefs use a number of different approaches. Some of these approaches seem more like indoctrination or propaganda, even when motivated by unselfish caring and concern. Others seem like no approach at all. All of them can be used ineffectively as well as effectively. Most of these approaches can be grouped into the following categories:

1. *Teaching values through pronouncements, rules, and warnings:* Many times adults simply tell young people what to believe. This may occur very openly or it may be much more subtle. In school, for example, it is common to begin by giving children a set of classroom rules. There may or may not be discussion of these rules, but the fact is that the children are told that these rules have to be obeyed. The rules tell them what is right, what is wrong, what is good, what to admire, and so on. Values are also taught very directly when certain behaviors are expected in children. Teachers, parents, and other adults imply what is good and bad by the behaviors that they demand or expect. Values are taught directly through home and school rules, requirements, and individual and group orders and state-

ments. The teacher says, "Stand up straight! Do your homework! Work carefully and neatly!" The teacher wants and expects work to be on time and complete. The headings have to all be alike. Paper and writing utensils have to meet certain standards. Children are to be quiet except when the adults wants them to talk. All of these actions imply compliance to authority, responsibility, taking pride in work, and other attributes that constitute at least part of being good. Young people vary in the extent to which they may be influenced by this way of teaching. It is fairly clear that they will not easily believe something that contradicts values they have learned earlier or what they want to believe. At the same time, a constant and unvarying repetition of the same message or of the same expectations has a conditioning effect. For instance, when children are quieted whenever they speak out in class, when they are required to sit in the same seat every day, or when at the same hour and on the same cue they are required to get out a particular book and turn to a prearranged page, they grow to believe that this is the way things are supposed to be. When behavioral expectations are accompanied by a consistently applied punishment and reward system, over time behavior and beliefs fall into line. Some systems of classroom management are based on this approach.

2. *Teaching values through examples and models:* Children like heroes and they want to be like their heroes. Their heroes include people they know, people they see in television and movies, and people they read about or hear about. Characters in nearly every story children encounter serve as models for children. Children are watching characters from history, from school reading books and library books, from comic books, and from television and movies every day as models. Even the toys such as Barbie dolls and G.I. Joe action figures, that are advertised for children become models of ideals.Simply put, these models or heroes are exemplars of some set of ideals and values. When used in school, the modeling approach involves getting children to look at figures in stories and history as the kind of people that they should aspire to be. As a way of teaching values, it involves making children more aware of people of accomplishment and principle and makes children feel more positive toward these people.

Modeling may sometimes occur as an unconscious process on the part of teachers. They share their own admiration, their own personal heroes with such enthusiasm that it communicates infectiously to the children. We also should not ignore the fact that the teachers become models themselves. As they work with their students, these children grow to like and admire different qualities that they see in their teachers. Teachers, for children, are often models of fairness, of a caring personality, of intelligence, of dress, and so on.

Teachers may also unconsciously or consciously be using a modeling approach when they hold students up for praise or when they display students' work. They are saying to the children that this is the way I want you to be.

The most obvious use of modeling in the social studies involves identifying heroes in history, heroes from real life today, and heroes from fiction or from radio, motion pictures, or television. Teachers do this by reading to children, by telling stories, by encouraging discussion, and by having children read. Teachers who use this approach most effectively present desirable heroes in exciting ways and bring out the most admirable qualities of these heroes.

Among the major plusses for this approach is that it makes school more interesting and positive and may even make the teacher seem more aware of the real world in which the children live. Schools tend to ignore the many positive characters in television shows and in movies, and this is one place where this set of child-selected experiences can be brought to good use. Folk tales are rich in heroes and can provide a way of helping children to see qualities that are admirable while examining cultural values and beliefs. Most children's fiction involves protagonists who represent the good versus antagonists who are perceived as bad.

A major danger of the modeling approach with real-life heroes is that real people all have weaknesses, shortcomings and even vices. Whenever we deal with heroes we risk later disillusionment. Children find out that some of the stories that they learned as "truth," stories that even their teachers thought were true, are merely legends and are probably not true at all. The George Washington stories about throwing the dollar across the Potomac and chopping down the cherry tree are prime examples. Even worse, children may discover that the heroes they thought were perfect have made bad mistakes, shown prejudice or other very negative emotions, or been unfair or even dishonest. It is often difficult to maintain admiration for what heroes have stood for when their imperfections and humanity are revealed. Disillusionment with a hero may also mean rejection of the positive values he or she represents.

The problem is that there are no infallible heroes. This may be an argument, at least, for reliance on mythical and fictional heroes. These kinds of models have a distinct advantage. Their lives are limited to the stories in which they appear. Hidden flaws cannot be discovered outside that context. But the advantage is also a limitation. Most story heroes lack depth and because of this lack they do not always seem real enough to serve as models. The best solution seems to be to continue with a combination of historical and fictional heroes, teaching children to admire the positive while recognizing the shortcomings and weaknesses of their heroes.

3. *Teaching values through stories with morals or lessons:* Another way of approaching morals, values, and world views is through stories and examples that speak directly to particular values. A story is told with a lesson embedded in it. Typically, the stories show how to behave or how not to obey in situations where a decision has to be made. Often in these stories right behaviors and actions are rewarded and, of course, wrong behaviors bring undesirable consequences.

Fables and parables have been used to teach right and wrong for thousands of years. This approach is most effective when the listener or reader is provoked to think by the story and then through discussion and thought discovers the lesson embedded in the story. Obviously, the lesson in the story can be too difficult to figure out or too obvious. When either is true, the approach is not very successful. It also fails if a lesson runs contrary to the existing world view of the audience and when the story seems to be an attempt to force a belief that they do not want to accept. The story approach offers a lot of possibilities for the teacher. Most importantly stories have plot, characters, and settings all factors that make them both interesting to listen to or read and, at the same time, memorable.

Nonfiction or fiction stories provide a way to look at different cultures, different times, and different beliefs. Every folk story tells a great deal about the culture from which it came. It shows what those people believed and, more importantly, what they thought was worth teaching or passing along to the younger generation.

Stories offer opportunity for discussion and thinking, for questions, for focusing on alternatives, and for comparison both with other stories and with personal experiences. Students can learn through dramatizing experiences with stories, through looking at character motivation, through examining alternative outcomes and beginnings, and through looking at the author's viewpoint, for example.

4. *Teaching values through examining personal actions of self and others:* One of the ways that teachers can help children to develop their values is to give them experiences where they can become more reflective and analytical about what they do themselves and what they see. The teacher needs to get children to examine more carefully the occurrences of everyday life, how they acted and felt in particular situations, and the reasons behind these feelings. This kind of values analysis involves looking carefully and sequentially at the details of what happened, making special note of behavior, then looking at the causes or reasons contributing to that behavior as well as the outcomes of it. The analysis does not end there. The next step is to speculate about alternative possible behaviors and consider what might have been more reasonable, moral or right, and effective in the situation. There must be constant reminders of what the principle people involved did and did not know at the time.

One of the outcomes of this approach is that it gets students to look at their own lives instead of just two dimensional characters in media, storybooks, and history. The teacher may begin with autobiographical anecdotes or description of events in the classroom that the students have experienced. The autobiographical stories serve as models to provoke examples from the students and as one way of communicating the real humanity of the teacher. Often the stories point out times when the teacher did not act in the best way. If the teacher can share an embarrassing moment, it may have a releasing effect on the students. The shared class experiences need to be carefully selected, however, and developed as a group effort. The teacher should not be using the approach as a way of criticizing or scolding students. Rather, it should be an honest joint exploration of an event that was not exactly satisfactory in its outcome. Used well, the approach also has a bonding effect for the class.

Usually the approach goes through a series of definitive steps beginning with a narrative description of the situation, which is then discussed from the standpoint of identifying the central issue, concern or problem. This last may require considerable time because it is critical to really get a clear vision of the heart of the matter. The next step is to look at all sides of the matter, examining the most minute detail and looking for things that may appear trivial, but, upon examination, are critical. This is essentially an information gathering stage. That information is then examined and sifted to remove the clutter of irrelevant or unimportant observations that are not needed for judgment. The final stages take the students through tentative judgments that are evaluated and appraised before final assessments are made.

5. *Teaching values through problem solving:* Many of the approaches to affective teaching that have been developed in recent years have involved problem solving. They begin with dilemmas or conflicts where decisions are demanded and ask the learner to make a judgment and then explain it. Both the moral reasoning approach, which involves moral dilemmas, and clarification approaches are essentially of this type.

Moral reasoning approaches, popularized by Lawrence Kohlberg (1979,1984), involve the development of a sense of justice through a series of progressive stages. The basis of Kohlberg's approach is that individuals can be guided and accelerated these stages, developing their reasoning ability, by thinking about a series of dilemmas in which there are no clear-cut right and good actions to take. In essence, the individual has to choose between alternatives where it is a matter of determining the "lesser of evils." An example of such a dilemma follows:

In the 1840s, a boy traveling by wagon train to Oregon became the head of his family when his parents sicken and die. His family is running out of food when he sights some game. If he stops to hunt, the wagon train is going to move on without them and the winter may close down on them in the mountains. If he does not hunt, he and his brothers and sisters may starve. Should he make camp and go after the game or try to keep up with the rest of the wagons?

If they are shown a few of these dilemmas, the students can create their own. The dilemmas themselves, which can be designed to age level and to relate to content studied, are involving points of departure. The essential position of the Kohlbergian research is that the development of moral reasoning occurs through exposure to such dilemmas and that growth is both irreversible and important in influencing moral behavior.

Values-clarification approaches are designed to help students become clearer about why they act and think as they do. The essential view is that people should reflect their values in the way they act, but they do not always do so. The reason they do not is that they are not really clear about what implications their belief systems have for their lives. The approach confronts students with decisions that simply have to be reasoned out or clarified. Teacher questions that probe the reasons for feelings and decisions are at the heart of this technique. The student is often confronted with open-ended situations where the question of what the meaning is becomes most important. Students may be asked to set priorities, choose from among alternatives, and examine choices. The overall concerns are, "What do you choose and prize?" and "How would you act?"

Both of these approaches allow adaptation to practically any topic or theme under study. They allow the student to examine questions of right and wrong as well as other values in the past, in other cultures, in hypothetical and fictional settings, in current events, and in their own lives.

LOOKING BACK

Individual values have a close relationship to our personal world view. They have an impact on decision-making ability and especially on every aspect of evaluation. Teachers should expose children to many types of values based, decision-making activities including those in which children determine alternatives, those in which they choose alternatives, those in which they are required to distinguish fact from speculation, conclusion from opinion, fantasy from reality, and truth from falsehood, those in which they determine relevance or adequacy of evidence, and those in which they project trends.

In the social studies, teachers need to be most concerned with values related to living in a democracy, values implicit within a multicultural society, and those values related to school success and successful functioning of the classroom. Teachers develop values through a variety of approaches including direct teaching, modeling, moral stories and lessons, and examination of personal actions and the actions of others.

SELF-TEST

1. What are some of the decision-making skills?

2. Why is there a need for multicultural education?

3. Why are values so often taught very directly?

4. What are some different ways of modeling values?

5. What are some stories that you know that teach values?

6. Under what conditions is a problem-solving approach to teaching values effective?

REFERENCES

Engle, S. H. (1960). Decision making: the heart of the social studies. *Social Education*, 24 (November), 301.

Kohlberg, L. (1985). *The meaning and measurement of moral development*. Worcester, Mass.: Clark University.

Kohlberg, L. (1984). *Essays on moral development: Vol.2.The psychology of moral development*. New York: Harper and Row.

SUGGESTED READING

Lockwood, A. L. (1991). Character education: the ten percent solution. *Social Education,* 55 (April/May), 246-248.

Richburg, R.W., and Nelson, B.J. (1990). Using a historical incident to focus on value information. *The Social Studies*, 81 (March/ April), 80-83.

10 Using Simulation Games and Other Types of Drama in the Social Studies

LOOKING AHEAD

Drama is not just something we can have children do in teaching. It is a light under which we can look at and evaluate all that we call teaching. Saying that teaching has dramatic impact is just another way of saying that what we were calling education will be remembered; has commanded interest and response; and will affect how students think and feel about people, places, and events for a long time to come. The range of dramatic techniques available to the social studies teacher enables him or her to make the problems approach come alive.

This chapter examines the importance of and uses for drama. It attempts to show how problem solving is a natural and intrinsic element of drama and how dramatic techniques can be a vitalizing and energizing force to a problems approach. The chapter offers a description and examples of a wide variety of dramatic techniques. These examples and descriptions can be models for activity development for a variety of topics and levels and show the wide range of problem solving experiences available.

CAN YOU? DO YOU?

Can You

- Tell how the teacher is a *stagecrafter*?
- Tell how drama is a problem-solving activity?
- Identify several reasons for using dramatic activities?
- Describe several different forms of mock trials?

Do you

- Know what *dramatic tension* is?
- Know how to use a variety of dramatic techniques in the social studies?
- Know the difference between role play and sociodrama?
- Know what a guided fantasy is and the purposes of this technique?
- Know what an *in-basket* game is?

THE IMPORTANCE OF DRAMA IN THE SOCIAL STUDIES

The longest-running stage show in the world is not *Cats*, or *Les Miz*, or *Phantom*. It is not *My Fair Lady* or *Fiddler on the Roof* or even *The Mouse Trap*. Yet it is a piece of theater that is acted on thousands of times as many stages as all of these put together. In all of these productions, this show is done at only a fraction of the production costs of a Broadway play. I am speaking, of course, of the show that is staged daily in classrooms everywhere, a piece of theater that can be filled with dramatic tension; is rich in plot and character; and is couched in suspense, comedic genius, and pathos. It is a show in which teachers everywhere have the opportunity to direct, produce, and, at their best, costar. I say "at their best, costar" because the very best teacher dramatists make the students the real stars.

Every classroom, every school day, every lesson is a dramatic experience. If the teacher does the job of stagecraft well, the classroom experience is going to be interesting, exciting, and eventful, a memorable time filled with just the right level of plot and suspense, an opportunity for some very unusual learning. If the teacher has no flare for the dramatic, then the classroom is likely to be a somewhat lifeless and unexciting place where only routine learning occurs.

Drama can provide a perspective for conceptualizing teaching, but in order to see this you have to see drama as more than putting on a play or even a category of techniques that teachers can use in the social studies. You have to think about drama as a way of looking at the entire learning thrust of the classroom. That thrust is the product of the emotional atmosphere, the teaching style and range of the instructor, and the kinds of activities in which students are engaged. When dramatic tension is the focus of the classroom, then there is a kind of positively and electrically charged atmosphere that can be felt. This kind of tension is the distinguishing feature in the very best classrooms regardless of the teacher's style. It is an almost visible glow of anticipation that can be seen in every aspect of the classroom. It is evidenced in the way students come into the room, in what happens when class is begun, in how small groups and large groups are handled, in the things that contribute to order and management, in the kinds of assignments that are made and how and when they are made, and in when and how oral reading is done.

The dramatic tension of the classroom is as much a part of little mysteries, surprises, and suspense that teachers plan as it is of role plays and staged productions. The teacher promises a surprise. A mysterious visitor is coming. A kindergarten class that I know of built excitement for several March days over the strange visits of an invisible leprechaun who left activity materials and green tracks (made of construction paper) whenever the class left the room. Such mysteries also are intrinsic to the content of the social studies, often in the form of provocative questions, problems, and anecdotal descriptions. What happened to the Roanoke colonists? Was Booth aided in his assassination of Lincoln by Washington insiders? What happened to Hitler or to Merriwether Lewis? What can be done to preserve the ozone, the rain forests, and the various endangered animals? Teachers are always performers in the drama of the classroom, but their roles and the ways they play them may be richly varied. There are teachers who are wonderfully dramatic solo performers, good storytellers, and powerful mood setters. There are others who develop their own dramatic flare best while interacting with their students. Some have a way of evoking passion and excitement and curiosity in a class while remaining quietly in the background. Others seem to be mostly organizers and catalysts to unleash the impassioned thoughts and feelings of the student. You can be a good teacher without being a ham, but not without enthusiasm and a flare for lighting the flame in others.

Mostly, those teachers who create the dramatic atmosphere are stage managers. They provide students with a dramatic vision of history, of culture and of human relationships. They allow them to experience and to become involved in the conflicts and controversies, the personalities and plottings—in effect, the drama - implicit in the very name *social studies*. They make students aware of the dramatic moments of the past and of the present, the elements of conflict, climax, comedy and tragedy; plot or story; suspense and resolution; setting, character, and dialogue. As stage managers, teachers can also utilize a number of dramatic techniques that get children involved, provoke curiosity and give reason for research, develop a sense of event sequence, develop skills of oral and written expression, and develop sensitivity to the feelings and ideas of others. The use of drama as a teaching approach makes the social studies come alive. Most importantly, drama can stimulate research and often give purpose and meaning to gathering and studying data.

Only when the perspective of drama is understood is a teacher really going to be able to use the spectrum of dramatic techniques purposefully and effectively. Dramatic techniques are almost always involving. In almost every type, a variety of problem solving opportunities occur. Fortunately for teachers, there are variations of drama that can be done with almost any ability level and require amounts of time varying from a few minutes to weeks. The amount of teacher centeredness and control also varies and children can be moved slowly from dependence toward independence in planning and carrying out dramatic activities. Over the next few pages, about a dozen different dramatic techniques will be described with examples.

SIMULATION GAMES

Perhaps the most familiar of the social studies dramatic techniques, for those who know the literature of the field, is *simulation gaming*. Simulation games have become part of the culture. Fantasy simulations are played out recreationally by young people worldwide and there are many well-known computer games that are described as simulations. Many popular board games, including the perennial favorite, Monopoly, have elements of simulation gaming in them.

Essentially, simulation games are structured decision-making activities in which students assume roles and then solve problems. Participants are given problem scenarios and additional information related to the problem and their roles. Their job is to come to the decision points in the game and then make the best choice among the options available. Decisions and actions of students playing the games are limited by sets of restrictive rules. These rules make simulations more patterned than other role-play activities. The decisions often result in consequences and, are more often than not at least some chance is involved in those consequences. The problem scenario itself, which serves as the beginning point and the heart of the games, may be based on some very real current or historical situation or on a hypothetical one.

To recap, the critical and necessary elements of a simulation game are:

- Problem scenario based on some model of the real world

- Role playing

- Decision making

- Rules that limit how roles are played

- Consequences from the decisions

- Some element of chance involved

Like any school activity, simulation games used as a teaching technique should be more than just for fun. Both the choice of games and the way that the gaming activities are conducted is critical. There are several important considerations in choosing and playing such games at any level. Perhaps the most critical of these is that the game should serve an important curricular purpose. Let me put that textbook type phrase into understandable language: When children play these games they should be learning something. The games should help them understand better. Once that is the prime consideration, other concerns follow logically. The students ought to be aware of and understand what they are doing. The game should be one that students truly enjoy and they will immerse themselves in the issues and the content. The best games provoke questions, reading, and research. All of these considerations should make teachers aware that how the teacher sets up the game and follows through after the dramatic game playing is complete are critical to using simulation activities effectively. These are often referred to as briefing and de-briefing, and few simulations have much meaning or learning value without them.

Samples of Simulation Games

At the elementary level, simulation games need to be relatively simple. The amount of reading required in order to play the game is a factor that needs to be controlled to fit the abilities of the particular group of children. It is usually advantageous to use games that can be played in one day (from about ten minutes in the early grades to just under an hour in upper elementary and middle school) depending on the attention span and involvement level of the students. This reduces the possibility of students continuing the game in unsupervised settings. Another factor that the teacher may want to consider is the ability of the children to work independently. This factor is the all important one if a game is played with less than full teacher control.

Game 1: THE PRESIDENT'S CABINET

MR. PRESIDENT, WHO WILL YOU CHOOSE?

The president's cabinet helps in the decision making and directs the day-to-day operations of the executive branch of the government. While the first president had only five members in the cabinet, more recent presidents have had far larger cabinets.

Following is a list of some of the various cabinet offices held over the years. Which five of these do you think Washington would have had on his first cabinet?

State	Commerce	Housing and Urban Development
Labor	Defense	Transportation
Energy	Justice	Attorney General
Education	War	Health and Human Services
Postmaster General	Treasury	Health, Education, and Welfare
Interior	Attorney General	Navy

President George Washington had the same problem as every other president when it came to selecting the people to help him take on the job of chief executive. Who should he ask to serve on his cabinet and in what jobs should he place them? Because his cabinet had only five members, the choices, even among the people that Washington had known and worked with, were many. Following is the list of Washington's cabinet offices and brief descriptions of some people who might have been considered.

MR. PRESIDENT, CHOOSE WHO WILL SERVE!

Pretend that you are George Washington and make your choices and placements for your cabinet. Before you begin, you will need to answer one question. In choosing a cabinet, Mr. President, which factors do you think are more important? To help you answer this question, nine of the factors Washington might have consider are identified on the following list. Rank order the factors (plus one factor of your own) to get your mind-set to making your final selections among the ten finalists for your Cabinet:

- ____ Represent all regions of the country on the cabinet.
- ____ Choose the people who are best qualified for the jobs.
- ____ Represent the small states as well as the large states.
- ____ Select friends who are loyal and true to you.
- ____ Favor people who have great political influence.
- ____ Have people with the most experience in government.
- ____ Reward those who gave outstanding military service.
- ____ Have people who have opinions and views similar to your own.
- ____ Include people who have outstanding accomplishments.
- ____ Other _____

Cabinet Offices

State

Treasury

Attorney General

War

Postmaster General

Potential Cabinet Members

(The teacher may want to assign each of the people under consideration as roles to students and let them try to make a case for themselves for a particular cabinet post.)

1. Boston bookseller; forced to flee Boston in disguise in 1774; Revolutionary War general; served as an artillery officer with Washington's army; developed a reputation for being able to move equipment and supplies quickly; known as sound, solid, and dependable.

2. Revolutionary War general; served with distinction and bravery; considered a strong, brilliant leader in battle who men would die for; fought guerilla-type warfare from the swamps of his native state for a considerable period of time while British were in control of the area.

3. Strong-minded, clear speaking champion of individual rights; opposed to a central government that is too strong; extensive experience in dealing with other nations; took a leadership role in Congress during the Revolution.

4. Supporter of a strong national government and a strong executive branch (may even want a king rather than a president); revolutionary war officer of Washington's personal staff and strong supporter of Washington; good organizer and thorough planner; wants to establish a national bank and be sure that the new nation has a strong economic base.

5. Supporter of strong central government; southerner from a powerful state; lawyer by occupation; took a leadership role in the approval of the U.S. Constitution; keen observer and careful record keeper.

6. Elder statesman with ambassadorial experience; had a strong role in both the Declaration of Independence and the U.S. Constitution; extremely well liked; inventive and scientifically curious; writes extremely well and has many publications.

7. Outspoken critic of the U.S. Constitution and defender of states' rights; spirited public speaker whose words caused many to support the Revolution; experienced as a state governor and long-time member of the state legislature; has real vision for the future.

8. Lawyer from a powerful northern state; took a key role in the effort to gain separation from England and helped in the writing of the Declaration of Independence; considered uncompromising and unyielding but a man of principle; advocate of a strong central government.

9. Boston merchant; Harvard graduate; served in the Revolution, first as a captain and later as a colonel; strong supporter of the U.S. Constitution, first Commissioner of the U.S. Treasury, 1785-1789.

10. Virginia lawyer; aide de camp to Washington; governor of Virginia; member of Congress; attended Constitutional Convention but refused to sign; urged the ratification of the Constitution on the grounds that the union was necessary.

The students may want to compare their choices to Washington's and know the names of the people who were candidates. This is one case where it is really not so important that their choices line up with the first president's.

Actual Selections (First Term)

State	Thomas Jefferson (3)
Treasury	Alexander Hamilton (4)
War	Henry Knox (1)
Attorney General	Edmond Randolph (10)
Postmaster General	Samuel Osgood (9)

Not Chosen by Washington

Francis Marion (2)

James Madison (5)

Benjamin Franklin (6)

Patrick Henry (7)

John Adams (8)

Game 2: WHAT DO WE NEED IN OUR NEIGHBORHOOD?

Pretend that you are planning a new neighborhood with a shopping center. There is room for only ten businesses in the shopping center but there are spots for four other businesses at other locations in the neighborhood. It is important to know that you and your family, as well as other people in the neighborhood, may have to travel a long way to get those services and goods not offered in your community. So, be very careful as you choose the fourteen different types of goods and services you want. You also want to take care as to where the businesses are located within the community. Be very thoughtful as you place them on the map so that each business is at exactly the right spot.

Here is a list of potential businesses.

Appliance and furniture store	Garden supply store and plant nursery
Auto supply store	Hardware store
Bank	Hobby shop
Barber shop	Hospital
Bicycle shop	Ice cream store
Bookstore	Jewelry store
Bowling lanes	Miniature golf
Candy store	Music store
China shop	Pet store
Clothing store	Post office
Convenience market	Produce market
Craft store	Restaurant
Delicatessen	School
Dentist	Service station
Department store	Shoe store
Doctor's office	Skating rink
Drug store	Souvenir shop
Dry cleaner and laundry	Toy store
Eye doctor	Variety store
Fabric and sewing store	Veterinarian
Fast food restaurant	Video store
Furniture store	Video game arcade
Grocery store	

WHAT DO WE NEED IN OUR NEIGHBORHOOD?

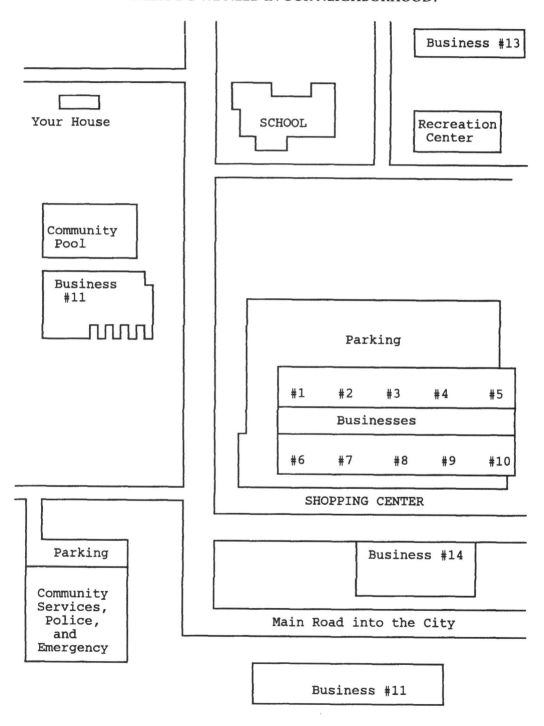

Game 3: ESTABLISHING A COLONY

AN IN-BASKET GAME

In-basket games are prioritizing activities. They are based on the notion that quite often, life choices require us to decide what we must do first and what can be put off or done later. In-basket games begin with a list of activities or jobs that a single individual must do. The central question is, "In what order should these jobs be done?"

In this in-basket game, you are the leader of a group of colonists who have come to the new world during the seventeenth century. You have sighted the coast and sailed along it for several days, finally dropping anchor in a quiet cove. There is a likely area for a colony just ashore and a small river flows into the sea here. The area does not appear to have any permanent settlements, but you have seen natives peering at your ship from shore. You have no idea whether they are friendly or hostile.

You do not own your ship, but have hired the ship along with the services of its crusty old sea captain who wants to hurry you off his ship, so that he can return home to take on other cargos. A number of tasks face you. The following is a list of some of them.

- ____ Send scouting parties to explore the surrounding area to be sure that the best possible site for a colony was chosen.

- ____ Find fresh water to replenish the ship's stores.

- ____ Send a group to try to meet with the natives who have been seen looking out from the shore.

- ____ Hold a meeting of all the colonists to decide on the rules of government for the new colony.

- ____ Land all passengers from the ship.

- ____ Pay the captain what is still owed him for the voyage.

- ____ Draft a letter to the patrons of the colony telling of your safe arrival and suggesting what you will do now.

- ____ Determine your exact location and how far your colony is from other new world colonies.

- ____ Build a stockade for defense.

- ____ Start building shelters for the colonists.

- ____ Plant crops.

- ____ Send out a hunting party to find fresh meat.

- ____ Disembark all passengers.

- ____ Unload all supplies.
- ____ Plant the flag of your country on the shore claiming the land for your sovereign.
- ____ Hold a Thanksgiving celebration.

Game 4: NUCLEAR WASTE DISPOSAL

For this game you will need a large map of the United States and one of the world. The scenario is that there is a need to dispose of certain waste products from nuclear reactors and other sources. These waste products are radioactive. Children are divided into five groups, one representing the Congressional Committee that will be making the recommendation and the others representing various potential sites. The Congressional Committee and the four area groups meet as groups first to plan strategy. Then the Congressional Committee listens and asks questions while each group makes its case indicating why its area should not be chosen. Then the groups all meet separately again, the Congressional Committee to make its final decision and the area groups to come up with a contingency plan in case their area is the one chosen. This plan may include a set of safety recommendations, recommendations regarding specific site priorities, and some recommendations about how the amount of nuclear waste might be controlled (recycled, etc.).

Congressional Committee
The committee is made up of seven members of congress, one from each of the regions being considered and three from unspecified other areas of the country. A chairperson and a secretary are appointed. The chairperson should be an uncommitted individual. It is the job of the chairperson to keep the hearings flowing smoothly and to present the final recommendations of the Congressional Committee. The four options that the committee is considering are the following:

1. Burial of the waste in sealed containers in a southwestern state that has a small population.

2. Burial of the waste in sealed containers in a southeastern state relatively close to the majority of the facilities producing the waste. There is, of course, danger of spills and contamination whenever radioactive materials are moved.

3. Disposal of the nuclear waste by putting it in sealed waterproof containers that are then taken out to sea and placed on the ocean floor in a specified site, away from major shipping lanes or ocean currents.

4. Disposal in airtight sealed containers at a specific site in a mountainous area in a northwestern state with a low population.

Group 1: Southwestern State

They feel that their state does not get much, if any, benefit from the plants producing the nuclear waste. Neither does it profit from the products, which are largely military in nature. This state is one of the few areas of the country where pollution has not yet become a problem and they wish it to remain that way. They also point out that their state has many Native Americans in it and that putting the waste disposal site there would be yet another blow of oppression and discrimination against that population.

Group 2: Southeastern State

Their state has a potential high population growth as part of the sunbelt. They feel that as a producer of nuclear products for the nation that their population is already exposed to enough danger. They also know that their population density already far exceeds that of the two western states.

Group 3: Coastal State

There is great fear in this state that no containers can be designed that can withstand the sea over time. If the waste is disposed of in this manner, it is believed that eventually leakages and seepage will bring about further damage to coastal plant and animal life and pollute the coasts themselves. This area already has one of the biggest pollution problems in the nation.

Group 4: Low Population Northwestern State

The severe weather of the mountainous region and the difficulty of burying anything in the rocky area make the container problem a serious one. Falling rocks or cold weather could damage a container very quickly and a nuclear leak problem would then exist. This is a nearly pollution free area and the population is very independent and wishes to stay that way. They also feel that the creation of this waste is not their problem, and that the people who benefit from the nuclear energy produced should be the people who have the waste product disposal site.

Advantages and Benefits, Problems and Limitations

A major strength of simulation games is in the interest and involvement that they generate. Students become impassioned about the games. That very quality also means that simulation games can really stimulate students to do some meaningful research, meaningful because they want to do it and because, for once, they feel some purpose for that research.

The major emphasis in simulation games on problem solving and decision making is another important plus. Simulations offer perhaps the best vehicle available for practicing problem solving. One of the reasons for claiming this is that, although the emotional stakes and commitment may be high, the consequences that come from decisions are only vicarious ones. This allows students to practice their problem-solving skills in relative safety. Carefully conducted debriefing sessions can really strengthen the development of problem solving. Such sessions are both analytic and reflective.

The down side of simulation gaming cannot be ignored. There is no denying that games can be very time consuming in the classroom. They often take time away that could be spent in acquiring factual knowledge. In the light of the turn to more performance-based assessment, this may not be considered such a negative as it once was. Nevertheless, for the teacher whose concern is more slanted to how much content students learn, this does pose a distinctive disadvantage.

There is also a possible problem in the amount of preparation time required of the teacher. The teacher does have to limit this, and simulation games often require a lot of thought and preparation as well.

The major problem of games, though, really is in what most proponents consider to be their greatest strength, the kind of emotionally involved commitment students give to them. The competitive nature of many of the games may also develop and encourage some values and feelings that may be very contrary to the spirit of cooperation and working together. That emotional commitment may also cause some unwanted carryover into relationships among students. One thing that has to happen during debriefing if this danger is to be avoided is a definite and convincing closing down of all phases and aspects of roles that students have taken during the game play time.

MOCK TRIALS

The activity of the courtroom offers many possibilities for drama. Because the justice system is so integrally important to understanding democracy and the democratic process, various kinds of dramatic activities can be built around the legal process. This can be useful in helping students understand the constitution and the legal system as well as the various conflicts and controversies that have been and continue to be important issues. Understanding the legal system seems nearly as important as understanding the democratic process itself and developing the knowledge and attitudes needed to participate. Most people will be involved in the legal system several times in their lives, and the more students learn about the law and the courts and how they operate the better prepared they will be to deal with these legal encounters throughout life.

By far the most used dramatic activity related to the legal process is the mock trial. Mock trials enable students to reexamine history and to look at questions of right and wrong as they relate to the law and the legal system. Mock trials can take numerous forms and be developed with varying thoroughness and detail depending on such factors as the teaching purpose, the ability level of the students, and the time available. There are at least nine forms of mock trials.

1. Re-creation of real trials from the past: We attempt to re-enact the trial as it took place. The more thoroughly we research it and the more preparation we do the more completely this can be done. Because of the court record keeping system, almost exact reenactments are even possible if desired. With elementary and middle school children, of course, giving the broad picture of what happened is more likely to be more comprehensible.

2. Staging trials from the past with open verdicts: With this type of mock trial, we want to see if a jury of students is going to come to the same decision that was reached at the original trial. When comparisons are made, the question is always going to be why the verdict was the same or different.

3. Hypothetical trials of historical and contemporary figures who have never stood trial: With this type of trial, the student's sense of justice and fairness or even their natural curiosity is served, as well as their biases. Trials of historical characters like Oswald, Hitler, and Custer have been the subject of speculative movies and novels. The question is what kind of evidence and testimony might have been given if the figure went to trial. Figures from centuries ago, such as Attila the Hun, Brutus, King John of England, Jack the Ripper, or Ivan the Terrible, might be tried. More recent figures, such as Richard Nixon or Harry Truman (the atom bomb), also give insight.

4. Creating cases to retest a landmark decision of the Supreme Court: The emphasis is on discussing the issues and the particular circumstances of the original case an then attempting through discussion to come up with a parallel case that might cause the Supreme Court to offer a modern opinion.

5. Trials related to current controversies and issues: The cases come right out of the newspapers and news broadcasts, and relatives and friends have information and opinion. The issues of current events become relevant and important to young learners as they try to make their own case.

6. Reenactment of trials suggested in fictional books: Trials are a popular subject in fiction. Having children develop the detail to enact one of these trials can help comprehension and test their creativity.

7. Fantasy trials of story and book characters: Moral themes are almost universal in children's fiction. Putting a fairy tale character like Jack or

the Wolf on trial can be a delightful learning experience. The advantage is that children are very familiar with the story line and the characters. The trial gives them a new perspective on the events of the story.

8. Creation of a new crime scenario and then staging the trial: This is a totally creative experience in which the children create a crime, a victim, witnesses and clues, and an accused perpetrator of the crime. The teacher can exercise some control by a discussion in which specifications regarding the nature of the crime are carefully drawn.

9. Development of a classroom court to try discipline offenders: Several systems, ranging from very simple to very elaborate, may be used to put members of the class on trial for breaking the classroom rules. The major benefit of the exercise is that children develop clearer, more meaningful ideas about such issues as reasonable doubt, the relationship of punishment to crime, and punishment as a deterrent to crime. The technique has been used successfully by some teachers as part of their classroom management plan.

Selecting a Jury

One of the activities that goes on in courtrooms is the process of jury selection. Children will learn something about trial by jury by going through a modified version of this process. As part of the process, the teacher may want to bring up the reasons that a potential juror might be excluded from a jury for cause and why and how attorneys can excuse jurors without telling the reason.

Jury Selection for the Trial of Goldilocks
Goldilocks is on trial for illegal entry, burglary, and vandalism. For this activity, there are 14 potential jurors. The rest of the children serve as bailiffs, court stenographers, and teams of attorneys for the defense and prosecution. The lawyers are given only the names of the jurors while the jurors are given the additional defining material that indicates what some of their biases are.

Instructions to the Attorneys
Each team of attorneys (beginning with the attorneys for the defense) will get to question as many jurors as time allows. All attorneys should realize that some jurors have had experiences that will make them predisposed toward the case. No more than two attorneys on each team may actually ask questions. We will begin with a five-minute period in which the teams confer. In that period, the team should decide which jurors they want to question most, what questions they want to ask, and who will do the asking. (Attorneys not asking questions need to take notes.) The questioning

period will be 10 to 12 minutes long. The defense will be allowed to question one juror, asking no more than three questions. The prosecution will then have a turn and may continue asking questions to that juror or go to someone else. The defense and prosecution attorneys will go on alternatively until time is called. At that point the teams will have five minutes to confer. They may then recuse, or exclude, up to three jurors each. A straw vote will then be taken among the remaining jurors to see how they would decide the case.

Prospective Jurors

*   Little Miss Muffet is afraid of almost everything, but she does understand people who love a good snack.

*   Little Boy Blue tends to be a little lazy himself.

*   Big Bad Wolf thinks that it is perfectly all right to go in someone else's house, as long as you knock first. He is more fond of pigs than of little girls.

*   Gretel has a history of being lost in the woods.

*   Cinderella has had to deal with broken objects before.

*   Sleeping Beauty has had to deal with uninvited guests even at her own birthday party.

*   The Giant has had some problems with uninvited guests.

*   Snow White has had some experience sleeping in a bed in a strange house.

*   Beauty has had to pay a high price for trespassing herself, but she is very fond of beasts.

*   Rapunzel has had a hair loss problem due to her own hospitality with uninvited strangers.

*   Rumpelstiltskin has tried to adopt a stranger's child himself.

*   Mary Contrary likes to garden and is not too fond of people who trample her flowers.

*   Pied Piper is very fond of children.

*   Puss in Boots understands meeting a challenge.

Other Trial Related Activities

There are various other activities that can help children learn about the legal system. Role playing a crime with various witnesses giving independent accounts of what they saw can teach children that people see and remember events differently. Visits to law school mock trials or to one of the mock-trial competitive programs put on at the high school or visiting a courtroom can be real learning experiences if carefully planned. Classroom visits by attorneys, judges, and police officers are also profitable if such guests can relate to the children. Students can examine laws and go through the process of debate and enactment of a particular law. They can go through structured-writing exercises to write trial briefs.

DRAMA THROUGH READING: GUIDED FANTASY, CLASS ACTION DRAMA, READERS' THEATER, AND DRAMATIC READING

The dramatic power and eloquence of the printed word can be used to create images and suspense when read aloud. Here are two techniques in which the teacher does the reading and two in which the students are the readers.

Guided Fantasies

Guided fantasies, also called visualizations, are dramas in which even the most shy children can participate because they require no acting, only good listening concentration and sensory imagination. The students are asked to sit with their eyes closed and to envision as vividly as they can a particular scene as it is described by a reader. If some of the students are really expressive readers, they can be involved in this capacity as well as being listeners. This is especially true in the upper grades.

Basically, this activity has the teacher reading and the children listening, but the teacher wants a very different kind of listening here. The teacher wants the children to get the feel of what it is like to be in another time, another place, or another time in another place. She wants them to be able to see it in their minds, to smell the smells, to hear the sounds. What she wants, in short, is a very imaginative sensory kind of listening, the kind that involves the students and makes them want to interact with and know more about what is being described.

The readings need to be fairly short, certainly within the concentration span of students. They need to be very descriptive, sensory, and specifically detailed to the point of being graphic. The scenes that they describe should, of course, be relevant to the curriculum. They should help students envision the settings, the culture, and the sequence of events. In essence, you want them to smell the smoke of the battlefield, the stench of the prisons, the perfume of the flowers, and the aromas of the feast spread before the king. You want them to almost hear the sounds of the royal court, the noises of battle and of the marketplace, and the voices and clatter that fill the city and the streets. In their minds' eyes, you want them to see as clearly as they can the panorama and the detail of everything. The scenes described can be historical or contemporary. What is important is the amount of imagery they create, so it is important to get the students involved. Step out of the story to tell them to breathe in the smells and ask them what they are smelling. See if they can add detail to the vision. Reread short segments of the description that are particularly strong in the images they create. Pictures and objects and things to touch, hear, and even smell, can be examined to add to the intensity of the sensory experience and to increase input into the discussion from students.

As a follow-up activity, the guided fantasy can be turned into a planned pantomime with assigned roles. Through the pantomiming activity, done while the fantasy is read aloud again, students can intensify the visualization and express the images they have seen in their minds.

Example: The Tornado Opening

(Something like the first paragraph here needs to be standard to establish the kind of mood and attitude desired. Children might be seated in a circle or perhaps on the floor so that there is a sense of closeness in the group. At its best, the technique allows the listener to totally immerse him or herself into the images being created and suspend disbelief in their reality.)

Close your eyes and let your mind go blank for a minute. Now I want you to begin to see a picture in your mind. Try to make this picture as clear and as filled with vivid detail as you possibly can.

It has been an uneventful April day in the town of Xenia in central Ohio. It is a quiet kind of old-fashioned town most days. This part of Ohio is fairly flat and you can see from one end of town to the other. The carhops at the local drive-in rootbeer stand are taking orders. Along with other girls and boys, you are waiting for a ride in front of the school. The air seems strange, kind of heavy and oppressive, and there is a quietness in the air that does not seem normal even by the standards of a midwestern American town. Though it is not raining, dark clouds are hanging low and daylight seems to be going early.

Something catches your eye. A couple of miles distance to the southwest, a huge darker cloud has formed and seems to be revolving. In minutes, it is funnel shaped. Because you have been listening to radio weather, you know that conditions are dangerously right here in the "tornado alley" part of America today, so you have no doubt at all. That cloud is now a tornado! And this one looks like a bad one headed right into town.

You run back into the school screaming, "Tornado! Twister coming and coming fast!" Looking out the window of the school, you and other students and teachers can now see with horror a terrible fearsome twisting cloud only a few hundred yards away. Everyone hits the floor in terror as the tornado slams into the building with screaming force. Crashing, banging, and grating sounds fill the air along with the screams of terrified people. The air is raining rocks, slabs of concrete, tree limbs, bricks, and great chunks of earth that have been ripped from the ground. Daggers of broken glass twirl through the air everywhere. The huge beams of the school are falling everywhere.

The tornado funnel moves across the town at a rate of 40 miles per hour. It leaves a trail of destruction and rubble. Wood-frame houses in its path are crushed or swept from their foundations. Huge old trees are torn from the earth and hurled in the air. The air is filled with objects, from furniture to cars and trucks, all now being hurled with monstrous force.

The black twisting tornado hits the rear of a train moving through town. Several train cars are thrown from the tracks across the main street where they crash into the red brick post office, a museum, and a restaurant.

Finally, the destructive tornado passes. Thirty three people have been left dead and hundreds injured. Over 1300 buildings have been destroyed. Of course, you don't find this out until later. For now, you can only see the awful damage everywhere. You and the rest are left dazed and unbelieving, but you feel lucky to have survived.

(Based on accounts of the destructive tornado that swept the midwest on April 3, 1974)

Class Action Dramas

You may have done these little stories and called them by a different name or had no name for them at all. What they involve, more than anything else, is specific listening skills. But there is drama in them, too, or at least opportunity for expressive fun. Students have to listen carefully to the story as it is read. When they hear a particular word or phrase they respond in just the way that they have been instructed. The words and actions usually involve very rudimentary drama and usually even the shyest child will participate in most roles.

The results are usually fun and funny. The stories themselves are often rich in stereotypes and misinformation, and they convey a lot of ideas so blatantly exaggerated that they cannot be missed. Often these ideas are made to look ridiculous by their portrayal in the stories. Thus, the stories can be very provocative and are often good departure points for discussion of issues and values.

For these stories, an individual, a group, or the entire class may be required to respond. The teacher decides based on the type of action required and the nature of the class. The first job is to assign the roles within the group. It is usually good to rehearse before doing the entire story. The story should be read with as much excitement and expression as possible, but the rate has to be regulated to allow everyone to see, hear, and participate in the responses.

"Rutabaga Bones and the Golden Cat of Felina"

Word-Phrase/Character	Action and/or Words when Heard
Rutabaga Bones	Salute and proclaim, "I found it!"
Professor Ima Manx	Expressively say, "I *want* that cat!"
Golden Cat	One person holds two fingers like cats' ears and strikes poses while others frame that person as if taking a photo.
Dr. Fang Doberman	Give an evil laugh, like a villain.
Cat	Say, "Meow!"
Expedition Shout,	"Here we go again!"
Meow River Say,	"Splish! Splash! Hiss!"
Crocodile pool	Make jaw-like motions with arms and say, "Crunch!"
Rapids	Very fast, boys say, "Water lilly! Water lilly!" At the same time girls say,"Rub-a-dub! Rub-a-dub!"
Great Falls	Shout, "Look out for the waterfalls!" (Holding out the word *falls* and trailing off like someone falling.)
Hairball Desert	Pant and stick out tongue in thirst while groaning, "Water!"
Catsears Mountains	Sing, "We love to go a wandering along the mountain top."
Snake pits	Do snake hissing sounds while writhing.
Lions' dens	Roar while acting like the MGM lion.

Rutabaga Bones was the greatest adventurer and explorer of the modern world. He was better at finding things, especially old things, than anyone in the whole world. When the Museum of *Cat* History in Meowvia discovered an ancient map showing the location of the ancient kingdom of Felina and of a fabulous *Golden Cat*, naturally they sent for *Rutabaga Bones*.

"Bring back that *Golden Cat*," said *Professor Ima Manx*, the Curator of the Museum. She knew that *Rutabaga Bones* could not resist a challenge. Even so, she insisted that he take his arch rival, *Dr. Fang Doberman*, along with him. *Dr. Fang Doberman* was the world authority on the *Golden Cat*. He had been chasing cats around the world for years, but *Rutabaga Bones* always got there ahead of him.

The *expedition* started up the *Meow River*. *Rutabaga Bones* led *Dr. Doberman* and *Professor Manx* and the rest of the *expedition* through the *rapids*, past the *crocodile pool* of the *Meow*, up and over the *Great Falls* of the *Meow*. Following the map, *Rutabaga Bones* directed the *expedition* over the *Catsears Mountains* and across the *Hairball Desert*. At last, they reached the fabled, fearsome Valley of the Felines. The *map* led them through *snake pits* and *lions' dens* to the Great Temple of the *Golden Cat*. At each step of the journey, *Rutabaga Bones's* resourcefulness and his ready Argentine Bolos saved the *expedition* and, of course, *Dr. Doberman* and *Professor Manx*, from being destroyed. *Rutabaga Bones* was always just in the nick of time.

True to form, the minute the *expedition* found the Great Temple of the *Golden Cat*, *Dr. Fang Doberman* showed what a low cur he was. Barking a sudden order, *Dr. Doberman* sprang forward, a pistol in his hand. Ten of the members of the *expedition* threw off their native worker disguises revealing themselves as armed Canine elite guards from the dictatorship of Mongrely. *Dr. Doberman* grabbed poor *Professor Manx*. Unless he took a chance on *Dr. Manx* being shot, *Rutabaga Bones* was helpless. "The *Golden Cat* will be all mine," growled the snarling *Dr. Doberman*.

Suddenly, from the Temple of the *Golden Cat*, a low hissing was heard. Before *Dr. Doberman* and the Canine elite guards even realized what was happening, a hundred giant cats sprang from the doors of the temple and down the great stone steps in front of it. Cats were all over the *expedition*. *Dr. Doberman* and the Canines were running for their lives. Thinking quickly, *Rutabaga Bones* reached for *Professor Manx's* hand. With a sudden flick of his bolo, *Rutabaga Bones* caught hold of a high stone overhanging the temple. Holding the end of the bolo, he and *Professor Manx* swung up over the giant cats and the Canine elite guards who were trying to get away from them. Without looking back, *Rutabaga* and *Ima* rushed up the steps and into the Temple of the *Golden Cat*. In the very center stood the great statue of the *Golden Cat*. They were about to grab the statue when suddenly it spoke to them.

"I'm ashamed of you, *Rutabaga Bones* and *Ima Manx*!" said the *Golden Cat*. "You really shouldn't steal a relic."

Rutabaga Bones and *Professor Ima Manx* jumped back startled. Then they answered together, "You know, you are absolutely right."

"So why don't you buy a nice replica in the souvenir shop?" suggested the *Golden Cat*.

So, that is exactly what they did even though they thought it was overpriced. Wrapping their replica carefully, *Rutabaga Bones* and *Professor Ima Manx* left the temple and traveled back past the *snake pits* and the *lions' dens*, across the *Hairball Desert* and over the *Catsears Mountains*, over the *Great Falls* of the *Meow*, past the *crocodile pool*, through the rapids and down the *Meow River*.

From that day to this, no one ever saw *Dr. Fang Doberman* again. Everyone else became fabulously wealthy from the adventure. *Dr. Ima Manx* and the Museum of *Cat* History printed copies of their ancient map of Felina which sold like hotcakes. When the tourists who bought the maps found the Temple of the *Golden Cat*, they bought hundreds of the *Golden Cat* replicas, enabling the Temple to make a nice profit. As for *Rutabaga Bones*, he made his fortune rescuing people from *snake pits, lions' dens, crocodile pools, rapids*, and the *Great Falls*. He also set up a water concession on the *Hairball Desert* that makes big money. In the off-season, of course, *Rutabaga Bones* seeks new adventures.

Readers' Theater

Readers' theater involves turning a story that is written in narrative form into a play. A group of students reads the story and then plans together how to alter it so that it can be read as a play. This approach emphasizes drama as a planning process. The students have to think out how they can change the way that the story is told. To do so, they have to develop a thorough understanding of the characters; a feel for the setting; and a mental map of the purpose, themes, and the plot line or sequence. They literally rewrite the story, putting in dialogue to cover narrative passages. They are made to think about what character would be most likely to relate the information and how it can be fitted in as conversation or as monologue. Of course, one of the natural tendencies is to fall back on the device of a narrator, but ideally the use of this voice should be prohibited altogether or kept at a minimum.

Because the focus of dialogue is human interaction and monologue is really a way of revealing inner thoughts, dreams, and concerns, this technique has a lot to offer to the social studies. Of course, some stories are better suited than others.

Stories that place a lot of emphasis on character, those that are written in the first person, and those that are already rich in dialogue usually take less adaptation. For social studies content purposes, folk tales, biographical episodes (such as those in the books of Jean Fritz), historical fiction (such as *Nettie Goes South*), and stories which emphasize culture and human relationships (such as *Ming Lo Moves the Mountain* or *Frog and Toad are Friends*) are most useful.

After the story is planned and usually rewritten, the students can try reading through it different ways running through it several times. This can allow different people to express themselves in the roles and allow rewriting and rethinking different parts of the story.

Dramatic Reading

There is a wealth of short dramatic material that children can read expressively. These can be fun and either funny or serious, depending on the material. The trick is finding and/or adapting (which most often means cutting down to a reasonable length). For adaptable or abstractable material, popular descriptive histories and historical fiction are good sources. Good material can also be found in popular history and geography magazines such as *National Geographic, Smithsonian, Cobblestone*, and others. It is also productive fun for students to prepare their own readings as creative-writing assignments and creative-reporting exercises. The teacher needs to set it up so that more than one student reads the material aloud. That way, they can begin to envision the range of expressive possibilities. Among the separate categories of readings that can be done brags, cliff-hangers, character monologues, in-role reports, first-person poems, expressive poems about human feelings, and historical poems are briefly discussed here along with some examples of the less familiar types.

Brags are good comic devices. They are humorous partially because boasting is considered inappropriate behavior in mainstream society and partially because of the use of exaggeration that is implicit in all bragging. In reality, most children's social interactions are filled with boasting claims from the stereotyped, "My father can beat your father up!" to the "dares" that are so common to youth society and on to the name dropping of adults. Brags involve strength, ability, status, possessions, and relationships. Bragging has become and continues to be an art form in some societies (including that of frontier America).

Written brags make excellent oral reading devices. They invite competition and imitation. They make excellent models for creative writing, and they can incorporate a great deal of knowledge of a culture. Here are two brags from fictitious inventors. They might be used in a unit on invention and discovery or one dealing with a period of history where invention was a major theme. Have the students read these to see who can read most expressively. Then have them write their own scientist brags.

Brags

PROFESSOR IMA CHEENIUS

Of course, *I* am the greatest inventor of all time! *My* inventions will one day be household words. Why, *I* have inventions in process right now that will make life easier for everyone, save energy, repair the ozone, cure cancer, get us to other planets, make clothes and shoes and cars that will never wear out, and solve the energy shortage. And here is a little secret, I am inventing an engine that will pull smog out of the air and run entirely on the pollution in it. Too much for you! Well, try this! I am going to invent instant water to save the world from water shortage. All you need to do is add water. Can you believe how clever I am? I just don't know what I'll come up with next, maybe chewless gum or a math pill that helps children get their math homework done twice as quickly! Why, next to me, Edison was a bulb head and Newton was a fig cookie. Bell was a ding-a-ling and

Marconi was pasta. And, just between you and me, I think Franklin flew a few too many kites in the lightning. I am just *so* clever!

Dr. I. Hahva Ben Wrob

I have had *so* many ideas you just couldn't believe it. But every time I come up with an invention, someone always copies it and gets to the patent office ahead of me. The airplane, that was my idea, only mine flew constantly at four feet off the ground. If those Wright boys hadn't gotten their patent filed first, we would never be having all these plane crashes. And how about the telephone, mine again! My phone only let you talk one way, too. You called and talked. The other person just listened. Think of the time that would save! And you would never have to listen to those stupid answers people give either. Television, another one of mine? You bet! I gave that one a lot of thought and effort. My television was a little large, though, somewhere near the size of Yankee Stadium, but it had a six-inch picture! I just don't know why those guys at the patent office laughed so hard. They could at least have waited for the new season. I tell you that I am always being robbed! Do you think that it's space aliens spying on me? Maybe there is a hidden camera in my laboratory. I know! I'll start putting all my notes in code! Wait! I feel another idea coming on, a machine that thinks, that you can program to do what you want it to! What do you mean, someone has already invented the computer? I've been robbed again, I tell you!

Cliff-hangers are readings in which the central characters are depicted in impossible situations, dire straits from which it may seem impossible that they can ever extract themselves. I like to design these as problem-solving readings. After they have been read aloud a few times to try alternate expressions, have the students try to suggest ways out of these truly solution defying situations. Generally, the decisions do not involve moral dilemmas so much as insurmountable difficulties. They can really test the students' problem-solving thinking to the limit. One thing that these discussions can teach is, when faced with many impossible problems, one has to look at them individually *and* together, often beginning with the initial task of identifying the least impossible one to solve.

Cliffhangers

THE SEA CAPTAIN EXPLORER

There I am. My ship has run aground in totally uncharted waters. There is a gaping hole in the hull and even if it were fixed, there seems to be no way to get this heavy ship back out into the water. Speaking of water, there isn't any, and thirst is a terrible killer at sea. The stores are in short supply and we've been eating wormy ship's biscuits for a week. The crew, which is made up of the worst cutthroats that ever signed sailing papers, has been grumbling and refusing to take orders. The sailors are beginning to plan a mutiny, and some pretty nasty looking types are starting to edge toward me with cutlasses and belaying pins in their hands. Out of the jungle-like growth just a few hundred yards away, a large group of hostile looking natives, wicked-looking spears at the ready, are moving toward the beached ship and me. Out to sea and moving toward us, I can see a fierce seasonal storm, the kind that can pick my poor ship up and break it entirely on the rocks. It is coming fast. The only path of retreat is the sea, which will soon be stormy. But that may not be the worst part. Out on the bay, I can see a half dozen black fins slicing through the water. What are you going to do?

THE NEW COUNTRY EXPLORER

There I am, climbing the mountain trail where no Englishman has gone before. The mountains tower all around me, and the only trails are those made by animals. A single misstep along a narrow ledge and I go crashing down through underbrush and scrub trees, hitting every rock as I go. Desperately grabbing at trees and rocks I try to break my fall, finally sliding to a stop only inches from a 200-foot drop-off. Badly bruised and shaken, I try to struggle to my feet only to find one leg twisted grotesquely underneath my body. For a moment there is no feeling at all in the leg. Then the pain hits me with a jolt and, in a cold sweat, I nearly pass out. Just then, I hear a snarling growing noise. The hair on my neck stands on end as a giant brown and gray grizzly bear rises on its hind legs not more than a hundred feet away. Pitifully, I struggle to drag myself away. Suddenly, there is a whizzing sound and an arrow thuds quivering in a tree trunk a few feet away. I look up to see a party of dreaded Blackfeet warriors with bows drawn on the ledge above me. It is at that exact moment that I hear the warning rattle of the rattlesnake at my feet. So, what are you going to do?

Character monologues are readings that reveal the history, philosophy, or plans of an individual. Shakespeare is filled with them, Caesar, Hamlet, and so on. Browning's poetry as well as the writings of people like Dickens, Poe, and Twain contain other examples. Children's books, from humorous treatments such as Sid Fleischman's McBroom series of tall tales and Judith Viorst's Alexander stories to serious historical fiction is rich in usable material. In addition, there are many usable primary resource materials, particularly letters, diaries, and newspaper accounts. Generally, first-person writing is best, but individual examples should be judged on their own merit. Whatever the examples used, they should help children get a feel for the person and his or her cultural context and value system.

In-role reports represent one device that can be used to get the students to write their own dramatic reading. In-role reports bring a refreshing change from standard student reports. It has been common practice for decades for students to copy reports directly out of an encyclopedia or some other reference and then read with little comprehension what they have copied. With in-role reports, students take a character role and give the report from the perspective of that character. Characters may be real or created. Students have to pick a point in time for the character and report as if they knew nothing from that point on. For example, someone taking the role of Lincoln on the first of April, 1865 would know nothing about the assassination and might even end the report by describing plans to see "An American Cousin" when it plays at Ford's Theater. The point of these reports is to get into the feelings or perceptions of the characters involved.

Orally read poems are extremely effective dramatic devices. Poetry is one of the most personal forms of writing. It expresses feelings in their most essential form. Poetry is also designed for oral display by its very nature. A number of kinds of poems are excellent material for dramatic and expressive reading. *First- person poems* are especially useful and, when their subjects are historical and geographic characters, may even be a very different type of in-role report because they are more likely to express feelings than facts. The humor poems of Jack Prelutsky and Shel Silverstein as well as the poems of such serious writers as Walt Whitman are really superior dramatic devices. They are lively, relatively short, and very intense. Expressive poems about human feelings are also good oral-reading material and can provoke interesting discussions. Finally, historical poems, particularly narrative ones, bring a certain epic quality to the past, conveying pageantry and drama as well as presenting a picture that conveys strong emotions and values.

ROLE PLAYS AND OTHER STRUCTURED DRAMA TECHNIQUES

Role Plays

Structured role plays are dramatic activities in which character information and a scenario are provided to the participants. Some device is used so that the sequence of the drama is controlled, more or less, by the teacher.

Example of Structured Role Play

Create two groups of six to eight students each, the Rollercoasters and the Merry-Go-Rounds. Other students can be observers or the activity can be duplicated if space and control variables are favorable.

Scenario: The Rollercaosters and the Merry-go-rounds live in neighboring villages, but their cultures are very different and neither knows much about the other. The Rollercoasters have decided to invite the Merry-go-rounds to a big Getting-to-Know-You Party. The fact that noone in either village speaks the others language causes some problems but the invitation is finally sent and understood. Their are some differences in culture, however, that may cause the people of the two villages to believe about what one can and cannot do.

Only the Rollercoasters know the following:

* You honor your people by always letting your guests eat first.

* The most honored people (your guests) are always served apples.

* Your teachers have taught you always to wear something blue.

* You must give a gift to a guest.

* During a meal it is impolite to talk or stand, but just before and after the meal, everyone shouts, "Yeow!" very loudly several times.

Only the Merry-go-rounds know the following:

* It is impolite to start eating before your hosts take a bite.

* Apples are a forbidden and profane food. Any of your people who eat apples are thrown out of the tribe.

* Blue is a sacred color of the sky and sea to be worn only by the most holy person in the village. When anyone else wears blue it is a terrible wicked thing.

* It is rude to take gifts from a host

* When one is a guest, a good Merry-go- round does everything he or she can to please the hosts.

* One is silent before and after meals, but, while eating, a polite guest shouts, "Gooba!" and jumps up and turns around after every bite.

The role-play event involves the party. It can be played two ways, either with the two cultures able to speak to one another or with both ignorant of the other's language. The role play can be suspended at any moment with a "freeze" signal for discussion of questions about the nature or culture or about the culture clash that is occurring. The obvious problem for the role play to resolve is, how can the different cultures resolve their differences

Sociodramas

Sociodramas involve acting out the solutions to problems. The major difference between role play and sociodrama is that in sociodrama you are yourself. The essential problem situation begins, "If you were in this situation what would you do and what would you say?" Quite often the problems are essentially of the sort that children themselves encounter such as someone wanting to copy their homework, seeing someone cheating or stealing, meeting someone new, relating to someone who is very old, getting directions when lost, giving "how to" directions, making a complaint in a store, or going to the principal about an unfair rule. But children may be projected into situation in which they are asked how they would act in parent or career situations if they were involved.

Picture pantomimes require prints of paintings showing historical or legendary events or people in action in cultural settings. Children look at the painting and isolate and focus on two or three motions they see that they can do in sequence. They then do these motions and each person's response is discussed, at the same time drawing out the meaning and explanations of the paintings.

Story Play is a technique in which stories are acted out without prewritten scripts. The story line, at least to begin with, is a familiar one. The children have a solid understanding of "how the story goes." This is either because the story is an extremely familiar one or because the teacher has taken them through the reading or the telling of the story a sufficient number of times to give them a good sense of who and where in the story the characters are and where the plot line goes. The children then plan how to play the story and then act it out based on their plan. The actual dialogue is improvised as they go. The children can do the story as it is written, experiment with different endings or different twists on the plot, try putting the story in different contexts (doing parodies such as a modern version of "Cinderella" called "Successerella" based on economic problems, for example).

Usually these story plays are done not for an audience but for the experience of doing them. Children delight in having these videotaped or in doing a radiodrama on audio tape. They also can profit from the opportunity these dramas afford for experimenting, redoing the same stories, using different students in the same roles, treating closed-ended stories as though they were open ended.

One device that can be incorporated into these story plays is story cards. In essence, the teacher or the students in the planning process create a storyboard of the story. Each story card on the storyboard represents an advancement of the plot, a different scene or an event in the sequence of the story. For example, the first card from "The Brave Little Tailor" might read, "While working in his shop, the Little Tailor swats at some irritating flies, killing seven of them; and is so proud of his feat that he goes out to seek his fortune." All of the story cards are then put in a stack on the chalk ledge and revealed one at a time as the story play is enacted. This gives students a better metacognitive map of the sequence of the story. It keeps the drama moving, too, and when the students themselves are in on the planning of these stories they learn about sequencing and writing a story. This enables them to develop a sense of the importance of sequence in any chain of events.

Story cards allow students to plan and create new endings as well. Most importantly, they give the children an experience in drama that can be the basis of discussion. After the children become familiar with using the story cards as a way of developing and pacing the drama, they can use them to develop entirely new story dramatizations. They can dramatize how a story goes with a set of story cards such as the following, improvising from the meager information given and even creating various endings because none is given.

1. The expedition was alert for any sign of danger as the horses moved at a slow trot along the dusty trail.

2. The explorers were looking for a route that would lead them to the Pacific Ocean.

3. From the dense undergrowth, the captain of the expedition felt hostile eyes watching his small party.

4. In a small glen, a spring bubbled up out of the rocks and there the party stopped for a refreshing drink.

5. The captain felt rather than heard the footsteps on the path behind them and turned to see a large party of armed natives moving toward him.

6. The small party of explorers was helpless to do anything but follow the natives back through the undergrowth.

7. The walls of the strange city loomed high in front of the party, catching the explorers by surprise.

8. Where the explorers had been expecting primitive natives, they found a people who were far advanced in every way.

9. The explorers were led into the magnificent halls of the king's palace.

REENACTMENT

Hobbyist reenactment groups across the country work yearly at staging authentic Civil War and Revolutionary War battles. In various historic sites, local preservationists and employees go through the motions of living and working as early settlers as a part of the attempt to show visitors what life was like. Various plays and other performance pieces are staged at various times by theater groups. When teachers have children participate in any form of reenactment, they find that the children can become very motivated to do the needed research. That purposeful research aimed at doing an authentic and accurate job in a reenactment role can be, defensibly, one of the most invaluable experiences students ever have.

The adult reenactment groups create at least one misconception about reenactments that they are something that young children cannot do. This is, of course, far from correct. What is true is that the kind of reenactments that children can do is altogether different.

The general guidelines for any reenactment begin with the selection of some event that will put the children in touch with the historical and cultural world heritage. The event should be one that children can reproduce with *some* faithfulness to history, but it should also be one with an internal sequence that is simple enough for the students to follow. Another consideration also might be that the event should be one that they can reenact without doing any violence to one another. (Battle scenes, so popular with reenactment hobbyists, are almost always excluded by this consideration.) The event should be one in which the sequence of actions by participants can be researched and reproduced.

Among the events that reenact well with young children are ceremonies and cultural rituals (greetings of two people, home entry rituals, tea ceremonies, a military group from a particular period setting up a camp, etc.), historic document development, and exchanges and land sales (the Louisiana Purchase, the Purchase of Manhattan, etc.), and parades and celebrations (women parade for the vote, labor movement picket lines, etc.). Once the event is selected, the students need to do basic research, identify the sequence of events, and then plan how they are going to replay the event. If possible, I like to go through the reenactment once before the research and then again after the research is complete. It gives the teacher and the students a better sense both of what they know to begin with and of what they have learned. It also gives some ideas about the kind of questions that need to be answered in the research. During the planning period, the teacher needs to help children discuss the meaning of what they are doing as well as the things that they cannot accurately or fully portray.

INTERACTIONAL DRAMA

Interactional drama involves an outsider or outsiders playing out a scenario from a historical context in front of the children. The actors, usually in costume, play in such a way that they draw the children into the dialogue, either by asking direct questions or asking the students about what they think (in such a way that they solicit both opinions and viewpoints). The dramas are not scripted and are usually open ended, leaving the children the job of solving problems and conflicts the actors have brought to them.

Though interactional drama usually involves no role taking by the children, the success of the technique depends on *suspended disbelief*, the ability of students to think and act as though what is happening is real instead of just pretend. Suspended disbelief is what enables anyone to enjoy a play, a movie, or a television program, thinking of the characters as real people instead of as actor playing people. To make this happen in interactional drama, older classes especially may need to be coached beforehand. Convincing actors who stay in role and know their material are essential. It may be helpful but not essential to use actors who are not recognized by the class.

It may be best if the historical persons who visit the classroom for these dramas are not famous figures. In general, famous characters are more difficult for the children to believe, especially if the children already have a physical image of how the person looks in mind. Ordinary people or less well-known historical personages are easier to impersonate. There are a number of ways that the visitors can work:

- *Interview*: The visitor gives an introduction of him or herself and then answers children's questions. The actor must really has to have a good background on the character to do this and the children will do better if prepared so that they can ask better questions.

- *Storytelling*: The visitor, in role, tells stories about his or her life.

- *Eavesdropping*: The visitors have a conversation staged so that the children seem to be overhearing something they were not meant to hear. (There may be a "freeze" signal that causes the actors to seem to become statues while the teacher and the students talk about what has been said.)

- *Recruitment*: The different actors, taking different sides, try to get the children to side with them.

- *Confrontation*: The actors are set up to have a conflict. One of the characters wins the sympathy of the children and gets them to help defend him or her against the adversary.

Following are a few sample scenarios that indicate some of the kinds that might be used for interactional dramas:

- The time frame we want to take the children to is September 1776. Two revolutionary figures enter, arguing. One says that Washington's situation is so hopeless that he ought to retreat from Long Island, burning New York City behind him so the British cannot quarter there for the winter. The other argues that this is too drastic because it would destroy a lot of American property and leave many people homeless. The other replies that two thirds of the property in New York belongs to Tories anyhow. Both try to recruit the children to their side.

- Two people dressed in turn-of-the-century garb enter, arguing. One thinks that women should be given the vote. The other is convinced that this is the wrong thing to do. The two (I prefer for them both to be women) try to recruit the children to their view, limiting themselves to arguments of the period.

- A young man (or woman) dressed in ancient garb sneaks into the room looking frightened and wary. He claims that he is a Roman slave and that his master was killed in his home during the night. Because the murderer cannot be identified, Roman law says that all the slaves of the household can be executed. He asks the children to hide him. After he hides, a burly Roman enters looking for the runaway slave. He tries to get the children to reveal the hiding place. When the young man is found, the teacher convinces the Roman officer that they should debate the law right there in the classroom before he is allowed to take the young man away. (It is admitted in the debate that the circumstances of the death indicate that a much stronger man than this youth and probably an assassin from outside the house committed the crime.)

EFFECTIVE USE OF DRAMA

Drama in the social studies can produce the kind of memorable Camelot moments that students will carry with them throughout their lives. It can help develop the research drive in lifetime students and make research purposeful and important to even marginal ones. It can make the classroom an exciting place to be, and can help students remember historical and cultural concepts and facts that they would otherwise forget. It can teach about social interactions and develop self-concepts in a way that traditional "lecture, read, and recite" social studies can never do. However, dramatic activities can be a waste of time, if not a disturbing and disruptive force, for students and teachers alike. The difference lies in the way the teacher handles drama.

If drama is to be effective in the social studies, the teacher has to first feel comfortable with it. He or she must be attracted to dramatic techniques and feel very positive about his or her potential to make the entire classroom a more exciting and interesting place. Teachers should avoid using techniques that make them feel they are losing control of the classroom. Because dramatic techniques require high student involvement and sometimes include student planning and student leading in different directions, they may do just that. Teachers also need to feel that what they are doing with drama is solid and purposeful. Drama cannot be used as a mere time filler or entertainment. It has to have curricular importance and value. The teacher has to feel that and has to communicate that effectively to the students and usually to parents and the rest of the school as well.

Drama requires preparation and, if there is a first rule of effective use of drama in the classroom, it is, "Be prepared!" The teacher has to know what he or she is about, find the right material, plan and structure the dramatic activity, and lead the students through planning and rehearsal and up to the dramatic enactment moment. The plan and the material cannot be developed along the way. The teacher who shoots from the hip with drama is likely to fall flat or, worse, waste a lot of valuable learning time.

Drama only works in a conducive atmosphere. That atmosphere is one that is open and experimental and charged with exciting stimuli. It also offers emotional security so that children feel safe psychologically. To take the kind of personal risks that drama demands, children have to be sure that their peers will not be ridiculing or demeaning them for their efforts. No child wants to appear to be foolish or ridiculous. Paradoxically, some children will act silly on purpose to avoid looking silly while trying to be serious. The safe conducive atmosphere for drama comes only with a series of positive experiences in which the teacher slowly edges the class toward dramatic expression that involves more risk taking.

LOOKING BACK

Teaching is stagecraft and teachers who have a stronger sense of the drama of the classroom are going to add suspense and excitement to their teaching. They will create a dramatic atmosphere and give children visions of history, of geography, of culture, of government, and of society that is vivid, interesting, and memorable. Teachers who want to involve students in the drama can plan any of a large variety of activities in which they can act and pretend in order to understand.

Simulation games involve students in usually competitive ways and combine elements from games and role play. Though there are many types of simulation games, the ones most suited for social studies are those which can be understood and played by children within a short period of time. Simulation games are most effective when played with a definite learning purpose and when children understand that purpose.

Another related form of dram in the classroom is the mock trial. Mock trial activities range from recreation of historic trials to invented trials of fantasy characters. One form of mock trial involves the class in invention of everything from the crime to the witnesses.

Among the many other forms of drama that can be used in social studies instruction are guided fantasy, readers' theater, various types of dramatic reading, class action dramas, story play, sociodrama and role play. These teaching techniques can all be related to children's literature and to the past experiences of children. Such drama activities become memorable experiences themselves, and that experience can provide the basis for

Increasing attention has been paid recently to two forms of drama requiring background research. Historical reenactments involve studying past events in detail and trying to recreate them. In interactional drama actors, in role, attempt to draw children into a problem discussion related to issues and events of some historic period.

SELF-TEST

1. What is a simulation game?

2. Set up an in-basket game for one of the following three individuals:

    • The Abbot of a Medieval Monastery under attack by Vikings

    • A wagon master of a wagon train traveling to Oregon in the 1850s

    • The chief of a village in Africa that is in fear of being raided by slavers in the 1700s

3. Describe three types of mock trials.

4. What is *readers' theater*?

5. What is the point of class action stories?

6. Why is humor used in so many of the dramatic techniques?

7. What is the difference between role play and sociodrama?

8. What is story play?

9. What purposes do different dramatic activities serve in the social studies?

SUGGESTED READING

Chilcoat, G. (1989). The melodrama and the American slave experience. *The Social Studies*, 80 (November/December), 325-239.

Turner, T.N. (1990) *Stand Up and Cheer*. Glenview, Ill.: Scott Foresman.

Turner, Thomas N. (1979). Variations on a theme: three simulations based on the fallout shelter model. *The Social Studies*, 70 (November/ December), 281-285.

Epilogue

Textbooks don't often have epilogues. This one does. I want to give this book some closure, make it more of a whole for you. I intended the book to be a very practical, readable one, full of adaptable teaching activities, ideas, and suggestions. Your own reflections on the ten chapters can be the test of that intent. I also wanted to put across some messages that I think are very important. There is a passage in one of Conan Doyle's wonderful Sherlock Holmes stories when Holmes refers to the clue of the dog that barked in the night. When his uncomprehending audience reminds him in perplexity that the dog did not bark, Holmes says, with some satisfaction, that that is precisely the point. Sometimes the most significant things slip by us simply because nothing calls our attention to them. It is for that very reason that the most important messages go unnoticed, that I want to review them in this epilogue.

First, there is the message of the wholeness of teaching children. Because the total child is the concern of the social studies, the goals and purposes that the social studies program is centered on should relate the child's general knowledge, the development of language and other skills, and thinking. Every part of the child's own world, from what goes on in the family to what occurs in the neighborhood, to the music, television and movies that the child watches and listens to and the books that he or she reads influences that child's ability to understand the knowledge of the world that we are trying to teach.

Second, there is the message that a problems approach to teaching is one that allows both the teacher and the child to be active in the learning process. The theme in this message has been that social studies should be motivating, stimulating, and involving. Problem solving is learning how to learn. It is moving toward independence in learning, and it is both natural and preparatory for what happens later in life.

Third, and most important, there is the message that teachers who are responsible for the social studies need to be purposeful, thoughtful, and focused in what they do. To put it another way, teachers need to be problem solvers themselves. This means that they will have to look at new and different ways of using teaching tools from computers to textbooks to literature, and that they may need to look at these tools differently. It also means that teachers need to look very carefully at the ways that they use both their own time and that of their students.

Index